The Homegrown City

The Homegrown City

Reclaiming the Metropolis
for Its Users

Matias Echanove and
Rahul Srivastava

V

VERSO

London · New York

First published by Verso 2026
© Matias Echanove and Rahul Srivastava 2026

The manufacturer's authorized representative in the EU for product safety
(GPSR) is LOGOS EUROPE, 9 rue Nicolas Poussin, 17000, La Rochelle, France
contact@logoseurope.eu

1 3 5 7 9 10 8 6 4 2

Verso
UK: 6 Meard Street, London W1F 0EG
US: 207 East 32nd Street, New York, NY 10016
versobooks.com

Verso is the imprint of New Left Books

ISBN-13: 978-1-78873-013-6
ISBN-13: 978-1-78873-015-0 (UK EBK)
ISBN-13: 978-1-78873-016-7 (US EBK)

British Library Cataloguing in Publication Data
A catalogue record for this book is available from the British Library

Library of Congress Cataloging-in-Publication Data
A catalog record for this book is available from the Library of Congress

Typeset in Minion Pro by MJ & N Gavan, Truro, Cornwall
Printed in the UK by CPI Group (UK) Ltd, Croydon, CR0 4YY

Contents

1

The Cities We Build, the World We Live In

Perfect Plans and Imperfect Cities

This book is about imperfect cities and the people who inhabit them and improve them over time. We tell the story of individuals and groups carving space for themselves, appropriating and humanizing it at every step. We look at habitats from the point of view of those who shape them through use. We take journeys in space and time and attempt to demonstrate how seemingly mundane everyday acts produce habitats full of vitality and relevance. We write about lived experiences that transcend the logic of the plan. We describe how cultural relations and economic needs generate urban form. We observe how social processes leave their marks on space. We assert the importance of valuing and consolidating what's right before our eyes rather than speculating on a future that we have no means to anticipate, control, or plan.

We dedicate this book to ordinary residents: the homemaker who manages to create an affordable space in an unaffordable city; the local mason taking pride in the house he built in a favela of São Paulo; the owner of a tiny house in Tokyo who spends his weekends fixing his deck with materials bought around the corner; the migrant who shares a room with eight others in a basement in New York; the mother who runs tuition classes from her one-room house in Mumbai; the Californian geek who turns his parents' garage into an office defying zoning codes; the artists in Tbilisi who create a live–work studio in a former factory; the collectives who manage to repopulate abandoned buildings in Brussels; the teenagers in Parisian suburbs who run a business from their bedrooms and street corners; the family in Nairobi raising chickens and selling them right outside their home in a crowded settlement. This book is dedicated to the efforts of the quiet majority of urban dwellers all over the world who make the most of whatever space they manage to access and, in the process, provide it with new functions, meaning, identity – and, yes, beauty.

In many parts of the world, this majority builds houses, pushes street carts, invests in education, celebrates festivals, and engages in local politics in the shadow of skyscrapers along highways and bullet trains. It lives with little capital, uses inherited skills and shares resources in cities with increasingly fractured economies. This book builds on experiences we gained in a great variety of user-generated environments in Asia, Europe, and America, with a special focus on Mumbai, a city that expresses this reality more than any other, in a context full of social contrasts and urban tensions.

This book is also aimed at those who keep dreaming of the city of tomorrow, of a new urban landscape with affordable housing, inclusive technologies, and social justice: architects and architecture students everywhere who are looking for direct ways of engaging with the world around them, and planners, engineers, policymakers, and researchers, who often struggle to apply what they learned in school to real-life contexts.

Urban professionals carry forth a relatively recent legacy of concepts, tools, and techniques, now more or less universally declared acceptable for an identifiably modern city. The kind of urban planning we see today is still shaped by our agrarian–industrial heritage. This involves spatial configurations in which work, residence, and recreation are separated and then managed in various permutations and combinations.

From a scenario where villages could once be multifunctional spaces – in which farming, herding, manufacture, and active trading networks (with urban nodes) were coexisting activities – diverse activities have been reduced to centre primarily on farming. Farming now mirrors industrial operations, with large, plantation-based, single-crop systems deeply connected to global trade becoming the norm. The urban is defined against the rural, yet its structure remains an extension of a relationship with our surroundings based on the domestication of the ecosystem and the control of agrarian populations. The process of urbanization is narrowed down as one that marks the shifting of a population from a rigidly defined rural space to a large city. All nuance reflecting more complex configurations, such as rural–urban networks, densely populated forest-dependent regions, and village-towns, have been flattened out.

We keep on imagining and developing dense cities which are fed by industrial farms located in the distant periphery, notwithstanding the fact that alternatives to this picture have always existed. There is, for instance, growing research-based evidence that the Amazon forests were once densely populated with their own distinct urban networks that did not destroy the forest habitat but worked with it.[1] This experience is far removed from the urban planning paradigm in which city dwellers, from São Paulo to Shenzhen, live today, and which is very much based on a Western worldview. Whenever it is not, it is considered a failure. Japanese urbanism, which has managed to retain neighbourhoods that do not quite fit in the dominant model has for many years been dismissed as inadequate and substandard, when in fact it was based on gradual and small-scale improvement, with less dramatic shifts than those we are used to seeing in the name of urbanization.

The control of the state remains significant everywhere, particularly in Asian megacities. The forces that shape our cities are largely financial though, with the state acting as a facilitator for private capital. The coming together of administrative control and financial power leaves little scope for local populations to plan and manage their habitats. The arrangements that once gave dwellers some level of control in the making of their homes, villages, and neighbourhoods have given way to large construction projects and master plans. This means that the financial logic of producing settlements has also changed, with less user-driven local development and more investor-driven development. Urban planning rules and regulations have only made it more difficult for inhabitants to contribute to the development of their habitats. The relationship between people and their immediate surroundings that once defined urban development, has been replaced by norms and rules that have turned active agents into consumers, with little scope to use their immediate environment as a resource.

The norms structuring the evolution of cities around the world today have largely been developed in the twentieth century, which saw substantial global economic and urban growth. That world may have been divided along irreconcilable ideological lines, but there was a tacit agreement about how cities should be planned. A city like Berlin, which is overlaid by footprints of two ideological moments, socialist and capitalist, reveals a surprisingly similar template for neighbourhoods that grew around both sides of the wall.[2] Over the twentieth century, cities as historically, culturally, and ideologically different as Berlin, Beirut, Belfast, and Jerusalem followed a dominant trend in the way they were reshaped.[3]

Whether it emerged out of capitalism or socialism, the dominant architectural form linked to mass housing was the rectangular building block, vertical or horizontal.[4] This form could embody capitalist dominance, with the most successful people sitting on top of the others. Multiplied several times and stacked in rows, it could symbolize socialist egalitarianism. In either case, the rectangular building block was seen as an expression of order that contrasts with the imagined chaos of pre-modern cities. Well-aligned buildings along roads and infrastructural grids that brought hygiene, light, and modern comfort to the masses. The building block became synonymous with efficiency and rationality and remains so to the present day.

Unfortunately, by extension, every building that did not look rectangular and geometrically aligned became anachronistic and suspicious. Planning departments endorsed and promoted a specific typology, which prioritized the mass production of housing. New materials and technologies allowed the government and the private sector to build cheaper and bigger buildings that loosely reflected the values and aesthetic of modern architecture. Along with sparking a process that nearly destroyed pre-modern artisanship, it reinforced the trajectory that discouraged local inhabitants from engaging with their built environment.

A contemporary manifestation of the same impulse is threatening to destroy architectural practice as well. The process in which artisans, masons, and others involved with construction work with a master builder (architect) dependent on this larger constellation of skills and trades quickly transformed to one where the artisan was either redundant or reduced to a small, easily replaceable technical help. Subsequently, the role of the architect was also diminished and increasingly distanced from the actual processes of building.

Today, there is an increasing tendency for engineers to prefabricate and piece together buildings, following standardized metrics. Who needs an architect when you can order a building from a catalogue? Design is often seen as superfluous, and when architects are involved, it is usually to maximize the return of the investors, either by optimizing space to the fullest extent or by providing a design that may increase its market value. What is lost in this paradigm is, of course, any attention to the context: the landscape, the ecosystem, the history, and the culture of a place; the needs, means, and aspirations of the existing population.

While some cities have long resisted a complete takeover by industrial developers, we can safely say that big corporations won the battle against smaller artisanal builders. In Tokyo, until the mid-1990s small, unincorporated contractors who had inherited traditional construction practices, preserved through apprenticeship and guild systems for centuries, constructed as many new buildings as did large corporations. Eventually though, regulations biased in favour of larger builders made it extremely difficult for artisanal-scale construction to survive anywhere. The only places where small-scale construction is still thriving are cities where people are too poor to afford what developers supply or in neighbourhoods where people are rich enough to afford bespoke design and craftmanship.

In Mumbai for instance, nearly half of the population lives in small houses that have been built by local contractors, while a fragment of the population enjoys the luxury of beautifully crafted weekend homes across the bay. The rest live in substandard but expensive mass-produced housing.

While industrial construction techniques have helped raise standards, particularly when it comes to the provision of civic infrastructure, much has been lost as well. And there is no reason why the various qualities that were brought about by modern architecture – light, ventilation, infrastructure – could not be provided with a different approach to construction for those living in the poorer settlements as well.

This only demonstrates how the principal casualty of the modern regime is primarily the end-user: the resident-inhabitant, once a co-creator of her dwelling. Through this act of co-creation she managed an economy of construction that was affordable because it included – besides finance – skills and a familiar form of habitat that was socially endorsed by a supportive community, and often relied upon local, accessible materials. The industrial process either reduced her to a passive consumer of a mass-produced living space, condemned her to live in a poor-quality home, or relegated her to a narrative of homelessness.

The value of urban space

The quantification, commoditization, and trading of built space has led to phenomenal urban development in North American and Asian cities, with some emblematic successes such as New York or Shanghai. It has also been responsible for the pushing around, impoverishment, and disempowerment of countless urban dwellers. In the next chapter we present its extreme expression in Mumbai. This is where we can clearly see how speculative urban development directly impacts people's lives, usually for the worse.

When space becomes a commodity that can be bought and sold like any other, neighbourhoods lose their humanity and people lose their agency in the production of habitat. In theory, urban planning departments ostensibly exist to control urban development and protect the common interest. In practice, urban planning and real estate development work together to produce cities that may look good on paper, but which are socially, economically, and environmentally unsustainable.

Process matters. When dwellings are conceived in purely quantitative terms – the value of space calculated in dollars per square foot – they become qualitatively neutral, but also much more difficult to adapt to different needs. The use value of space cannot simply be equated to its exchange value. Use value derives from the way people inhabit space, generate relationships within it, develop it to serve their needs, and beautify it as they make it their own. This process unfolds over time, sometimes over generations, eventually creating a kind of value that is as real as it is intangible and unquantifiable. It suffices to walk through the streets of Jerusalem, Rome, or Varanasi, and feel the energy contained in urban forms that have been carved over centuries.

Yet it does not require thousands of years for space to generate meaning and value. A stroll through South Mumbai, where nineteenth-century Victorian architecture meets twentieth-century Art Deco buildings, easily indicates that. These grand heritage landmarks are imprinted with layers and layers of use: museums, galleries, and graceful gateways merge into a rich palimpsest of everyday appropriation. South Mumbai's monuments have, for several decades, absorbed the ordinary resident, user, and urban dweller in ways not always expected from its architectural language. A staircase, an entrance, and the arcade are full of unanticipated activity – used mostly for trading and resting. Niches, folds, corners, and alleyways live and breathe such uses and overwhelm most of the city's public spaces. It is not so much the architecture that makes the character of a city but the way people appropriate it and make it their own.

When great architecture is fully appropriated and imbued with new meanings derived from use, then of course it is an occurrence to be celebrated. The best way to appreciate the old colonial quarters of Mumbai and the life that animates them is from the vantage point of a busy corner, sipping a *chai* expertly brewed by a street vendor who looks as old as the buildings around him. The building's grand architecture blends into a sea of cabs and motorbikes, screeching and zigzagging around commuters rushing to work in their iron-pressed white shirts and colourful sarees.

Oftentimes, urban space generates value well beyond the price of the land. Shenzhen's electronics market, Huaqiangbei, isn't exactly considered a heritage site – at least not yet. Still, it has become so central to the city's economy and culture that one cannot imagine the metropolis functioning without it. The market's use value is so high that no matter what the monetary value of the land it sits on, this monetization cannot compensate for its loss. It is thanks to this market that new products are invented, and business connections get constantly made in Shenzhen. One day, it may attract more tourists than makers, and it will be considered a heritage site, which will change its value, meaning, and relevance. But for now it is still one of the vital organs of this young and innovative city.

Similarly, thousands of central neighbourhoods in cities around the world are vital to the people who inhabit them yet are threatened by a form of speculation that has no relationship whatsoever to what is happening on the ground. On the contrary – their current use is considered a liability. While on-site houses and businesses may represent years of investments to those who inhabit and exploit them, to the real estate developer they represent only the cost of clearance.

Inhabitants of neighbourhoods that have consolidated over decades without much planning – for example in Shenzhen, Mumbai, or Lagos – are often considered to be temporary dwellers who will eventually have to leave when the real estate interest comes home to roost. From the point of view of the mainstream urban planner, these places simply must be redeveloped. They have been firmly entrenched as aberrations from an ideal modern-city form.

Even in the most successful cities, however, observations reveal routine cracks between ideals and actuality. A prosperous city at the cutting edge of technology and business, such as San Francisco or Seattle, must face the challenge of homelessness, which rises alongside its economy and rental prices. Glitzy Cape Town, rebuilt on a fresh bout of inclusive political ambition in a post-apartheid nation, finds itself struggling for water. Most inhabitants of Mumbai live with the burden of uncertain citizenship and a half-hearted legal acknowledgement of their homes. The marginalized majority never quite knows if it belongs to the city where it lives. European cities need to deal with density stress generated by the presence of newcomers who need accommodation in a space that is perceived by oldcomers (yesterday's migrants) as saturated, already too diverse and populous for comfort.

Between aspiration and experience

Whether they live on the preferred end of the urban spectrum or its opposite, most people have to deal with a cross-wiring of lived experiences. Even if we exclude dramatic or extreme examples in cities confronting unimaginable stresses and infrastructure strains and just focus on routine urban administration and practices in the most ordinary of cities, we find a great richness of experience to learn from, which thrives between the ideal and the real, the planned and the emergent.

The universal quality of inhabitant-centred experience emerges from the inherent, immediate, and persistent tension that exists between incremental consolidation and large-scale urban planning. One is opportunistic and contextual, the other strategic and speculative. These two forms of intervention have many names. In bureaucratic speak, they are often described as bottom-up and top-down. Bottom-up development is usually seen as grassroots and community-driven but inadequate and backward. Top-down planned development is considered expert-driven and technically advanced but often cold and remote from the daily reality of end users. The top-down approach is increasingly opening itself to participatory approaches, which should, in theory, bring users' expertise into the plan.

Our experience has taught us to be suspicious of these polarities. Most of all, it suggests a fake sense of balance, as if there were a middle ground – an ideal space between bottom-up and top-down practices. We prefer to imagine a new practice that works beyond spatial and architectural considerations, operates at different scales simultaneously, and stimulates creative engagement throughout the life cycle of urban projects. The fundamental arena for this practice is the human dimension – not only from an experiential point of view but also in relational terms. The resident, the user, the entrepreneur, the planner, and the policymaker can all relate at an interpersonal level, which can break through the most rigid bureaucratic hierarchies and social boundaries. We believe that the resources, skills, and will we need for such a practice already exist around us. We need simply to give them space and harness them.

A new way of conceptualizing and developing urban environments may, however, require some creative destruction of the rigid models that have imposed themselves in modern times. What we are up against is a practice in the public and private sectors that finds much comfort in drafting urban and financial plans that are blind to context and usage. This approach will resist with all its might any alternative way to think about planning. Its practitioners will refuse to engage with a complex reality for fear that it will make *their* lives more complex and challenging. Urban planning produces its own complicated set of rules and regulations, codes and zoning, exemptions and incentives to make sure that the process stays as obscure as possible to end-users. The practitioners may agree to complement their own 'expertise' with insights from 'users' expertise only to absorb them into a bureaucratic black box that will shred any innovative idea to pieces, ultimately generating only more of the same generic urbanism. This is done in the name of modern, rational, sustainable, and inclusive cities.

An increasing number of people around the world live in master-planned neighbourhoods, which have been developed following bureaucratic processes, financed by real estate investors and maintained by professional agencies. The delivery of such mass-produced habitats has been streamlined and optimized to the point that they can be effortlessly reproduced again and again. This normative urbanism, seen as the expression of modernity, has been reproduced with industrial precision all around the world. In South Korean and Chinese cities, the model has been perfected by conglomerates such as Samsung and LG, which are aggressively exporting their methods, even as they are being questioned at home. The South Korean government is now seemingly interested in preserving whatever is left of the homegrown fabric of its cities. Community associations are increasingly demanding urban regeneration strategies that do not involve the destruction and reshaping of their low-rise habitats.

The system in place for the delivery of such housing, though, is full of loopholes and collateral. The housing created through the process of established norms and procedures is usually expensive, often alienating, and nearly always environmentally unsustainable. These developments are wired into existing industrial and market structures rather than responding to the needs of their future inhabitants. They are financed in ways that produce debt and financial insecurity. Even the richest cities seem incapable of producing enough affordable housing for their citizens. As the case of Seattle shows, corporations such as Amazon that attract top-tier workers are ready to fight tooth and nail against any form of taxation that would address their impact on rent.

It seems paradoxical that municipal governments in rich cities often lack resources to address civic needs, but it follows a deadly logic of competition between towns to attract large firms. Those who offer state-of-the-art infrastructure, tax breaks to corporations and low income tax usually manage to win over the biggest players.

In related moves, the inability of municipal governments to provide affordable housing has led many cities to outsource its delivery to real estate developers. Mumbai has been praised for its slum rehabilitation scheme, which presents itself as a public–private partnership.[5] In fact, it provides highly valuable building rights, often on public land, to developers, in exchange for their redevelopment of slums into substandard mass housing, where families of eight people or more live in one-bedroom apartments.

Cities across the world experience a multiplication of stresses in the face of urban growth. As cities take on an ever more central role in the global economy, what follows is an increase in issues of housing, huge disparities of income, a fractured quality of life in neighbourhoods, poor-quality construction that becomes expensive to maintain, traffic congestion, low air quality, and long commutes in crowded public transportation.

When such civic issues are successfully managed, relatively speaking, a city's internal divisions, concentration of wealth, and economic exclusion may cause other kinds of stress – mainly social tension or civic violence. Civic spaces from Chicago to Paris to Delhi are brimming with conflict, and many of them are linked to a broken social contract and the ever-increasing geographical and economic polarities that have become dramatically common in urban contexts. In this scenario, it is understandable that the middle classes keep looking for safe spots, preferably fenced and guarded.

The human/nature relationship

Many people seek to resolve the contradictory impulses that draw them to cities in search of human interaction or professional opportunities and the opposing drive that compels them to run away from conflicted, crowded, expensive, and polluted urban centres. The suburban home has long been the holy grail of successful urban life – a spacious family house at the edge of the city, close enough for a daily commute but far enough from the hustle and bustle: one or two cars in the garage, trees and tomatoes in the garden, a bedroom for each child, and perhaps even a sense of community in the neighbourhood.

The problem, of course, is that this desire for something that was once visualized as an ideal garden city but became manifest as dreary suburbia has only caused more infrastructural stress and environmental damage as it throws more concrete around city centres and puts more cars on the road. Despite the rise of ecological consciousness in most cities, we have not yet found ways of producing environments that merge human and natural habitats in ways that benefit both. We have failed to produce human habitats that contribute positively to the ecosystems in which they are embedded. It is almost taken for granted that human presence in dense concentrated living is anathema to sustainable ideals. The most we can do, it seems, is reduce the harm we are causing by certifying buildings as environmentally friendly.

But there is no reason to think of the relationship between humans and nature only in terms of pollution and exploitation. Humans have been living in forests, deserts, and mountains for thousands of years and have not always been a destructive presence. On the contrary, humans are often custodians of nature – the only species that can decide and manage to afforest an arid region or maintain the balance between different animal and vegetal species, keeping a check on excesses to preserve an ecosystem's diversity. Forests have been densely inhabited, regenerated, and sustained through human intervention as much as they have been destroyed through indiscriminate use and abuse. This complex legacy is with us in the lives and experiences of people who belong to indigenous histories, environmental experts and modern-day adventurers who live, to the best of their abilities, according to these knowledge systems. We could harness all of this and much more. But so far, what we have created instead are urban systems that run on the exploitation of natural resources and pollute the world in the process.

What we want to emphasize in this book, perhaps paradoxically, is that everything that exists around us, no matter how damaged and toxic, must be seen as a resource. Imperfections in our cities appear as such because they are viewed through the prism of an unrealistic urban norm; but imperfections help us understand the world as it is and provide an archive of experiences that can become the foundations for a stronger, more effective practice. Imperfect habitats are those we should learn from. They are places where people have no choice but to find solutions to the problems they are confronted with. Well-planned neighbourhoods, on the contrary, can only teach us how to reproduce and maintain the existing order, even if that order is utterly unsustainable. To us, ready-made solutions are dangerous and ineffective.

The truth of the matter is, we can neither wish the present away nor promise magical transformation. It is necessary to be particularly sceptical of the promise of social and urban utopias, however tempting they seem – especially utopias that plan to eradicate poverty wholesale or vow to reduce the number of slum dwellers by tens of millions through massively funded big-bang projects, or that make promises to 3-D print cheap houses for the poor.

We should not fall for such prophecies of radical change, especially when the proposed change implies a fundamental transformation driven by experts operating from remote labs and studios. In fact, such utopias become the chief urban problems facing us today, including spatial exclusion, social conflict, civic alienation, and countless environmental abuses.

Leaving utopia – the journey to reality

Political utopias are always based on the idea of the future as something fundamentally different from the present. Yet according to Bruno Latour, we lost the future somewhere in the second half of the twentieth century. Sci-fi images of flying vehicles, vertical cities, and a world controlled by a ubiquitous intelligence – whether of alien origin or man-made – belong to the 1960s (along with lava lamps and Ball Chairs). Belief in the possibility of engineering a future that would be totally different, for better or worse, is at the root of the largest undertakings of the twentieth century, from fascism to capitalism, from communism to ecotopias. The fundamental problem with most utopias – and what makes them attractive in the first place – is that they fail to acknowledge the local contextual exigencies that act as their foundations.

At their pinnacle, some of these political utopias have produced huge bureaucracies, state or corporate – sometimes with success in eradicating hunger and homelessness, but at other times unleashing reigns of terror and environmental devastation. They have all, at some point or other, triggered massive urban development projects. Their experiments made us believe that we could go from plan to reality at the gigantic scale of a city, if not a nation. Today, however, we see the tattered remains of many ideological utopias strewn around their corresponding urban totems – from Los Angeles to Hong Kong, from Berlin to Moscow – all of them afflicted by conditions deemed problematic that have been brought about by their own idealistic intentions aimed at wholesale transformation.

According to Plato, *if* our built environment followed the laws of good proportions, just measure and harmony, then our citizens would surely behave justly, and the life of the good city government would be assured. In reality, this has never been the case; yet we don't learn. As soon as a new centrally planned city materializes, it becomes evident that even the greatest masters of architecture and the most expert teams of professionals cannot anticipate life, which spills out over their grand plans and visions. Planned cities shift ground thanks to the inhabitants who come to occupy them in ways that could not be fully anticipated. New settlements pop up in places not expected, and new populations and habitats grow in unplanned crevices among the shadowy spaces that inevitably emerge between the perfect straight line drawn on the plan.

It is not that the authorities do not try to control the force of independent human will. China has tried for decades to restrict rural–urban migration; demolition of habitats deemed illegal is routine in Africa, and security cameras monitor possible appropriation of public space all over Europe. There are countless ways in which we are coerced to conform to the bureaucratic imagination and follow lines drawn to direct our movements. Such attempts at control continue to rage in urban planning and administrative offices, either with brute force or sophisticated rhetoric. There are few things that excite the bureaucratic planner more than being able to decide exactly where pedestrians will be directed to cross the road and how they will be physically prevented from exercising their free will. This is, of course, always enacted from a moral high ground –for the greater good of people who really don't know what's best for them.

The fundamental behavioural assumption of classical economics, from which all others derive, is that individuals are rational and intent on maximizing utility. The fundamental assumption in urban planning seems to be that people are irrational and unable to assess what's good for them. Planners seem to believe that when it comes to the collective, decisions are better made from the top. But we have learned from Jürgen Habermas that rationality is primarily relational and communicational. He believes it is possible for a group of people who agree on basic rules of communication to come up with solutions that are optimal for the circumstances.[6] Unfortunately, we still seem to be light years away from this kind of approach to planning. The current approach reduces people to consumers who need to be sold a clever scheme.

The smart city, for instance, represents a new kind of planned urban utopia – one of efficiency, orderliness, and safety – complete with tokenistic greenery, glitzy malls, and autonomous cars. In reality, it is a summation of all previous governance ideals – the pure distilled spirit of urban utopia, as it were. It aims to keep all the failures of the past outside the technological bubble within which it defines itself. It promises to be pure of intent at every level – especially through ecological aims, technological savvy, and social inclusiveness.

If there is any testimony to the failure of the twentieth-century urban imagination, it is this little miniature smart city in a glass bottle of well-meaning but superficial intentions. It twists the debates of scaling up into a scaling down that reduces its ambition into what is essentially an acknowledgement of the failure of grand utopias. The problem is that it pretends to be such a utopia and its effect is exactly the opposite; and it suggests there is total control but the reality is anything but. Such a city cannot deal with the small economic and ecological crises that periodically toss it around, because the ocean on which it floats is made up of the very same crises.

The idea that we can plan our way to the future has been responsible for countless ego-fuelled man-made disasters. Our present generation must deal with the mess left behind by those who believed they could produce and control futures (dreamt up in the past). Latour says that there is no more future. What we are left with is really an *avenir* – what is to come.

In the present world, most people *don't* have the luxury of buying into readymade schemes that sort out safety, space, movement, and the quality of the immediate environment. Most people *cannot* afford to live in the smart city or the gated community. They cannot drive to work. They cannot call the building manager. They have to fix the pipe themselves. They don't have retirement plans. They cannot buy into a utopian life that fends off the messy reality outside their gate. They must deal with what's coming to them.

And now the circle that encloses them is becoming bigger; it is beginning to include everyone. Europeans and North Americans cannot shield themselves from migrants. Smart cities will need to deal with the excluded majority that surrounds them, and gated communities will suffer from the water crisis and environmental disasters like everyone else. Urban planning cannot protect anyone from what's coming to us. In fact, it is a certain kind of planned development that is itself responsible for what's happening to the world now. And what is coming to us is more of the mess we are already dealing with.

Dysfunctional cities; highly volatile markets; polluted, unpredictable, and uncontainable nature; more conflicts over basic resources; continuous rises in worldwide inequality; massive movements of population; and an ever more concentrated and paranoid global wealth – all of this is almost certainly upon us, as we have been reminded countless times. What we don't quite know, however, is in what specific form or magnitude it will affect us. The predictable nightmares are periodically listed in social media spheres: typhoons; riots; political coups; widespread social exclusion; terrorism. But an accurate profile of what is yet to come remains unknown.

We can only guess; and since we don't really know, it is nearly impossible for us to protect ourselves. In fact, when we try to protect ourselves – and we do seem obsessed with protecting ourselves from the mess we create – we often land up reducing some of the freedoms and comforts we have managed to gain over the last century. This is being experienced today in debates related to safety and surveillance or the promise of economic progress being conditional upon sacrificing freedom. Such bargains seem to be spreading, along with neoliberal economic structures and technological expansion. They are openly encroaching upon the freedoms and comforts that modern economies once promised us and to some extent delivered. More than just encroachment, they are threatening to reverse the political liberation of old bonded contracts that shaped modern lives.

The problem, perhaps, is linked to the hardwired incompleteness of the modern project. The twentieth century never fully actualized its ideals and promises. In spite of trying so hard, we were never modern, as Latour keeps reminding us.[7]

It is this heavy acknowledgement that allows us to navigate the maze of articulations and intents, practices and promises, rhetoric and reality that surround us today – webs that emerged from contrary, incomplete intentions, and gestures that continue to entangle us. From the vantage point of the twenty-first century, we can see more clearly how cross-wired our political ideals and practices were – progress, democracy, colonialism, fascism, capitalism, communism. They all collided and tripped over each other. Their shared and contested ideals were employed in a way that was always debatable; no wonder that today, the more we try to free ourselves, the tighter the knots that bind us become.

All the same, it is not easy to give up on utopian thought. Social aspirations become part of our identity and provide us with a moral compass. For instance, the utopia of a post-capitalist world where the means of production and wealth are shared remains a valuable dream. At the same time, the moral expectation of this moment has also led us to abstain from actively engaging with the world as it is, especially its imperfections.

Urban planning theory is still dominated by academics who denounce the existing world order as one integrated system and see any engagement in urban practice as complicit. They fear it only serves to reproduce existing power structures. Academic planners usually advocate abstract principles of equality and justice, knowing very well that these are not available in our world: plans based exclusively on these principles are doomed to failure outside the controlled studio or classroom conditions.

While we fully sympathize and agree with the critique of the system as it is, we don't think it is wise to locate oneself outside the world. An engagement with the world is necessary, no matter how corrupt and toxic it is. Change comes through practice. New ideas, especially in the field of urban planning, emerge from interacting with the world. Engagement with a toxic world does not mean that we are bound to contribute to its toxicity. But it is through practice, especially when it is embedded in community, that we can attempt to detoxify and transform.

For this to happen, we must be immensely creative. We must not fear using whatever means are at hand – from local markets to state agencies, from critiquing the totalizing rhetoric of the left to valuing its ideals, from dealing with the anxieties of those who are vulnerable to right-wing manipulation to working creatively with exchange mechanisms that make up daily life, incorporating technology but rejecting the manipulation of surveillance and control. Trading skills, monetizing knowledge, developing new techniques, and absorbing new processes and technologies must all be part of our practice. These are all tools for improvement.

How exactly does such a practice work? What is the nature of the imperfection we are referring to? Where does it exist? How does a non-utopian practice work, and how can it be prevented from becoming dystopian? These are some concerns that our line of argument spontaneously generates, constituting the subject matter of this book.

Reclaiming locality

Our own practice is always located in a specific place. Categories such as 'urban' or 'habitat' do not exist as abstractions but are invariably located in time and space. This means dealing with the concreteness of a specific locality at every level of consideration. Every human arrangement inevitably and naturally produces its own context. A context is a combination of its material, physical, historical, economic, and sociocultural dimensions.

As anthropologist Arjun Appadurai explains, localities are actively produced by inhabitants and expressed as neighbourhoods. They are arrangements that have an awareness of other places – neighbours – which exist around them.[8] Localities are not bounded units. They are always infused by varying scales of operation, be they class-inflected, regional, national, or global. These have expressions and institutional arrangements of their own. However, any notion of scale should not relegate locality to one end of a spectrum that spans degrees of the regional, national, or global. This would inaccurately reduce the local to a subset of these categories.

Rather, it is important to see locality as the real frontier of engagement and practice that makes it possible for all scales to operate. In our reading of Appadurai, the idea of locality can be seen as integral to the production of context – *all* contexts. Even the most global of arrangements operate at some level of locality – whether in an airport or a generic office complex. Local space is infused by history and human presence that have contributed to its creation and influenced its existence in some form or the other. Anchoring places through location immediately brings in aspects of agency, citizenship, and engagement. This is a world in which people do not simply address themselves through generalities of class or national position, but as actors who shape their immediate context.

Even when modern societies are conceived as part of large-scale systems (that have themselves been scaled up by technology and modes of mass production), we have always managed to evoke specificities of place within those generalizations for one reason or another. Examples include factories doubling as spaces for the proletariat to meet and generate class consciousness, or streets and open grounds acting as sites of congregation and worship of nationalist symbols, or sports events as favoured dramatic sites for advertising global logos and brands, or cities with competitively tall buildings becoming totemic symbols of corporate success.

What we need to understand is that we live in a world of multiple and networked localities and neighbourhoods. Most humans live and operate from a sense of locality in which they are embedded. It is this vision of locality that makes us look at our practice firmly in terms of immediacy and engagement.

Finally, we must resurrect *inhabiting* as an action that is available to us all. Inhabiting is necessarily an act of resistance against decay and the status quo. There is nothing passive about it; it is a fundamentally relational, political, and creative act. Inhabiting means shaping the environment so it becomes hospitable and productive. This relationship does not have to be a hostile takeover of space. In fact, it means that the land does not always need to be cleared and dug before it can be used. The creative inhabitant, just like the creative architect, is someone who sees locality as a resource that can be nurtured, besides being the context that we collectively create for ourselves.

This book emerges from over a decade of close interaction with such creative inhabitants and from such active contexts. It is both a moment of reflection and a consolidation of our convictions based on years of practice.

2

Speculative Versus Intensive City

The high-rise and the slum

Cities such as Mumbai, São Paulo, and Lagos are often presented as schizophrenic urbanscapes where emergent islands of modernity are surrounded by an endless sea of informal shacks – or the other way around, as globalized cities, which cannot seem to get rid of residual underdevelopment. Either way, this image depicting a city sharply divided between opulence and poverty is used across the political spectrum to justify redevelopment projects in the name of modernization or equality. The intuitive but misleading parallels – that slum equals poverty and high-rise equals middle class – coupled with an inability to recognize the variety that exists in between these extreme urban archetypes, has allowed countless acts of injustice to be perpetuated in the name of slum upgrading and redevelopment projects. In the process, the ongoing incremental development of so-called slums in many cities has been curtailed, with dramatic consequences for the concerned populations and for the long-term social, economic, and urban sustainability of the city.

Mainstream notions of what a world-class city should look like and a tendency to understand urbanization from the point of view of form rather than process have given a free ride to the real estate industry. This is why it is important to interrogate the typologies of the high-rise building and that of the slum and propose a new planning paradigm based on neighbourhood life and local economic activities, including the production of habitats themselves.

Unplanned neighbourhoods in many cities have been a victim of old-school urban practices that are increasingly detached from the reality they are supposed to improve. These include the imposition of outdated concepts and typologies, a total incapacity or unwillingness to understand developmental dynamics at a local level, as well as a stubborn and anachronistic predisposition to segregate spatial uses (working, living, leisure). A more grounded understanding of so-called slum habitats and the socio-economic processes that generate them may help produce viable alternatives to the perpetual loop of slum demolition and reconstruction that preclude inclusive and sustainable urbanization.

We must also analyse the typology, social meaning, and political economy of high-rise apartment blocks, which is presented as the only possible architectural response to slums. This provides the backdrop to our concepts of the intensive and speculative city, which reflect the conflicting logics determining urban development in cities such as Mumbai and São Paulo – and which reflect the challenges faced by cities around the globe.

We attempt to show how the extreme urban typologies of the slum and the high-rise are ultimately produced by the friction between the use value of urban space and its exchange value as a tradable commodity. These concepts also emphasize the importance of not simply reading the city through its formal expression, but rather of paying attention to the generative processes at work in the city's morphology.

The fact that different logics are at work in urban development is no news; nor is the fact that these logics are often in conflict. Architect and urban historian Rahul Mehrotra describes India's brand of urbanism as one where two worlds are compressed against one another: the 'kinetic city', temporary and in motion, and the 'static city', monumental and aspiring to permanence.[1] This echoes Kevin Lynch's theoretical distinction between the 'city machine' that is planned and engineered as opposed to the 'city as a learning ecology', which develops locally and from within.[2] In the same vein, Donald Richie described Tokyo as a principally lived city in contrast to the designed cities of the US.[3] In addition, many theorists, including sociologists Saskia Sassen and Manuel Castells, have considered the relationship between the formal and the informal processes within global cities, pointing to the fact that, far from merely coexisting in distinct universes, these were mutually dependent and supportive.[4]

Much has also been written about 'top-down' planning versus 'bottom-up' processes, especially from an activist point of view, with Jane Jacobs as the charismatic figurehead of a grassroots, people-centric approach to urban development. The debate is now often put in terms of participation and exclusion, with the kinetic, organic, lived, informal, bottom-up city on the one hand, and on the other, the static, machine-like, designed, formal, top-down planned city. The former is the city that is being produced every day, incrementally and in a piecemeal fashion by the multitude. It is inclusive at one level but also messy, dysfunctional, and substandard, often represented as a sprawling slum. The latter is a city planned by experts: efficient, rational, modern, but also expensive, exclusive, unsustainable, and alienating. Its icons are the high-rise building, the air-conditioned shopping mall, and the parking lot.

There is indeed a long-lasting schism in urban studies between those theorizing the city from the point of view of its spatial organization and structure, and those who are interested in issues of urban justice, economic development, and planning. This schism also runs through the list of authors we just referred to. Architects and urban designers tend to focus on physical form, while sociologists and planners usually explore the processes at work in urban development.

When Castells and fellow Marxist planners use the word *form*, they mean it in the sense of social and economic structures rather than physical urban typologies, or morphological responses to the context. Thus the observations of scholars interested in social processes and physical urban form often overlap but rarely converge. This has led to a great deal of confusion in the field of urban studies, culminating in the disciplinary split between urban planning, focusing on the social, economic, political, and legal aspects of urban development, and urban design, which draws from fields of architecture and landscaping. As a result, in spite of a broad-ranging interest in so-called informal habitats, we rarely see theories or design schemes that recognize the validity of the typologies that emerge within them.

Specifically, the issue of housing for the poor has long been caught in the fault lines between form and process. While economic deprivation and social exclusion lead to all kinds of creative – if unsatisfactory – urban solutions in slums, mass-produced housing rehabs are symptomatic of ideologically based political and architectural responses to complex social and economic processes.

An understanding of these processes is crucial to explain why the high-rise is not always a solution to the needs of a highly populated and dense city (as its spatial logic presupposes), but can well become an ideological tool used by a political economy of construction that ultimately contributes to producing a surplus of empty flats alongside a multitude of de-housed people.

Conversely, once shorn of its extreme manifestation as a civically challenged, violence-prone category, the typology of the slum can be seen to hide within it a great variety of built forms (high-rise, low-rise, high-density – and facilitating several creative uses of environment and space), eventually managing to absorb surplus populations better than any mass housing scheme, however counterintuitive such an argument may appear. This is why we see the question of form, typology, and diversity of habitats, rescued from the binary of the slum or high-rise, as crucial to providing practical solutions to the global urban housing crisis.

Narratives of inequality and other binaries

Richard Burdett, the chief organizer of the Urban Age Conference that travelled through Mumbai in 2007, opened his presentation with an image showing a world-class, high-rise building, surrounded by a slum.[5] The building stands like an island of modernity in a brown sea of shanties ready to swallow the structure at the next financial crash, or conversely to be redeveloped into a well-ordered mass-produced housing project once enough money has been accrued. Whether this photo was taken in Mumbai, São Paulo, Bogotá, or Istanbul is irrelevant. The same cliché has been used countless times in movies, documentaries, and articles about the global South. The inequalities generated by the world's economic system seem nowhere as visible as in the megacities of South Asia, Latin America, and Africa, where decades of foreign and domestic investment in real estate have produced globalized cityscapes in parts of the city, while others remain entrenched in supposedly pre-modern living conditions.

Juxtaposed thus, the slum and the high-rise look as if they belong to different worlds, coexistent but irreconcilable. The slum appears anachronistic: a living ruin from a not-so-distant past, when modernization and urbanization in the national context were stuck in a time lag, enmeshed in Third World conditions. The juxtaposition is seen as representing two faces of the same capitalist coin, simultaneously producing poverty and wealth.

The slum and the high-rise have often been described as deadly enemies whose mortal combat can potentially bring about the downfall of urban civilization as we know it. The dramatic exposition of this urban fantasy is provided by Mike Davis in the dark conclusion of his review of slum literature:

> Night after night, hornetlike helicopters and gunships stalk enigmatic enemies in the narrow streets of the slum districts, pouring hellfire into shanties or fleeing cars. Every morning the slums reply with suicide bombers and eloquent explosions. If the empire can deploy Orwellian technologies of repression, its outcasts have the gods of chaos on their side.[6]

This imagery was brought to cinematic life in the 2009 movie *District 9*, which envisioned a scenario where monstrous alien visitors get stuck in a township of Johannesburg. Filmed with a handheld camera in a deserted section of Soweto, *District 9* uses the physical reality of slums as well as the politics of spatial control as special effects.[7] Slums, townships, shanties, or favelas offer a potent backdrop for classic gangster plots, feel-good movies, sci-fi fantasies, and political commentaries (as in *City of God* [2002], for example, or *Slumdog Millionaire* [2008]). Slummy landscapes work as a visual stimulant for cinema creatives who sense vitality amid the deprivation, while developers, governments, industrialists, and some architects see them instead as a last frontier of wilderness that needs to be conquered and domesticated.[8]

Expositions of urban misery and the corollary imperative of bold, urgent action satisfy everyone – from government officials to nongovernmental organizations, including builders and architects. The sense of urgency and the need to do something has led to countless well-intentioned (and less so) schemes by governments, NGOs, and international institutions to alleviate the condition of slum dwellers. In 2005 the UN Millennium Project aimed 'to achieve significant improvement in the lives of at least 100 million slum dwellers by 2020', proposing a mix of strategies relying mostly on massive government intervention, market-driven solutions, and the involvement of slum dwellers themselves.[9] It is now obvious that such seemingly progressive schemes aiming to improve the life of slum dwellers develop severe fault lines, particularly at the interrelated levels of concept and implementation.

Questioning the category of slum is not simply a matter of responding to rhetoric. It has important consequences for the people affected by slum alleviation, rehabilitation, and redevelopment projects and beyond, including those indirectly affected by the development of new slums in their cities. Countless redevelopment projects across time and in all parts of the world have been justified by labelling neighbourhoods as slums. Here is Jane Jacobs denouncing an urban renewal in the West End of Boston during the 1960s:

> I talked to two architects in '58 who helped justify the destruction of the West End. And one of them told me that he had had to go on his hands and knees with a photographer through utility crawl spaces so that they could get pictures of sufficient dark and noisome spaces to justify that this was a slum – how horrendous it was. Now that was real dishonesty. And they were documenting stuff for it.[10]

Creating a version of what theorist Achille Mmembe, referring to discussions on African post-colonial history, calls *absolute otherness* is a well-known strategy for labelling old, contested, lived-in neighbourhoods as slums; the aim is to justify a wholesale takeover with massive investment because of the project's potential to generate profits.[11] In his view this is only a mild modification of the strategy that colonial powers used to justify imperial oversight of territories by labelling entire cultures as primitive, barbaric, or in need of enlightenment.

Similar strategies are used today to justify large-scale real estate projects in cities throughout Asia. The ongoing Dharavi Redevelopment Project (DRP), in Mumbai, has long pioneered the provision of housing to the poor by private developers. The project is subsidized by the revenue generated by clearing space released after squeezing (only eligible) existing inhabitants into tiny rooms with basic amenities in tall buildings with elevators that are expensive to manage. A part of the land is reserved to build rehabs for slum dwellers. The rest is used by the developers to build housing to be sold at market rate. In a city with an inflated real estate value this translates into massive returns.

The eligibility factor is another dark side of the process. It is a politically negotiated one and typically involves a dateline marking inhabitants' eligibility based on when they became residents. Since these negotiations tend to take a long time, there is always a lag, creating a significant cohort of inhabitants who have to move out and find another place to live when a project starts to materialize – until the redevelopment juggernaut reaches that new site. Experts have pointed out not only how ineffective the process is as a way to solve the so-called slum question in Mumbai, but also how it keeps generating new ones.

Already in 2009, the moves to transform Dharavi through initiatives such as the Dharavi Redevelopment Project never quite won the trust of the city. The project was denounced by a panel of experts appointed by the government as an unethical takeover. In an open letter to the chief minister of Maharashtra, they wrote:

> The residents of Dharavi have established not just homes but thriving businesses and livelihoods ... The residents of Dharavi are being offered free construction and the legalising of their status, but this is in exchange for (a) shifting into less than half (47%) of their original land area and (b) the destruction of their livelihoods ... the land thus released from occupation will be commercially exploited and significant profits are expected to accrue to both the Government and to the developers entrusted with the project. The project is being driven by personal greed rather than the welfare of the residents of Dharavi.[12]

The late Jockin Arputham, who was one of the experts in the panel as well as being president of the National Slum Federation, was quoted on the DRP as follows:

> There are so many contradictions and complications. Only 35% of the slum dwellers seem to be eligible for the project and the government has not [surveyed] 35,000 families living on lofts and first floors. To the social and economic destruction that such a redevelopment project implies, one should also add the perverse effect that throwing out hundreds of thousands of people out of their homes and work will have on the city as a whole. In which new slum will people go? Which streets will they be sleeping on? Whose jobs will they compete for?[13]

The inability of policymakers to understand Dharavi's enmeshed residential, productive, trading, and community spaces is proving severely detrimental to its planned future.

What the official gaze actually does is standardize the entire neighbourhood's experience into a legal argument about invalid citizenship; it has labelled the settlement as the city's biggest slum and in the last ten years has started to unleash a process in which real estate interests dictate the area's redevelopment. This process is eventually bound to evacuate a good percentage of the erstwhile population and reduce those remaining to fuel for a service-based economy looking after the needs of the new middle class ready to move in.

This extreme case of urban real estate abuse, denounced by prominent urban planners, social workers, and slum activists in Mumbai, is echoed at a much smaller scale, thousands of times over in slum rehabilitation scheme (SRS) projects, which allow private developers to redevelop slum pockets with the consent of 51 per cent (formerly 70 per cent) of the 'eligible slum dwellers' living there, in exchange for construction rights in more valuable parts of the city.[14] Unlike the DRP, this scheme has the merit of requiring the consent of a part of the concerned population. Yet this scheme has also generated millions of square feet of housing of the poorest quality that cannot be maintained by its residents over time. Moreover, the rehabs do little to solve the infrastructural, amenity, and health issues of the concerned population, as was demonstrated by Amita Bhide of the Tata Institute of Social Sciences, among other studies.[15]

Past projects have shown that the poor quality of rehab buildings means that within a few years they start to deteriorate, and in many cases become just as bad as the slum from which dwellers were initially rehabilitated. It has also been observed that a large percentage of the rehabilitated tenants were quickly forced to sell their new property in exchange for much needed liquidity, and subsequently found themselves with no other option but to return to a slum.

This scheme that lets the private sector produce housing for the poor through incentives by the government has sparked the interest of people around the world. However successful these types of public–private partnership can be at providing formal housing to the poor, the economic mantra of development through market liberalism has not yet propelled the masses to the nirvana of high-rise dwelling. No matter how eager the developers are, the demand for housing seems endless, especially as the city grows with each successive wave of immigration from economically or environmentally challenged parts of the Indian subcontinent.

One of the most important problems with the SRS is also one of the most overlooked. As the rehab project pretends to improve living conditions, it often disconnects rehabilitated slum dwellers from their means of subsistence, which in India is often completely dependent on access to the street. In Dharavi, for instance, virtually every structure with access to the street doubles up as a storefront or a small manufacturing unit. These activities cannot be maintained on the sixth or seventh floor of a high-rise building. Social capital, which is often leveraged by slum dwellers for income generation or subsidy strategies, has long been identified as collateral damage to rehabilitation schemes.[16]

The displacement (even in situ) from low-rise, high-density dwellings to more impersonal high-rise, high-density housing has a negative

Figure 2.1. A street in Dharavi, Mumbai (photo: Ishan Tankha for urbz).

impact on social networks. This could perhaps be mitigated by intelli-
gent design, but unfortunately design is never a priority for low-cost
housing. Thus, the move from slum-type structures to high-rise rehab
flats comes at a cost, which is both economic and social. Dharavi resident and social worker Bhau Korde expresses it more clearly than
anyone else could:

> They say they will redevelop Dharavi, but look at what they're doing.
> These high-rise buildings mushrooming all round us. People who move
> in are selling and leaving their flats already. They need money because
> they cannot continue with their livelihoods in these buildings. People
> living in these high-rises don't know their neighbours anymore. The
> street life and economic activity will be gone. They say this is develop-
> ment, but it looks just the opposite to me.[17]

The high-rise as symbolic value

Despite the drawbacks, we must acknowledge that many slum dwellers are not opposed to rehabilitation schemes and it is important to
understand why. The most obvious reason is that after having lived in a
situation of precariousness, where even the most basic infrastructure and
intimacy is missing, the shift to a brand-new high-rise apartment, with
running water, is a real improvement in living conditions. A less obvious
but equally important factor is the desire to obtain a legitimate status as
a citizen of the city, and of the country. Slum dwellers are typically called
squatters and encroachers by the authorities, indicating that they have
no right or status as citizens. Owning a flat means belonging to the city
at last. Thus the readiness to move from slum structures to a high-rise
often reflects not so much the meeting of essential needs as the desire to
achieve higher status in relative terms. Status is in turn a function of the
social gaze (or 'regard'), as Adam Smith once observed.[18] The symbolic
value of residing in a building in a city such as Mumbai, where most of
the population is said to be living in slums, is so high that it sometimes
prevails over other costs, such as distance from work or the breakdown
of social networks.

Officially though, the argument to move to a high-rise is made at a
more fundamental level: through the belief that such structures supposedly absorb more people on a smaller footprint of land, and this is
inevitably desirable in a dense, crowded city such as Mumbai. Architect

Charles Correa has critiqued this point effectively in his seminal work *The New Landscape*.[19] He points out that the maths is not as straightforward as it sounds. The higher you go, the greater surface of land you need to secure the trappings of a higher standard of living, which include open space, facilities for cars and wider roads, and other infrastructure. Such trappings also come with greater maintenance costs. Unless the economy and ecology of the whole city is strong enough, the high-rise structure, if presented as a stand-alone solution to solve the problem of low-cost housing, is a deceptive affair. It only releases land that is ultimately filled by more buildings and infrastructure.

Moreover, the higher the building, the higher the status and income of its dwellers, hence the more space they use per capita. This results in similar density levels to those found in the low-rise, high-density clusters of urban villages, or so-called slums. The only reason such disproportionate use of land is acceptable is because it yields more short-term gains. There is no justification to use the high-rise as a standard typology for social housing projects on the common but misguided assumption that they absorb more people per square unit of land. Shorn of a deep understanding of the complex patterns of spatial use by people of different economic needs and backgrounds, such policies only produce the same dystopic urban forms that have already failed in cities such as Chicago, Paris, and many other places whose policymakers have attempted to engineer solutions to their own chronic housing crises.

In Mumbai, there seems to be a necessary trade-off between living in a high-rise building and being a legitimate citizen versus living in a slum and being a squatter. In the former case, there is the offer of status and the provision of basic infrastructure, and possibly (depending on the schemes) access to capital in the form of a property; in the latter, there are economic opportunities, a social network, and (depending on the situation) a relative freedom to improve one's own habitat. It is our contention that this trade-off is produced by faulty policies, inadequate regulations, and vested interests that artificially turn housing into a scarce resource, creating markets for the construction industry and increasing real estate value.[20]

Already in the 1970s, the philosopher Ivan Illich rightly criticized the regulatory apparatus that makes it nearly impossible for the vast majority of people to build their own homes, making them dependent on a web of industries and financial institutions for the provision of loans needed for the purchase of living and working spaces.[21] Habitats built outside of any regulatory frameworks may seem utopian, but this is how most of

Mumbai was produced. This is also true of Tokyo after the Pacific War, when most of its neighbourhoods had been destroyed.[22]

Even without advocating for a world free of regulation, we can see how Dharavi and many so-called slums throughout Mumbai could benefit from an approach that would first recognize the value of what has been built incrementally over generations, including a mind-boggling network of ad hoc water pipes and sewerage lines. The urban morphology produced by a piecemeal development process of many settlements from Mumbai to Tokyo should not be dismissed simply because they have not been master-planned or because their looks do not conform to what we expect of modern neighbourhoods. Many localities in Tokyo have much in common with Mumbai's low-rise, high-density residential clusters, though one may, from a Mumbai vantage point, find it laughable to refer to Tokyo's neighbourhoods as slums. But if all that separates one from the other is the presence of civic amenities, infrastructure, and services, then why should Mumbai's neighbourhoods not also be provided those?

In fact, Tokyo's low-rise, high-density neighbourhoods represent a de facto alternative to the idea that urban planning needs a clean slate. The state of the art in urban planning, design, and architecture is dealing with the existing fabric, reinventing what already exists, and taking inspiration from unique situations, rather than clearing what is there in order to impose the kind of generic urbanism we know all too well. It is time we accept that speculation-driven urbanism does not produce affordability – only more crises. Affordability, sustainability, economic development, and a sense of identity come from the recognition of forces embedded in each locality and the support of local initiative, along with what Tokyo does so well: managing (rather than planning) urban space.

Use value vs exchange value of space

We observe that in the so-called slum economy, the value of space is optimized by its use as a means of production, which we refer to as *intensive* use, while in the so-called formal economy, the value of space tends to be disconnected from its actual use. Instead, the value of space increases with its tradability. We refer to this use of space as *speculative*. These two modes of valuation have a deep impact on urban forms and their uses. Moreover, they appear to be somewhat in competition, with intensive uses being aggressively preyed upon by promoters and developers of speculative spaces.

The typologies of the slum and the high-rise correspond to extreme versions of intensive use and speculative spaces. On one side, a plot of land in a slum cannot be left empty even for a week before being occupied and used. On the other side, we have an industry that can generate enormous speculative value on property by trading it multiple times while leaving it empty. In the speculative realm, empty space is more valuable than occupied space since it is more easily tradable. The value of such space is abstract to the extent that it relies on uncertain notions of what it may be worth in the future. It is determined by the broader economic and financial context rather than intrinsic values or the activities it permits. Since it is used as a commodity, the value of speculative spaces is thus contingent on the capacity of traders to define its boundaries precisely. Informal settlements with their fuzzy ownership patterns and disputed boundaries need to be mapped out and audited before they acquire any speculative value. This is precisely what slum rehabilitation schemes do: they transform intensely used spaces into speculative spaces.

The impact of slum rehabilitation schemes on urban form but also on ground-level economic activity can hardly be overemphasized. Turning one's own intensive space into speculative space is the trade-off being offered to slum dwellers who typically accept to move from a two-level structure, where they live and run business, to a new 225-square-foot apartment cell on the fifth floor of a building, completely disconnected from the street economy. They trade the use value of a means of production for the speculative value of a real estate asset. At the level of the city, this means that the process of formalization comes at the price of reducing the intensity of use and creating a clear distinction between living space and working space.

This fragmentation is typically presented as social progress. But in real terms it comes down to buying slum dwellers off their current economic activity and destroying a process of incremental development that has proved its worth by providing employment and housing to hundreds of thousands of migrants to the city. If we are to bring back any meaning to the concept of *development*, it is time we understood the intensive process of urbanization in cities such as Mumbai, with their successes and failures regarding slum rehabilitation.

Unfortunately, government officials, urban planners, and mainstream commentators are predisposed to a certain kind of land use and urban forms – in particular, high-rise structures with multiple, standardized units that have to absorb a maximum of residents at the lowest cost, on the smallest piece of land possible. The process is expensive and depends on the government to audit space, as well as on the market for subsidizing the redevelopment. It is shaped by the pressure not just to absorb surplus populations but simultaneously to supply more land for the real estate market. This land can then officially be used for speculative purposes. Whether it occupies huge footprints or remains unutilized does not really matter as long as it achieves the purpose of converting slum land to formal land.

A classic illustration of what typically precedes such a process, equally relevant today as in 2003, was the blueprint published by consulting firm McKinsey & Company on how to transform Mumbai into a world-class city within ten years.[23] Among other things, it called for dramatically increasing the supply of low-income housing and moving manufacturing to the countryside so as to turn Mumbai into a consumption centre.

The first obvious problem is that low-income housing is typically out of reach of the poorest segments of the population, and instead serves the needs of the employed classes. Moreover, moving manufacturing out of the city means depriving millions of self-employed workers of their livelihood and consequently making the provision of low-income housing completely redundant, since there is no way for them to afford it. A lot of manufacturing takes place not in factories but in sweatshops and home units embedded in homegrown settlements. Even industrial units depend on such spaces for ancillary services and supplying small parts that the factories need for their own production. This mesh gets disrupted the moment manufacturing is pushed out. The intensive use of space – typical of the live–work conditions of the poorest – comes under attack in the name of providing affordable housing.

'Vision Mumbai', the McKinsey blueprint, was sharply rejected by the city's activists and politicians. In fact, it became politically suicidal to mention the 'Shanghaization of Mumbai', a catchphrase that was widely circulated in the publicity of the report.[24]

When speculative logic prevails, the real estate and construction industries dominate urban development. This comes at the cost of local economic activities, including neighbourhood-based businesses, retail, and services. As urbanists are aware, construction is often mistaken as a marker of economic health, when in fact the construction industry may be contributing very little to the city. Real estate development artificially increases the price of space; rising costs make it particularly difficult for people who cannot invest but need homes to buy or rent at affordable rates. At the same time, this does not stop the mass construction of housing projects that find their markets in the world of investment or luxury. Locked-up homes and empty high-rises shouldering over-crowded tenements is a common sight in many cities where the real estate lobby has muscled its way through the corridors of urban power.

In fact, speculative logic is producing empty urban shells all around the globe, fed as it is by the same financial markets that periodically collapse under the weight of the bubbles they create. The skyline of Mumbai is full of spectral constructions waiting to be inhabited by an elusive Indian middle class. In this respect, Mumbai is indeed follow-ing Shanghai, which after years of speculative investment is feeling the impact of overproduction.[25] The most dramatic example of speculative development is of course Dubai, notoriously competing with itself to hit the sky and producing millions of empty square feet of office space along the way.

But this is not only happening in rapidly developing cities. The occu-pancy of the iconic and ill-fated World Trade Center twin towers in New York was at around two-thirds of capacity even after all its years of exis-tence before the tragedy of 9/11. Since speculative value is tightly related to status, which is measured in terms of height, investors and developers do not much care whether full occupancy is achieved. More floors add value to the whole building, irrespective of actual use.

The intensive city, on the other hand, derives value only from actual use. This creates space that, for better or worse, is optimally occupied round the clock, since it is used as a means of production in a context of economic survival. It is produced out of sheer need by local actors rather than real estate developers.

This intensive process generates an environment that may be lacking many aspects of modern comfort, but which is free from the imposi-tion of any spatial dogma – especially the modern rule that living and working spaces must be segregated. It ultimately produces a great variety of forms, structures, and styles in response to means and needs. It is this flexibility that allows for a higher degree of absorption of populations, especially when they are part of the informal economy or belong to the poorer segments. With time, neighbourhoods generated through inten-sive use can be retrofitted with high-quality infrastructure and become perfectly nice places to live.

Tokyo's urban morphology reveals what could happen in Mumbai if, instead of being eradicated, slums were allowed to consolidate into neighbourhoods. The contrasting examples of Mumbai and Tokyo show

how these cities are typically a mix of intensive and speculative forces, and how historical and cultural factors affect the degree to which the intensive and speculative logics merge or break away from each other. How exactly the interstices and overlaps between these spatial-temporal regimes are negotiated varies greatly, as we demonstrate in the next section. In Mumbai, the legacy of speculative planning ideals has produced a sharply divided cityscape. In a city such as Tokyo, on the other hand, a more ambiguous and syncretistic understanding of habitats has allowed a new model to emerge, where combinations of speculative and intensive developments coexist at various scales in what could be described as a harmonious and well-managed urban mess. We explore the case of Tokyo's homegrown neighbourhoods in Chapter 7.

Intensive city vs real estate speculation

The landscape of the intensive city follows a multidirectional logic. It allows for numerous temporalities to coexist, epitomized in different kinds of economic practice: rural, artisanal, post-industrial, or high-tech. It can tear itself down and build afresh. It does not have fixed templates or business models to follow, and therefore it is flexible in its approach to construction and rebuilding. Its built environment combines residential, productive, and recreational spaces, often compressed in the same space-time.

Dharavi is perhaps the best example of a settlement developed through intensive processes. Hundreds of thousands of actors over several generations have incrementally developed a fully functioning settlement and a vibrant economy. Yet careful observation shows that the intensive and speculative are not necessarily working in opposition, even in Dharavi. In fact, at a micro level, Dharavi is full of investment by its residents, who see in their houses an important asset that could take value over time. What prevents speculative value from taking over intensive use in Dharavi is the fact that property is insecure, which is both positive and negative. It ensures that residents cannot be bought out by speculators from outside the neighbourhood, but it also makes it more difficult for residents to invest in their own houses. Any investment must be quickly recovered through use.

The incremental development of Dharavi is contingent on a specific bet on the future by all of its residents and entrepreneurs. The looming redevelopment project backed by the government, for Dharavi, makes it difficult for residents and business owners to invest in their houses and shops. Given the uncertain future, many residents are renouncing improvement projects, focusing instead on the optimal exploitation of existing resources. Thus, real estate speculation in the form of the Dharavi Redevelopment Project (DRP) is slowing down another sort of ground-level speculation led by the residents themselves.

The reverse is also true, as the speculative economy continues to generate its own slums, which often become permanent and relatively autonomous. For example, countless shacks have been built around construction sites. In Mumbai, makeshift structures where construction workers stay accompany every construction site and become the starting point of a slum housing the population that serves the residents of the new buildings. The development of shelters and spaces and the presence of services and commerce are conjoined economic activities in their own right.

In fact, construction often triggers other economic activity in very direct ways. Its residents generate their own services, and stimulate a demand for sales of goods for homes and domestic needs that then become integral to the locality. This process is typical of construction projects in many developing cities. The long periods of construction mean the workers sometimes settle down for a few years and generate the creation of a settlement.

In a study of the urban development of Brasília, the anthropologist David Epstein observes how construction workers developed the first favela of this perfectly planned city. They had nowhere else to go and were able to find economic opportunities in the new capital. Interestingly, the improvised settlements of Brasília are reportedly much more vibrant than the master-planned capital can ever hope to be.[26]

Invariably, unplanned settlements are deeply connected to the metropolitan economy around them. Far from being parasitic, marginal, or self-sustained, they are constantly servicing the city. This relationship is usually recognized and valued by businesses and private employers, since it constitutes an indirect subsidy of their activities. Such a relationship of mutual dependency between large businesses and the local provider is again neither unique to Mumbai nor found only in the context of slums. The speculative city is full of cracks and contradictions. Saskia Sassen has described familiar informal systems operating in neighbourhoods in Manhattan, with their own deep web of local businesses operating in the shadow of the skyscrapers, providing printing, cleaning, and food services essential to the functioning of the city.[27]

At the street level also, the integration of the informal and the formal is done through trade and services. In cities with a high level of tolerance to street activity and bazaars, such as Mumbai and Tokyo, local economic operators play a major role to facilitate and support the overlap of these spaces and activities in such neighbourhoods. Tea stalls, fruit vendors, tailors, and clothes presses are a fixture of Indian cities and can be found at every corner of middle-class neighbourhoods in Mumbai. They occupy leftover and in-between spaces, and cater to the needs of residents at discounted slum prices. The same relationship exists inside the homes of middle-class households employing illegal immigrants as houseworkers, carpenters, and cooks.[28]

Reconnecting forms and processes

The relationship between urban and economic development goes both ways. This becomes clear when the morphology of the slums is tolerated and the settlement is allowed to improve over time, turning the slum into a neighbourhood. Narrow pedestrian streets, low-rise buildings, street activity, and village-like communal arrangements are celebrated in some contexts. Tourists love to wander, for example, into dense old European towns, which have preserved these qualities over time.

In some cases, this morphology is even artificially reproduced in planned suburbs. Old European towns and villages are used as models by so-called new urbanists. Unfortunately, these designed habitats usually end up as gated communities or cute-looking themed neighbourhoods devoid of economic substance. This is because the impulses and processes that produce such intentional townships are those of the speculative city. Houses are produced in bulk and sold as commodities. Their value is their market price. They do not support much economic activity within, nor generate much use value beyond being comfortable residential spaces. As much as they try to imitate the form generated by intensive processes in old European towns and villages, such townships belong to another urban and economic logic altogether.

We need to question both: the superficial reproduction of a certain morphology, as well as the dismissal of neighbourhoods that are produced by intensive processes. We cannot accept the form and reject the process (and vice versa). When the imitation is preferred to the original, and reproduction is elevated to the status of an art form, the point is lost. There have been many attempts to capture the nature of vernacular urban order, including in the lifelong work of Christopher Alexander.[29] The processes that energize such orders have often been ignored by architects and theorists of urban form, leading to a soulless new urbanism that is only as new as an imitation can ever be.

What would be genuinely new is an urbanism that acknowledges the invaluable contributions of local actors in the developmental process, and does not judge the quality of urban space on appearance alone but also recognizes the social, cultural, and economic dynamics it sustains, and which in turn sustain it.

Tokyo is here to attest that if these urban processes are recognized and validated, they give rise to environments that can be as developed, functional, and technologically advanced as any modern city, and perhaps more so. The case of Tokyo represents a counterintuitive notion of urbanism that overturns the simplistic categorization of urban habitats in terms of slums and modern cities. It's vital to recognize that such a binary view feeds directly into speculative development.

In contrast, an approach based on the legitimization of intensive processes can liberate thousands of urban neighbourhoods in Asia, Africa, and Latin America from being treated as slums. It can break through Davis's apocalyptic vision, which creates a devastatingly circular logic that traps millions of urban poor into a situation of victimization and criminalization.

Such breakthroughs are not easy. Numerous conflicting interests and visions must be constantly discussed, challenged, and reframed. How does one justify a multibillion-dollar investment in a high-rise that is not actually going to exploit all its vertical space? It is justified by speaking about the jobs its construction creates and its function as an investment magnet, even if some of it is always going to be dead space.

Conversely, why do some cities manage to create a huge stock of rental housing while others do not? Perhaps because they come from a history in which ownership is not prized over occupancy. Similarly, why do some cities retrofit up-to-date technology into mediaeval civic infrastructure so efficiently, while others struggle with this? Perhaps because their inhabitants do not expect to start from a tabula rasa, due to demographic factors and local resistances.

This inevitable, embedded context and specificity of urban life is what produces, at any given point in history, a wide-ranging template of urban choices. No matter how powerful the influence of speculation on the planning process, there are several context-dependent variables that it has to negotiate. That is why anyone interested in developing a healthy urban practice must identify and locate themselves within these contexts, and work collaboratively with the inhabitants who challenge and stretch the limits of these practices. One important move in this direction is to work at the scale of direct human engagement – which is typically the neighbourhood.

Seeing a city as a constellation of neighbourhoods is a strategic way of paying attention to the multitude of details, however uneven and sub-jective, that make up *places*. It is also about understanding the multiple scales which even the most gridlocked or master-planned city has even-tually to acknowledge. As long as human presence, lives, livelihoods, movements, and mobility are the main units of urban life, the scale of neighbourhoods has to be taken as a starting point, no matter what larger calculation you make. And eventually the multiplicity of neigh-bourhoods becomes the unit through which urban formations express themselves, sometimes as a holistic unity – one city – and sometimes as an amorphous, ever-expanding landscape. What the scale of the neigh-bourhood does is allow its inhabitants to become visible, and see their activities and roles, their aspirations and issues, as starting points for collaborative engagement.

What is needed is a sharper documentation of the hugely diverse existing urban forms, especially those that emerge from the shadows of planning regimes or slip below the radar of audit systems. Such forms demonstrate possibilities that must be recognized and named. Newer professional equations need to develop between practitioners and local contexts, so that it becomes absolutely normal for an architectural, design, or planning firm to have sustainable operations in São Paulo's Paraisópolis or Mumbai's Dharavi, as well as in a rich neighbourhood in that city or elsewhere. At a macro planning level, there is an urgent need to define the financial management of local resources, including real estate interests in planning urban agendas and unravelling urban economies tied to strong ownership or occupancy principles, so that a clearer articulation of objectives unfolds.

At the broadest simplified level of urban planning, we typically see a process in which a neighbourhood becomes an object for intervention by professionals. This is followed by a process in which the intervention has to be accepted – or debated and modified and then accepted – before being finally implemented in that location. Rejection is rare. When it happens it usually means a strong presence of conflicting but powerful groups – either because of economic or political clout.

An idealized version of this broad process would avoid the linear approach in favour of one in which visions, plans, and goals are created at the neighbourhood level, making its implementation a collaborative venture.

Of course, the detailing of this easier-said-than-done approach is no less daunting. Local interests are as powerful as larger statist or corporate ambitions, and at no level can one deny the overlap of local, regional, and global dimensions. The neighbourhood is not a bounded unit, in conflict with the regional or national: it is the site of battle and coexistence of all kinds of interests – each of which depend on the socio-economic composition which resides there.

Implications for planning and policy

The ongoing growth, development, and transformation of unplanned settlements can be better achieved by allowing their internal energies, resources, and skills to take over. So far, this internal tendency has rarely been acknowledged or incorporated into planned visions. This is because the narrative of informality makes all residents in such neighbourhoods into de facto squatters; it was also invalidated on architectural grounds, through the belief that its typologies and structures are dysfunctional urban forms because they do not correspond to a certain idea of what a world-class city should look like.

A cynical eye on the situation might immediately recognize the mark of greed and corruption. After all, such neighbourhoods often sit on prime real estate. Governments simply play the game of real estate investors and builders; their land grab is sold to the general public as a social project that will provide decent housing to eligible dwellers and liberate land for the middle class. But misreading urban forms, especially of homegrown settlements, leads even well-intentioned governments to destroy impressive self-developed and self-improving urban ecologies.

This is why it is important to understand such spaces, and to demonstrate how it is both inexact and potentially destructive to reduce them to the sole condition of a slum. Such reduction deprives settlements of any sense of legitimacy and therefore lessens their access to services and infrastructure granted to other parts of the city. To recognize this effect, we must go beyond an analysis of urban form alone to understand it in the context of the processes that generate it. This means challenging our assumptions, and understanding the neighbourhood not just as a physical space occupied by people (that can be surveyed in two dimensions) but as a multidimensional spatial-temporal experience produced by communities, individual histories, and productive activities.

We must learn to understand urban forms of certain neighbourhoods not as objects in space, but as the living expression of productive processes generated by the users themselves. If we could appreciate and communicate this simple idea in our studies, designs, and plans, we would be closer to solving ongoing urban and economic crises in many cities around the world, including rich cities in the throes of affordable-housing shortage.

Any study of generative processes in the context of the urban form in incrementally developing neighbourhoods necessarily includes an economic or productive dimension. This is particularly evident in the example of the tool-house (Chapter 8), which is a residential space as much as an instrument of production, meaning that upgrading it also improves its user-inhabitants' economic condition. Similarly, any construction activity is always necessarily an economic one, in as much as it involves productive skills, labour force, purchase of material, land use, and so on. When local actors get involved in the process of construction, the wealth generated by this economic activity is typically recycled in the local economy. In resource-deprived contexts, mutual help often becomes the currency of exchange for the local production of habitats. When this process intensifies, the local exchange and production of resources, skills, labour, and material give rise to the most improbable urban achievements. It is therefore important to make the overlaps between urban planning and economic development more explicit.

We must understand that cities are variegated spaces with differing economic activities that have evolved in distinct historical contexts. These different economic functions have as many distinct spatial needs that support them. If offices and financial centres that are connected to global markets need segregated office spaces with a high level of connectivity, informal manufacture and local trading need their own special physical expressions and typologies. Cities such as Mumbai have a large sector that includes manufacturing, trading, hawking, and consumption for a population with a low level of income and expenditure. This economy keeps the prices of services in the city globally competitive. The sector can only evolve and grow to provide a better support system to the city as a whole when it has a physical context that can satisfy its needs. If one looks at the economic activities as well as their necessary physical structures as dysfunctional, then large parts of the city can be destroyed with no real loss to the official, formal city. Yet the so-called informal sector is intimately tied to the so-called formal sector: the large labour force that it yields, from semi-skilled office staff to inexpensive-food providers – acting as a subsidized producer of goods for the formal sector – makes the so-called informal an integral part of the official urban economy. If this is recognized, then the spatial needs of such an economy also have to be recognized.

Such recognition will make way for a productive transformation of a significant sector of the city's economy into a more dynamic one. Tokyo's story, at least for the moment of its transformation in the post-war period, will reveal that such dynamism is something that transcends specific cultural and historical explanations of economic growth and may well show the way for many Asian cities, if not for those from other parts of the world, where the question of informality has become an integral part of a city's story.

3

The Road from Illegitimacy to Recognition

Where we stand

Asian and Latin American cities have for long learned to live with the presence of slums, and yet policymakers and planners have been reluctant to normalize them. Slums are highly populated yet politically marginalized, suffering from persistent civic neglect and hostility. How is it that a phenomenon that is so widespread and universal has not been integrated into formal city-making processes?

Municipal authorities are often unable to cope with demographic growth. Rehabilitation is simply out of reach for most cities, which lack the capacity to provide sufficient housing or retrofit existing slums. What we observe is a mix of acceptance and exclusionary policies that has become structural to many cities. Policymakers are unwilling to legitimize certain forms of urban development while actively making it very difficult for existing slums to improve over time.

In Mumbai, the authorities deliberately maintain the status quo. Slums can be equipped with basic infrastructure (community tap water and toilets), but little effort is made to consolidate them into fully functional neighbourhoods. In fact, the municipal government actively prevents them from improving by refusing residents the right to rebuild their houses, by making it illegal to build toilets at home or connect running water, and by constantly reminding slum dwellers that they could be evacuated any time. It leaves settlements with only one path to improvement: clearance and redevelopment.

The enormous human, economic, and urban costs of redevelopment have sometimes pushed planners to test alternatives. There were genuine efforts to promote in situ slum-upgrading policies in the 1970s and 1980s. The World Bank, inspired by the ideas of John F. C. Turner and others, financed ambitious projects in Indian and Latin American cities.[1] Although these schemes were not perceived to be successful at the time, they produced long-lasting results, which could have opened the way to more sensible policies towards slums (discussed in Chapter 5). Unfortunately, from the 1990s all the way to the 2020s, there has been a reactionary turn to a crude attitude towards slums. They are seen as urban failures that should be redeveloped sooner rather than later. Their inhabitants are not perceived as legitimate citizens, agents of change, and actors of their own development, but rather as rural migrants invading cities and squatting on government land. Instead of engaging with slum dwellers, municipal authorities incentivize real estate developers to replace existing settlements with high-rise social housing.

Yet, there is ample evidence that the skills and means to improve slums exist within them. We have worked with local builders in the most vulnerable parts of Mumbai, New Delhi, São Paulo, Bogotá, and Cali. Each time we have seen artisans of construction priding themselves in their work, gaining the trust of their clients one house at a time, and gradually transforming the slum, favela, or barrio into liveable neighbourhoods. In each of these neighbourhoods, we have seen sophisticated economies of construction at work, with industrial building materials reaching deep inside settlements; specialized skills embedded in the community are transmitted from one generation to the next. We have met countless inhabitants with a good understanding of construction, willing and able to contribute to the design of their homes. We have observed construction processes that are so lean and efficient that no large-scale corporation could compete. We have also seen how the urban fabric generated by residents embeds history, culture, and local networks.

Why do planning authorities and policymakers fail to see the value of such urban fabric? On what grounds do we justify the replacement of incrementally improving mixed-used neighbourhoods, in which residents have invested much effort and capital, with low-quality mass housing? Indeed, the problem is not just with the clearing of habitats that represent huge investment over generations – it is their replacement by substandard housing.

We know that mass housing, especially when it is high-rise and hyperdense, is problematic at all levels: urban, social, economic, and environmental. We have seen this typology fail in rich countries, which built

mass housing to accommodate the working-class and migrant populations in the twentieth century. Apart from a few notable exceptions, these
have created terrible living environments at enormous social cost. Policymakers have learned nothing from Jane Jacobs's stringent critique, made
over sixty years ago: 'Look what we have built ... Low-income projects
that become worse centers of delinquency, vandalism and general social
hopelessness than the slums they were supposed to replace.'[2]

What has been happening for the past thirty years in Asian cities
is a supersized version of the same failed mass-housing projects that
were built in Europe and the US in the second part of the twentieth
century. How is it that even after witnessing countless sad, sometimes
inhumane mass-housing schemes, decision makers still cannot let go of
an approach to urban development that we know has a stubborn tendency to create poor, sterile, and unsustainable living spaces? Why are
cities still stuck in a pattern that damages them and makes their citizens
worse off in the long run?

The answers seem to be: first, decision makers are not motivated by
the well-being of end users; second, most cities know how to deliver
mass housing, but not how to make slum improvement work; and third,
the vested interests of real estate developers dominate urban development, as we analysed in the previous chapter.

Slum dwellers have no say in the process, because they are considered
illegitimate. It is also simply easier to plan a redevelopment project than
an improvement scheme. The mechanics of mass-housing construction
are well oiled; it can be neatly planned by municipal services and their
consultants. Financial institutions know how to inject capital in the
construction of housing and collect interest on it. Architects know how
to optimize space and maximize returns for their clients, who are the
investors. Construction companies know the drill and can supply mass
housing relatively efficiently. In short, everything is in place to deliver
poor-quality urbanism on a large scale. Everyone seems to benefit from
it, except of course the people who will have to live in these buildings, and
except also the city at large, which gets degraded through these schemes
instead of being upgraded. The kind of urbanism generated through
planned redevelopment and mass housing turns inhabitants into passive
residents of lifeless buildings. Rather than supporting the consolidation
of neighbourhoods that are full of potential, this system produces no-go
zones and hopeless ghettos, with little scope for improvement.

It is surprising that few people question the politics of clearance
and redevelopment. Why don't we spend more energy on developing

alternatives? Why do professionals like us, who are convinced that upgrading makes more sense than clearance, struggle to create a practice around it? It took us years to develop solutions in India and Colombia; they are based on collaboration with residents and local artisans of construction and receive no support from the municipal authorities.

There is a huge industry around slum clearance, but very little incentive to upgrade – except, of course, for the dwellers themselves. These local resources are apparently invisible to policymakers, urban planners, and the media. If there is one key point we would like to make in this book, it is this: residents are much better than developers at improving their own neighbourhoods, and policies that recognize this will bring huge benefits not only to the concerned populations but to the city at large.

Slum dwellers, in particular, spend vast amounts to improve their homes, despite policies that often actively discourage them from doing so. They would spend much more if they could do it with the blessing of the authorities. It is not only that many slum dwellers lack proper security of tenure, even those who have it have to work their way through an unimaginable series of bureaucratic hurdles to get a permit to improve their homes. In fact, residents in some parts of Mumbai deliberately avoid making their house look good in order to prevent attention from municipal officers. People even make extra efforts to ensure that recently refurbished homes look old and shabby.

Sometimes an entire settlement is artificially maintained in a slummy state. Shivaji Nagar, in Govandi, Mumbai was planned as a resettlement zone in the 1980s. The municipality always treated it as a slum, harassing residents who, on their own, had managed to bring running water to their homes. Residents are not even allowed to cover the rainwater drains running through their streets. Shivaji Nagar's resident builders are experts at dealing with constraints that would make most architects baulk: scarcity of space and resources; muddy, marshy ground; and lack of municipal services. They can deal with the most challenging of obstacles, but the biggest inevitably remains the hostile bureaucratic and regulatory context, which incentivizes bribery and deception.

The improvement dynamics at work in marginalized settlements must be acknowledged and the government must provide badly lacking infrastructure and services. It is time for the authorities to revise their policies towards slums, recognize occupancy rights and cut the red tape, allowing residents to consolidate their neighbourhoods. For this to happen, the government must turn the page over several decades of failed slum rehabilitation policy and realize that the most sustainable path is the one that residents have carved for themselves.

Sadly, this is unlikely to happen. There is a deep prejudice against slums and slum dwellers. The word *slum* evokes the worst possible living conditions, yet it is used to describe a wide range of habitats. In India, it is used to describe any urban settlement that's dense, built locally, unplanned, and underserviced. A large part of the world population lives in neighbourhoods that fit this description, reminding us that these characteristics are not the exception but the rule.

The labels *slum* and *informal settlement* have been instrumentalized to justify discriminatory policies. It is time we radically reverse the way we look at dense, locally built settlements. Instead of understanding them from a technocratic planning standpoint, we must see them from within, from the point of view of the inhabitants and local builders who are actively engaged in improving their habitat. In order to do that, we should start by trusting our subjective feelings of being energized in the streets of Dharavi, Shivaji Nagar, Paraisópolis, Complexo do Alemão, Cazuca, or Siloé: small houses; crowded streets; shops on the ground floor; people walking purposefully to their homes after work, or taking a cup of tea through the window of a house doubling up as a snack corner; tired, smiling faces; neighbourhood conversations and squabbles – these are no villa miseria. They are human habitats teeming with life, struggling to consolidate, often conflicted, usually vulnerable, but also incredibly resilient in the face of challenges. That may sound trivial, but if we don't address our prejudices and preconceived notions about slums and slum dwellers, we – as a society – will stay stuck in self-defeating patterns. This is not a romantic vision but a grounded, pragmatic one, based on years of work in so-called slums. It is a vision that rejects the narrative of urban and social transformation through clearance and development, which cynically justifies eviction by evoking misery.

How many times have we introduced visitors to Dharavi, where our office is located (including people who live in Mumbai) and heard them say that it did not correspond to their preconceived notion of the place? We have often found ourselves in Indian and Latin American settlements that are supposed to be hell-holes, only to discover nice streets with kids playing, people going about their business, and always a few houses being rebuilt or improved by local artisans. This is not an idealized vision; rather, it's a reality that cannot be seen from a distance. No one is saying that things are perfect in Dharavi, Paraisópolis, Siloé, or Cazuca. These are all difficult, sometimes extremely difficult places.

People struggle economically; they have to deal with inadequate facilities and years of institutional neglect and structural violence. This does not cancel out the necessity of improving their habitat, with as much institutional support as possible. These neighbourhoods need the same service provision as any other part of the city. What they don't need is indifference, condescension, and paternalism.

Slum and prejudice

In *The Argumentative Indian*, Amartya Sen discusses the importance of 'acceptance' in India's multiculturalist tradition. Tracing its origin to the Sanskrit word *swikriti*, he presents it as an enduring feature of the subcontinent's social ethos. Sen describes how the 'inclusiveness of pluralist toleration in India has tended mainly to take the form of accepting different groups of persons as authentic members of the society, with a right to follow their own beliefs and own customs'.[3] He argues that in India acceptance of the other provided a fertile ground for democratic and egalitarian politics. He notes, however, that although it implies political equality, acceptance does not automatically extend to the 'promotion of social and economic equality'. India is marked by sharp contrasts between an inclusive political sphere and a polarized society. The persistence of a profound class and caste divide (and general lack of concern about the living conditions of the poor) is symbolized by the presence of shacks in close proximity to exclusive residential towers in Indian cities, an image that is often used to represent the heterogeneous reality of Mumbai.

Passive pluralistic tolerance easily mutates into fatalism and indifference. Acceptance lays the foundation for communitarianism and casteism. Slavoj Žižek argues that the global celebration of tolerance and multiculturalism conceals a form of 'racism with a distance':

> It respects the identity of the other, conceiving it as an 'authentic' community, but it fails to provide the ground for an inter-communal solidarity based on an understanding that the living conditions of the poorest are a matter of concern for society as a whole.[4]

In a lecture focusing on the condition of formerly untouchable castes and poor Muslim communities in India, anthropologist Peter van der Veer questioned the persistence of poverty and filth in Indian cities in the face of the country's economic rise.[5] He observes that economic growth and the rise of the middle class have not meant better sanitation for the urban poor. Looking at urban development through the lens of caste, he describes how the opposition between inside and outside spaces allows an upper-caste family to keep their house pristine inside while dumping their garbage just outside its walls. According to Van der Veer, in the village as in the city, in traditional India as in modern India, the outside must tolerate garbage and human filth.

Indeed, accepting the other as someone who belongs to a different reality in which separate standards apply contributes to perpetuating the sharpest inequalities. The maid who works in a luxurious residential building and lives in a shack next to it may be denied access to municipal water, but her employer may not consider this to be an injustice. This is because, no matter how close the bonds between the maid and the employer may be, the two belong to different worlds and cannot therefore perceive each other as equals with the same rights to the city. We can accept the circumstances of the other while categorically refusing such conditions for oneself. Indeed, the maid herself may well not complain: she might have accepted a historically rooted difference or feel forced to accept it for economic survival. The situation may not prevent her from being treated as a part of the family – as long as her otherness is constantly reaffirmed. The distance provided by caste ensures that there is no resentment or pity complicating matters between her and her employer.

We find an expression of this social equation reproduced on a larger scale – in the development plan of Mumbai, which leaves large patches of land blank, designating them as slum areas, which presumably implies that they are not worthy of (or not entitled to) being mapped. The word *slum* is used casually in academic and professional circles as a way to describe unplanned settlements where poor people live. In Mumbai, there is a clear overlap between caste and slums.

According to statistical data provided by the government, we can infer that a large proportion of slum dwellers are from Dalit (once derogatorily known as untouchable), indigenous, and marginalized castes, including poor Muslim and Christian communities.[6] In India, the word *slum* does not only describe a kind of habitat or living conditions but also indicates the social background of its inhabitants. Journalist and columnist Swaminathan Anklesaria Aiyar, points out that slums are 'entry-points of the poor into the land of urban opportunity' for those who come from a history of ethnic discrimination from rural areas. He even states, emphatically: 'We need more slums.'[7]

Aiyar, like most journalists, accepts slums as the de facto reality of low-caste and poor Muslim communities. He may not question why neighbourhoods where Dalits live should be called slums and treated differently to those nearby settled by other communities – yet he believes that the term gives an inaccurate representation. He points out: 'The census description of slums as "unfit for human habitation" is highly misleading. In fact, census data prove that slums are much better off than villages, which are presumably fit for habitation.' He backs this claim with evidence from the census:

> As many as 90% of slum dwellers have electricity, against barely half of rural households. Ownership of cell phones (63.5%) is as high among slum dwellers as richer urban households and way above rural rates. One-tenth of slums have computers, and 51% have cooking gas (not far short of 65 per cent of total urban households). Amazingly, more slum households (74 per cent) have tap water than total urban households (70.6 per cent).[8]

In light of such discussions, we are compelled to ask why we should call these areas slums in the first place. In other words, we must ask about the definition of a slum. Is it not, after all, simply a name for areas where marginalized populations live?

According to the United Nations Task Force in Improving the Lives of Slum Dwellers, a slum is 'a group of individuals living under the same roof lacking one or more of the following necessities: access to improved water, access to improved sanitation, sufficient living area, structural quality and durability of dwellings, and security of tenure.'[9] By this definition, many people in Mumbai and all over the world live in slums. Indeed, according to the UN, the number of slum dwellers has been steadily increasing to over 1 billion today, with 2 billion more expected in the next thirty years.[10]

The definition used by the authorities in Mumbai is equally broad. According to the Maharashtra Slum Areas (Improvement, Clearance and Redevelopment) Act, 1971, the competent authorities can declare a slum area:

> (a) any area is or may be a source of danger to the health, safety or convenience of the public of that area or of its neighbourhood, by reason of the area having inadequate or no basic amenities, or being insanitary, squalid, overcrowded or otherwise; or

(b) the buildings in any area, used or intended to be used for human habitation are –

(i) in any respect, unfit for human habitation; or

(ii) by reasons of dilapidation, overcrowding, faulty arrangement and design of such building, narrowness or faulty arrangement of streets, lack of ventilation, light or sanitation facilities or any combination of these factors, detrimental to the health, safety or convenience of the public of that area[11]

We do not contest these definitions; however, they must be contextualized. Their use may actually reflect a progressive policy agenda aimed at improving the living conditions of those who are most in need. When the act was written, having the place where they lived formally declared a slum area was for people to claim access to basic services. The act granted slum dwellers the right to be resettled in the event of a clearance. However, in practice this was and remains an insecure process.[12]

The power to declare a slum area and decide whether it should be cleared was – and still is – being used by some officials to extract rent or votes from slum dwellers. To date, there seem to be more incentives for the authorities to maintain the status quo and even at times to allow planned settlements to become slums than to improve them.[13] According to a report from the World Bank, the reason behind the failure of the ambitious slum-upgrading programme it financed in the mid-1980s (which we describe in Chapter 11) in Mumbai was political interference.

Instead of empowering slum dwellers to improve their settlements, the municipal government leverages the land value of slums on public ground to finance redevelopment, essentially privatizing public property. This created a developer-government nexus, which resulted in an increase of irregular activities that keep surfacing with not-so-surprising regularity.

The quality of housing produced through redevelopment schemes is usually poor. New buildings quickly turn insalubrious and maintenance is costly for their inhabitants. Many beneficiaries of the scheme may be tempted to sell their flats to middle-class families who cannot find anything better in their budget; then they move to another slum or leave the city altogether.

After decades of failed policies, about half of Mumbaikars still live in slum areas. Yet there remains no incentive for the authorities to improve the condition of existing slums. The default strategy is to let settlements degrade to the point that slum dwellers are ready to accept resettlement.[14]

Slums are raw material for redevelopment projects benefiting municipal officers, politicians, and promoters.

The alternative we propose is to abandon the slum categorization altogether and simply consider all parts of the city as legitimate neighbourhoods with an equal right to access municipal services. Securing the tenure of dwellings built on government land is straightforward and does not require ownership or privatization. The in situ upgrading schemes promoted by the World Bank in the 1980s allowed slum dwellers to create housing cooperatives, which is a perfect means to promote participatory improvement. The land on which slums are built can remain in public hands, which would avoid speculation, or if the government isn't willing, it could be placed in a public trust with a mission to hold the land.

None of this is rocket science, and versions of this have been proposed by many activists, progressive architects, and NGOs. What is required, however, is a much more nuanced approach to planning that involves the active participation of residents and municipal authorities in co-designed improvement programmes. Some slum dwellers associations already manage to collaborate and redevelop their own areas – something that is allowed in theory but extremely difficult in practice. Being in control of the process and the finance, they manage to produce much better housing than a real estate developer would.

Even in the absence of any programme or scheme, a lot can be done by simply allowing inhabitants to improve their homes incrementally. For this to happen, we must trust people's ability to come together and manage their own settlements. Having worked in Dharavi for over fifteen years, we have full faith in people's capacity to improve their own condition even in the most challenging context. This is what people have already done over generations. There is nothing easy or smooth about it, but what has seemed to prevail in Dharavi in times of hardship is cooperation and solidarity, not chaos and disorder. The amazing mobilization of local leaders and community groups during the COVID lockdown is a case in point.

We are convinced that urban planning departments must be involved at the local level, supporting the process without necessarily leading it. Getting involved does not mean dominating or imposing blanket solutions. A good approach must be found within existing dynamics, not imagined from the upper echelons of public administration, architectural offices, or universities.

In search of the slum

Dharavi's story is about consistently pushing back the boundaries of the slum. Go to Koliwada, its oldest settlement, and ask for the slum. Residents will say this is a 400-year-old village; the slum, they will inform you, is on the other side of Dharavi Main Road. Across, in the direction they are pointing, you will find a scattering of overgrown municipal chawls. Those tenants, who have been renting their apartments from the government for decades, will in turn point to their neighbours who live in structures that look exactly like theirs and insist that those are the slums, not their homes. Their neighbours will say that their houses are better than many middle-class houses in other parts of the city, pointing to their flat-screen TVs, high-speed-fibre connections, and video-surveillance systems to support their argument. They will direct you to the Thirteenth Compound, where the recycling industry is located. That's probably where the slum is – at least it looks and feels like one. Yet in the Thirteenth Compound people will say that this is an industrial area, not quite a slum, and perhaps those huts over there – gesturing to the edge of the settlement – are what you're looking for. You may finally see lines of shack-like structures, which fit your general idea of a slum.

That is the place where you might spot a little girl walking on a huge waterpipe next to what seems to be her home. You immediately recognize a picture you've seen a dozen times before – one that is frequently used to illustrate articles and documentaries on the apocalypse of urban life, the perfect symbol of a planet studded by slums. The girl may inform you that the redevelopment project for Dharavi is a threat, not an opportunity, if she cannot prove she has been living here long enough. In all probability, her family moved there quite recently, a few years short of the cut-off date that makes her eligible for a flat after redevelopment. In that case, she and her family would either move to a settlement far away or simply return to their ancestral village.

When asked what life is like, living in a slum, she would probably say it is tough – with open drains and very little civic infrastructure – but she would also invite you inside her house, introduce you to her family, shut the door and insist that the slum is now firmly outside. This is her home – complete with an altar to a popular saint, cooking utensils hanging on the wall, maybe even a TV in a corner, and schoolbooks on the floor – and to call it anything else would embarrass you. Especially when you accept a cup of sweet tea and are told that, for all its ills, this place is still better than the one left behind.

It may sound trivial to question the validity of the terms *slum* or *informal settlement*. Yet, without addressing the huge gap in perception between policymakers and the actual dynamics of incrementally developing neighbourhoods, there is little scope for constructive engagement, and inhabitants are facing destruction and hardship rather than a future they can build for themselves. Depriving people of their habitat is to deprive them of all the opportunities that come with access to the city. The vast majority of slum dwellers are not fresh migrants but urban natives who have occupied and invested in their settlements for years, often over several generations.

The way marginalized neighbourhoods are described in the media and in academic and professional circles matters. Perception directly impacts decision-making. Dismissing a settlement as a slum legitimizes clearance and displacement of the inhabitants – either for their own good or because they are perceived as squatters.

Such othering, indifference, and condescension needs to make way for recognition, empathy, and support. This is a serious task that should challenge ethnographers, architects, planners, and economists. Engaging with rather than dismissing slums is hard work; it means discovering and unlocking the cultural, social, and economic possibilities that have been concealed.

This work starts with interrogating our own biases. Are we calling a settlement a slum simply because it does not correspond to our preconceived notion of what a neighbourhood should look like? Does it look disorderly because we don't understand its structure?

According to French philosopher Henri Bergson, disorder does not exist; there is only order in disguise, which we have yet to discover.[15] The efforts of practitioners have so far mostly focused on proposing solutions to the taken-for-granted problem of informality, but often without much understanding of the dynamics at work in the settlements.

An illustration of this attitude is the '$300 house' project, which was initiated by two management experts from one of America's top business schools.[16] The project, which presented itself as a 'business opportunity as well as a charitable endeavour', aimed to benefit 'participating companies'.

> First, they will be able to serve the unserved, the 2.5 billion who make up the bottom of the pyramid. Second, they will create new competencies which can help transform lives in rich countries by creating breakthrough innovations.

The project organizers initially assumed that informal settlements were a prime market for their product, without any kind of prior study of the economy and practice of home building in any part of the world where the poorest '2.5 billion' people live. They also assumed that poor people live in 'self-built houses' that are 'usually built from materials that are available – cardboard, plastic, mud or clay, metal scraps and whatever else is nearby'.

The much-hyped $300 house project was wholeheartedly supported by the *Harvard Business Review* and praised by the *Economist*. In response, we published an op-ed in the *New York Times* in which we questioned the project's fundamentals:

> We work in Dharavi, a neighbourhood in Mumbai that has become a one-stop shop for anyone interested in 'slums' (that catchall term for areas lived in by the urban poor). We recently showed around a group of Dartmouth students involved in the project who are hoping to get a better grasp of their market. They had imagined a ready-made constituency of slum-dwellers eager to buy a cheap house that would necessarily be better than the shacks they'd built themselves. But the students found that the reality here is far more complex than their business plan suggested.
>
> To start with, space is scarce. There is almost no room for new construction or ready-made houses. Most residents are renters, paying $20 to $100 a month for small apartments.
>
> Those who own houses have far more equity in them than $300 – a typical home is worth at least $3,000. Many families have owned their houses for two or three generations, upgrading them as their incomes increase. With additions, these homes become what we call 'tool houses', acting as workshops, manufacturing units, warehouses and shops. They facilitate trade and production, and allow homeowners to improve their living standards over time.[17]

The $300 house project reflects the way parts of the city are taken for granted and dismissed, even by those who pretend to care for the people who live there and who present themselves as experts. The language used to describe neighbourhoods built incrementally by marginalized populations is partly to blame. New concepts and entry points must be generated, based on observations and engagement with various types of neighbourhoods in the city.

The narrative of informality

Ananya Roy proposes that new concepts must address the 'inevitable heterogeneity of Southern urbanism', and these are not limited to the study of so-called informal settlements alone.[18] According to her, the recognition of subaltern spaces 'tends to remain bound to the study of spaces of poverty, of essential forms of popular agency, of the habitus of the dispossessed, of the entrepreneurialism of self-organising economies'.[19] Indeed, if cultural diversity is celebrated as an essential feature of modern cities, diversity of built forms should equally be celebrated, or at least recognized. When it is not the case, a city such as Mumbai gets reduced to the extreme typologies of the slum and the high-rise, ignoring everything in between.

Mumbai encompasses a great diversity of habitats, including working-class chawls, colonial architecture, historical villages, and vernacular homegrown settlements. There is even a deep rural–urban continuum linking villages to so-called slums that have been built by people arriving from the countryside. The combination of domestic and economic activities within the rural home, for instance, was reproduced in the urban context. New settlements often developed around older villages. Dharavi grew up around the fishing settlement of Koliwada.[20] Older villages provided land for affordable housing on a large scale and their templates were reproduced in the thousands of habitats that emerged all over the city. Every community of migrants came with their own skills and forms of organization. The juxtaposition of these cultures is what makes Mumbai such a vibrant city. Dharavi is itself a kaleidoscope of communities negotiating spatial thresholds and economic relationships.

While we do not see heterogeneity as a specific feature of the global South, we share Roy's interest in 'theoretical projects that disrupt subaltern urbanism and thus break with ontological and topological understandings of subalternity'.[21]

The problem with using words such as *slum* and *informal settlements* in academic circles is precisely the danger of homogenizing a wide range of habitats and blocking a finer understanding of the processes at work in their production, including the way they relate to the city and global context.

In his influential writings, Mike Davis presents slums as expressions of capitalist oppression and as time bombs with insurrectional potential. They are sometimes presented as hyper-competitive deregulated markets where only the strongest survive.[22] International organizations and NGOs often inflate the numbers of slum dwellers by carelessly grouping all kinds of habitats under the catchall terms *slums* or *informal settlements*. An entire industry seems to be profiteering from fear of the informal. Urbanists are master-planning new futures, and architects designing low-cost solutions to house the poorest. Developers are building mass affordable-housing schemes for the poor and the displaced. Real estate developers see slum areas as raw material for land development. Writers, movie producers, and documentary filmmakers have long been inspired by slums for the sheer dramatic value unleashed by their extremes.[23] The narrative is usually that of a parallel anarchic world of crime and human misery.

While right-wing politicians describe them as unruly zones populated by squatters and free riders, progressive voices see informal settlements as an expression of urban injustice. Either way, there is an overwhelming consensus that heavy-handed government intervention is justified. Any suggestion that neighbourhoods qualified as informal are often well organized internally and well integrated into the city is dismissed as romantic. Even after decades of failed rehabilitation policies in all parts of the world, the planning orthodoxy is still that informal settlements are inherently problematic and should be replaced by formal housing.

Settlements emerging outside the regulatory framework and development plans are typically referred to as unplanned and informal, and even illegal. While the term *illegal* is fairly straightforward, defined by unauthorized construction on government land, *informal* is much more ambiguous, linked to normative notions of what the city ought to look like (the order we wish to see). What is informal is broadly speaking what lies outside the formal; informal neighbourhoods are thus perceived as the antinomy of the formal city.

What exactly constitutes the formal, however, is never questioned. Etymologically speaking, what is formal has a shape that can be recognized. When prefixed with *in*, the meaning gets inverted, and by extension what is informal is unrecognizable, strange, unpredictable, and thus potentially dangerous. At the extreme, the informal evokes the irrational, the uncivilized. Phantasmagorically, informal settlements are the anti-city – a contemporary version of the wild forests of the Middle Ages.

It is essential to overcome the myth of the informal if we want to integrate social and urban diversity in the fabric of our cities. Its myth falls apart when we focus on the processes at work in the formation of neighbourhoods that have developed outside of administrative control. What these neighbourhoods have most to reckon with is the language of such control – a language that judges, evaluates, and measures, and in the process identifies what falls outside regimes of control.

Spreadsheet urbanism

Anthropologist Marilyn Strathern observes that 'audit cultures' have become an insidious presence in our public spaces, institutions, and practices.[24] We couldn't agree more: this evaluative way of thinking has a huge impact on urban practice.

Audits and balance sheets work best with discrete categories, most often arranged in binaries, where everything, from living standards to environmental quality, is calculated in seemingly precise terms, buttressed by extreme types for greater legibility. Calculations need numbers with degrees of variation that eventually create maximum and minimum quotients. They thrive on polarities and value judgements. Auditing is always accompanied by evaluation. Acts of evaluation come loaded with values. Auditing systems work quietly, shaping institutional goals, educational agendas, and development objectives. They dictate urban planning through measuring resources and spaces in reductive ways.

In urbanism, audit-based variables are best represented in the all-pervasive though simplistic binary of cities: they are either formalized, planned, and managed on the one hand, or informal, unplanned, and ill-managed on the other. Quite simply, cities are either readable by auditing systems, or they are not. There are those that fit into the calculable space quotient that makes people live and work in specific ways, in recognized ways, in ways that themselves are tightly controlled; and there are those that don't fit. This dichotomy pushes all the living processes of what makes cities alive for everyone else – especially newcomers, the young, and the capital-deprived – into the space of the informal, the unreadable, the incalculable. These are people who make do, re-use, share, and find ways to generate the most they can from the spaces they inhabit. However, auditing processes leach away agency and dynamism from them through rules of control, creating a situation where some of the most exciting urban contexts with healthy local economies and great ecological quotients are seen through a lens of suspicion. The inhabitants of such places are persecuted, at worst, or at best their communities are deemed temporary and informal.

Governing mechanisms are unleashed to bring them back into the formal, audited fold. Consequently, this often creates self-identified, smartly planned neighbourhoods and cities that look increasingly like three-dimensional spreadsheets: cubes, grids, and boundaries, elevated into rectangular cubes on a vertical plane. Such buildings – in fact most buildings in such regimes – are essentially boxes stacked upon each other. They are easy to draw, audit and manage. They are even easier to fit into financial plans and investment portfolios.

We live in the age of 'spreadsheet urbanism', the spatial expression of urban planning merged with real estate speculation.[25] The result is a hard-shell city that forces its users to adapt to urban structure, rather than the other way around. Does it have to be this way? Do cities and neighbourhoods have to become increasingly standardized and generic? Unfortunately the forces at work are very powerful, with the state and the market driving our cities in the same dull direction worldwide. Voters and consumers don't get much of a say about the kinds of places they want to live in. They assume that what they see on hoardings, in urban planning offices, and in corporate created projects is all they can aspire to.

The problem with informality

The issue with informality is the concept itself. While the term identifies a certain reality, it also makes it impossible to see all the nuances that exist within the phenomenon it describes. Whether we use it as a negative or a positive, it hides more than it reveals.

At one level, the phrase *informal settlements* is a euphemism for slums. It means a settlement that was built outside the regulatory framework, without state oversight, perhaps encroaching on public or private land, and where people have poor living conditions. In this narrative, rules and plans exist for a reason; the implication is that if anyone can build anything anywhere, the result would be some of the conditions that have made rules necessary.

For example, zoning exists to prevent housing from being located next to polluting industries or environmental hazards (such as flooding or fire). Planning codes ensure that neighbourhoods are equipped with infrastructure and amenities such as schools and parks.

Yet it is important to remind ourselves that for rules and regulations to make sense – in the spirit of what rules fundamentally imply – then the same must apply to all.

There are several documented cases of disjuncture between the idea of rules as a system of rights and obligations based on the principle of equal treatment for all vis-à-vis the existing system, which favours those who have prior access to resources. In practice, we see a system biased in favour of actors such as large-scale developers who manage to circumvent the same rules (connected to flooding, environmental degradation, or fire) – a bias that has been well documented in cities as far apart as Mumbai and Los Angeles.[26] Cumulatively, such odds are stacked against people in need of affordable housing, and when they try to create their own settlements, they are hit with the rule book – invoking the same hazards and risks of flood and fire, if not a deeper outrage against their takeover of land otherwise reserved for profit-oriented development.

If rules can be understood to be operational in a space of adaptability to context, following the idea of adhocratic rather than bureaucratic principles, then many more pragmatic possibilities open up.[27]

Decent housing, with access to livelihood and acceptable standards of living, is a right for all. If the state cannot deliver it, then people should have the right to build shelters, homes, and neighbourhoods for themselves, even on public land and even if they fail to meet certain standards. In the absence of any other solution, such processes should at least be in the realm of the acceptable.

To be fair, in some cities, such as Mumbai, these processes are indeed accepted within established slums. Slum clearance requires the rehabilitation of the occupants. The question is: who can claim that right, and what does it really give access to? Rehab housing is often far away from places of work, or it breaks apart the conjoined living and working conditions that evolve in most slums over time, or is of poor quality. The result is that it leaves people worse off.

While migrant and poor populations are often blamed for the development of informal settlements, they are not the only ones developing without planning. The public bureaucracy is often too weak to impose a planned approach to development for all players. Real estate developers with deep pockets and political influence gain access to prime land and develop it without any regard for the provision of infrastructure and amenities, producing large-scale slums, in effect, even if they are not officially classified as such. A few suburbs of Mumbai were developed without water infrastructure being put in place. Middle-class neighbourhoods such as Mira Road had for years to rely on water supplied by trucks.

Entire neighbourhoods and even cities are developed without planning, not by slum dwellers but by investors who manage to convert farmland into urban land. Gurgaon in the periphery of New Delhi is a perfect example of unplanned development driven by aggressive real estate investments.[28] The failures and successes of the city, which has grown to become a major economic hub in India, are both expressions of the *lack* of interference from the state, for better or worse. It is worth debating whether development works better outside of the regulatory framework, when institutions are broken or inefficient.

Of course, the best-case scenario is a situation where the state, private actors, and citizens work together to ensure inclusive and participatory development, following sound planning principles. In practice, very few cities manage to do this. Even rich European and American cities fall victim to the nexus between investors and politicians, and what prevails are not policies in favour of ordinary residents but those that maximize returns on investment. Spreadsheet urbanism is a global reality. It affects Mumbai just as much as Seoul, Paris, New York, or Geneva.

When a settlement is designated as informal, we must ask whether the regulatory framework was fair and adapted in the first place. We must also consider whether informality, defined as absence of planning, justifies the destruction of a settlement. Clearance creates enormous stress on the families that have settled and invested in the construction of their houses and the development of their communities. Throwing thousands of people out of their houses creates significant tension in the city as a whole. In situ rehabilitation and local improvement are almost always a better and more humane solution, and should be preferred whenever possible.

While the negative bias towards informality is understandable, we must acknowledge it as a symptom and not a cause: it simply expresses the fact that so-called formal processes could not deliver adequate habitats. Cities should aim at improving their capacity to deliver housing and consolidate existing settlements; in this process, their best allies are the inhabitants themselves. For too long slum dwellers have been seen as enemies within, benefiting from informality. In fact, they usually desire nothing more than the improvement and formalization of their habitats. The rules must be adapted to the reality on the ground, not used as a tool of extortion by state agents.

If informal settlements are ones that were strictly built outside administrative control, most settlements around the world can be classified as informal to some degree. Any vernacular architecture that follows norms other than what is decreed by the civic bureaucracy could be considered informal. In Italy, France, Spain, or Portugal, masons regularly repair country homes in villages that were never built on the basis

of a plan. Even back in the 1970s, John F. C. Turner pointed out similar-
ities between self-help habitats in Peru and the United States.[29] Today in
American suburbs, repairs, extensions, and other maintenance work are
typically done by small contractors who may or may not be employed by
registered companies. The US construction industry is largely dependent
on migrant workers picked up by contractors on the side of the road.
At a seminar in Princeton, architectural theorist Mario Gandelsonas
observed that entire parts of Los Angeles, New Jersey, and many other
large urban agglomerations are built and used in informal ways.[30] Most
of the time, authorities turn a blind eye, well aware that the construction
industry is dependent on these ad hoc systems. Many New York homeowners would agree that some of the rules they are supposed to comply
with are extractive and don't make any sense. This is why so many people
choose to ignore them altogether.

In truth, rules and regulations have often been used to assert control
over urban land, not to benefit end users. They sustain the bureaucratic
apparatus and favour large actors over smaller ones. The unwillingness of
governments to accept the processes of development and structuration
at the local level reflects the will to keep certain power relationships in
place. The notion of informality itself is instrumentalized to maintain the
status quo and invalidate the capacity of local actors to take development
into their own hands.

A closer look at the concept of informality reveals that it was meant
to do exactly the opposite: it was conceived to bridge the gap between
ground-level observations and policymaking. The anthropologist Keith
Hart first used the term 'informal economy' at a conference on urban
employment in Africa in 1971 to describe an economy previously invisible to economists. Development economists from the West applying
their categories to poor countries were only able to account for jobs
in state and corporate sectors, thereby undermining all other forms of
employment. This produced unemployment figures of 50 per cent and
above, which did not match the reality that could be observed on the
ground. In Hart's words:

> Anyone who visited, not to mention lived in, these sprawling cities
> would get a rather different picture. Their streets were teeming with life,
> a constantly shifting crowd of hawkers, porters, taxi-drivers, beggars,
> pimps, pickpockets, hustlers – all of them getting by without the benefit
> of a 'real job'.[31]

Hart, building on observations made earlier by the anthropologist Clifford Geertz as well as his own, coined a term that would account for that invisible economy. The emphasis was thus on the fact that there was indeed an economy – that people were not unemployed; the point was about productivity, not informality. Hart reflected on the appeal of the concept, stating:

> The label 'informal' may be popular because it is both positive and negative. To act informally is to be free and flexible; but the term also says what people are not doing – not wearing conventional dress, not being regulated by the state.[32]

The term *informal*, however, came to be used not only to describe certain kinds of economic transactions, but also entire geographical areas or sectors. When Dharavi in Mumbai and many other neighbourhoods around the world are called *informal settlements*, their complex and diverse reality is reduced to a notion that evokes the absence of a regulatory framework and, by extension, the lack of a recognizable built form shaped by planning regulations, codes, and norms.

Well aware of the shortcomings of the term, especially when it is extended to describe entire sectors, Hart notes:

> The informal sector allowed academics and bureaucrats to incorporate the teeming street life of exotic cities into their abstract models without having to confront the specificity of what people were really up to. To some extent, I sacrificed my own ethnographic encounter with real persons to the generalizing jargon of development economics.[33]

Hart acknowledges that forms exist within informality: 'Any observer of an informally dressed crowd will notice that the clothing styles are not random. We might ask what these informal forms are and how to account for them.'[34] This calls into question the validity of the concept of informality itself. Accounting for 'informal forms' amounts to recognizing that they were not informal to start with. Isn't the idea of informal forms oxymoronic?

Living with the *informe*

Some urban practitioners see informality as a positive state of possibilities. In reaction to the failure of top-down urban planning to produce adequate cities, a generation of architects and urbanists took an interest in the informal, seeing it as a source of creativity and innovation. According to architect Cecil Balmond: 'Informal is not classifiable. Informal is nonlinear and complex. Embracing this complexity and not insisting on self-contained categories of definition is part of it.'[35] In line with the postmodern tradition, this school of thought rejects instrumental rationality as a guiding principle of planning and design practices.

A friend of ours, the architect Filipe Balestra, during his work in India in 2009, shared many positive sentiments to the word informal, which he defined as 'relaxed, anarchic, tolerant, friendly, confident, hopeful, strong, deep and open'. Informal for him was a state of mind and a way of life that he associated with the city of Rio, with its beach culture and hillside favelas. He used the word *informal* to express something about the way a place feels.

While we fully empathize with his sentiments, we have argued that this notion of informality does not do justice to the efforts made by those who inhabit those settlements *to get rid of* this informality. Socio-economic aspirations, shared goals of communities, and the gaze of the authority all contribute to these efforts. The narrative of informality is as much of an outside perspective as the contempt towards these same communities demonstrated by those who self-identify with formality. It becomes an academic concept, hiding more than it reveals. We can do better than endorsing informality as a countercultural design practice. A much more radical approach consists in recognizing that much of what the adjective *informal* is supposed to describe is neither marginal nor alternative, but rather mainstream and dominant. More and more people in the world, seen as an aggregate across nations and continents, live in these contexts.

We conclude our critique of the notion of informality as applied to urbanism by consciously going beyond positive or negative connotations. It is relatively easy to relate conceptually to informality, but it is another matter to understand what it means when it comes to design. Designing something that is informal seems like a contradiction.[36] Design is about giving form, and the informal implies the absence of it. Even when they praise informality, architects tend to become formalists again when it comes to design. Balmond 'actually advocate[s] certain formalistic processes':

> Informal has various levels of meaning for me. It does represent for me a modern dynamic. It is interesting that there was a movement around 1935 called the *informe* led by Georges Bataille. But for him it was about

formlessness and entropy. I am against that. I am for starting from initial motifs and making form in a generative process.[37]

Our interpretation of Bataille's concept of the *informe* differs from Balmond's. The absence of form does not necessarily mean entropy. It could also mean that there is something at work that has not yet been recognized – it could be a form in the making (that is, negentropy). Perhaps the *informe* is becoming something that only needs to be identified to become formal.[38] Turning the light on something, naming it and describing it, implies a certain engagement with the subject. It is an eminently creative process, which draws inspiration from the context. We could call the act of recognizing something that was previously unnamed *enformation* from the old French *enforme* – literally 'giving form'.[39]

Giving form is what design and planning are supposed to do: these practices shape urban space, thereby structuring civic and commercial interactions. Neighbourhoods that have not been planned or designed are assumed to be formless. Yet this is rarely the case. We find structure and function in so-called informal neighbourhoods all the time: market spaces, temples and ceremonial spaces, street and transportation systems, homes and shops can and do emerge through different form-giving processes.

Planning regulations set the norm for urban forms. But that does not mean that forms cannot emerge outside of the regulatory framework, through use, negotiation, and interaction. What produces informality is the inability of urban planners to recognize forms other than the ones they generate. In that respect, the world of planning and design is decades behind the world of art, which has questioned the authority of the expert in judging what constitutes an art form and what does not. The surrealist movement, and in particular the provocations of Marcel Duchamp and his ready-made art, posed a critique of the institutions that claim authority on what can be called art and what cannot. The surrealist review *Acéphale* founded by Georges Bataille celebrates the 'headless crowd', a phrase that could be used to describe the unplanned and locally developing neighbourhoods of Mumbai.[40]

Of central importance for architects, planners, and policymakers is the question of how to reconnect with neighbourhoods that have been following their own developmental logic for decades. Refusing to recognize that a settlement may have a form is a way of negating its claim to normality. From an analogous perspective, a shapeless human body appears monstrous; similarly, for planning experts, the idea of a neighbourhood without form is repulsive. Attributing formlessness and then claiming to give it form is what justifies acts of redevelopment. From this point of view, clearing is not destruction since there was no initial structure – just a slum, a nameless, formless space, a nothingness. Clearing the mess makes space for something.

As Henri Bergson argues, however, nothing is nothing.[41] Calling something informal reveals only our ignorance – our inability and unwillingness to see form – and this is what generates our bias.

The difficulty of investigating, recognizing, and engaging with existing and emergent urban forms should not be an excuse to dismiss them altogether. Academic research in particular has no reason to adopt and spread blindly simplistic notions such as that of informality; rather, its role is to observe and name phenomena precisely, to help build a common understanding. In the field of practice, the failure or refusal of urban planners and policymakers to recognize existing urban development practices and forms is causing a lot of human suffering and even political conflict, as local inhabitants resist planning projects. This does not only affect only low-income neighbourhoods in developing countries; it is a global problem affecting planning in cities as varied as Mumbai, Tokyo, New York, and Geneva.

At the same time, we frequently remind ourselves that a purely professional or academic description of form-generating processes may not be enough. Researchers and urban planners alone cannot produce satisfactory descriptions of dynamic neighbourhoods and urban processes, and the information they produce will typically reflect their biases and preconceptions. For this reason, information must circulate back and forth from the neighbourhood, through communication channels that include local residents as well as professionals. In this sense, recognition should be based on an interaction; it should be a participatory process and not reduced to an academic exercise or left to so-called experts ready to coin new terms and categories.

One should never force form out of the *informe*. Some things need to remain uncategorized, if only to allow for the ongoing possibility that what does not seem to have a determined form can still have purpose and function.

Ultimately, we can only recognize form by *engaging* in urban processes. Bataille's *informe* is here to remind us that it's fine not to name everything. Resisting the temptation to label is a creative state that can lead to the emergence of something new and relevant. Instead of naming, we can participate, and support the processes led by those inside the neighbourhood. Let's enter and join them, instead of sitting outside and pretending we know what things are and how they ought to be.

Engagement means walking into the neighbourhood, working with the inhabitants, and participating in their processes. When viewed from within, the slum dissolves and a neighbourhood emerges.

The will to form

Following this line of reasoning, it becomes easier to see that the slum is not a place but a concept. In fact, it is a concept that entraps many places. A place can change and improve over time; the concept may remain static and even condemn people to the reality it is supposed to describe. Houses may have transformed from walls made of thin sheets to those of brick, from one storey to three or four, from shelters to homes and businesses; and the streets that lead to them may have developed from dirt paths into paved roads. Yet the houses, the businesses, the roads are caught in the narrative of the slum. On the ground, people may have organized, structured, and formalized their settlement, but the map still indicates a slum area. The community's dynamism tends to be rendered invisible when an entire settlement is reduced to the heavily freighted concept of the slum.

For us, this dynamism indicates the will to form. It is a major driver at work everywhere but is rarely acknowledged as a positive evolutionary force in urban development. This omission reflects a prevalent inability to see such places as reservoirs of potential for urban transformation.

The truth of the matter is that internal efforts by a multitude of inhabitants eventually generate functional neighbourhoods, embedded in their cultural and ecological context. People's drive to develop their own habitat is as universal as the inherently creative actions of communities to produce their localities described by Appadurai.[42]

Patrick Geddes, an evolutionary biologist turned urbanist, saw human habitats as complex and multilayered. A passionate evolutionist, he recognized the internal dynamics at work in the formation of habitat. Rather than categorizing them as informal, he saw them as *in formation*: in process, constantly shaping up. According to Geddes, for an architect or an urban planner to intervene in an existing habitat is like performing surgery on a living body – one must be careful not to do more damage than good. This is why he advocated and practised what he called 'conservative surgery' in his urban projects: to do the minimum necessary to improve the overall functioning of the system without breaking up what works.[43] In his words:

> Local character is thus no mere accidental old-world quaintness, as its mimics think and say. It is attained only in course of adequate grasp and treatment of the whole environment, and in active sympathy with the essential and characteristic life of the place concerned. Each place has a true personality; and with this shows some unique elements – a personality too much asleep it may be, but which it is the task of the planner, as master artist, to awaken. And only he can do this who is in love and at home with his subject – truly in love and fully at home – the love in which high intuition supplements knowledge, and arouses his own fullest intensity of expression, to call forth the latent but not less vital possibilities before him.[44]

These words of Geddes are particularly resonant and meaningful when read in the context of his civic engagements in India more than a hundred years ago. Only someone who genuinely practised that respect for local character – who developed genuine affection for the world he was working in – could take it to the depth that he did.

Because Geddes had so much consideration for the way people organized their homes and neighbourhoods, nothing infuriated him more than the obliviousness with which civil engineers preferred to respect the straight line of their ruler rather than the curve of an actual street, especially when a pipe had to be laid. Of course he knew that engineers must bring infrastructure to underserviced parts of the city, but he reminded them that their focus should be on consolidating what residents had built for themselves rather than destroying it. A little detour, an extra curve, an overlay rather than a replacement may cost a bit more in the short run, but will preserve the fabric in a more inclusive way and may even reduce hidden costs elsewhere. Each place has its issues and idiosyncrasies, and solutions must be found in collaboration with residents, not at their expense.

The problem with the concept of informality is not just the concept itself, but the forced flattening of real places with rich and diverse ground realities. Henri Bergson avoided using concepts altogether because he found them to be static, unable to convey the life within the object, thus hiding more than they revealed. He preferred to use examples and analogies. He argued, for instance, that no matter how many photos you take of a street, nothing will approximate the experience of walking it. Viewed from inside, informal settlements do not embody urban disorder but rather order that is in the process of being revealed.

Most human settlements follow a logic of constant structuration as they adapt to their climatic, political, administrative, and cultural milieux. It is time we build a practice based on understanding places from within, with as few preconceptions as possible, except perhaps to hold a methodological bias towards *processes*. From within, we can recognize patterns in movement, which can be culturally embedded or universal. Recognition is a participative process. It requires an ability to see what is there and where things are going. It reveals the hidden order in apparent disorder. Most importantly, recognition must come from within; it cannot simply be granted from outside. It is a political process of self-affirmation through which citizens claim ownership of the habitats they have built over generations.

4

Homegrown Neighbourhoods

Neither accidental nor designed

From a hill, city lights seem to reflect the stars. Looking up into the night sky or down at the city from a height, one sees a multitude of twinkling dots. Each one is a world in itself. Taken together they compose a vertiginous constellation, which confronts us with the wonder of life. How did it all happen – stars and cities – and how come they look so similar?

We can legitimately be amazed at how humans collectively produce something that mirrors the beauty of the cosmos. Such a production is not the outcome of any singular grand scheme. Humans produce cities without following any script. Or rather, we could say that humanity has built cities over generations following a lot of unrelated, often contradictory scripts. The city, according to Patrick Geddes, is 'neither an accidental human product nor the result of a conscious decision to create it'.[1]

The city may look like a wonder of nature from afar, but of course up close it's another matter. Cities are where individual interests and collective purpose collide. Norms and regulations largely fail to provide a framework for urban development and safeguard the common good. Cities are produced by a multitude of self-serving individuals and groups fighting for space and survival, incapable of putting the greater good above their own interests. How do these contradictory impulses manage to produce something that seems structured enough not to self-destruct?

City lights glowing in the dark remind us that what we are contemplating is loaded with energy and power. With enough distance, roads no longer look like concrete infrastructure cutting through neighbourhoods, generating noise and polluting the air; they become undulating arteries carrying the electric juice that keeps the urban body alive. They seem like an unstoppable force of nature. Looking at the city from a distance makes us feel as though we have created something greater than us that we are now struggling to understand, let alone manage. Not only did we create the city, we are also keeping it alive and growing. From the bird's eye view, people are almost invisible, yet it is our collective power and our *will to form* that feeds this mighty urban monster. We created it and now it shapes our lives.

Does the city shelter us, or does it devour us? Is it a gigantic parasite eating up the earth, a cancerous tumour spreading all over the landscape? Is it something we should fight against or nurture? Is there any limit to its might, now that it forms just one planetary urban system connected by an endless network of infrastructure? Can we control it, or does it control us? Can the city be compared to a living organism with an independent drive to exist and an inherent capacity to evolve?

The structure of a city

The Metabolists, a group of architects active in Tokyo in the 1960s, reached the conclusion that the city was too complex an organism to allow large-scale interventions without the risk of disturbing its vital functions at the local level.[2] Instead, they thought it made more sense to build above it. Arata Isozaki designed megastructures that float above Tokyo.[3] Kisho Kurokawa built a metabolic tower for busy salarymen. It was made of studio-capsules, which could in theory be removed and upgraded over time. This avant-garde project lived and died. Some of the capsules have been saved and kept in museums and private collections, but the building was demolished in 2022. One of them, kept in a private garden, is still in use as an Airbnb room.[4]

The Metabolists emerged in the specific context of post-war Tokyo – when the city was growing at a pace never seen before. Tokyo was by far the largest urban agglomeration in the world and following a seemingly unstoppable development. The city was a patchwork of dense neighbourhoods, with tiny houses cramped against each other and huge constructions defying seismic risks; everything was connected by advanced transportation systems. Tokyo's development did not seem to follow any script. The administration was barely managing the city's growth and its attention was primarily on infrastructure development.

The Metabolist architects understood that there was no point trying to control this growth and all they could do was work with it. They saw themselves as facilitators in a process where urban form was shaped by the flow of people circulating and inhabiting the city.

This avant-garde group often produced architectural projects that looked metabolic but were rather static in evolutionary terms. Christopher Alexander indicated this shortcoming in his famous essay 'A City Is Not a Tree', which argues that what creates strong cities and neighbourhoods is the multiplication of points of connection between urban elements.[5] The structure of cities, according to Alexander, is that of a semilattice: systems enmeshed within systems in complex and dynamic ways. He distinguishes between natural cities built over time, where functions overlap creating an infinite number of connections and possibilities, and artificial cities, where functions are spatially planned and static, and which are 'from a human point of view, entirely unsuccessful'.[6] Planning and design can either permit the emergence of new connections or restrict it. Either way, it is not spatial structure alone, but rather spontaneous interactions that turn cities into what Kevin Lynch calls 'learning, evolving ecologies'.[7]

The evolutionary city

Geddes believed that there was a sense of commonality among all cities across the ages. Not only do all cities share a fundamental physical structure, as illustrated in his valley-region diagram; they also have a common social structure composed of specific types that exist in every city throughout history: people, chiefs, intellectuals, and emotionals. These roles according to Geddes exist in cities across history under different avatars and combinations. Cities take on new characteristics in different epochs – mediaeval, industrial, financial – but in the end, they all respond to fundamental and universal human needs.

As Geddes pointed out, the city may not be accidental, but neither can it be said to be the result of a grand plan. Rather, it is the result of an infinite number of interactions. It is precisely at the point of tension between accidental and conscious action that the city assumes its unique role in the evolution of mankind – 'the supreme striving of nature to balance the freedom of the individual and the continuity of the species'.[8] The city offers a space for individuals to escape from their communities, as well as the possibility for new communities to emerge. It provides a sense of continuity, together with the possibility of breaking away from it. It allows the new to constantly emerge out of the old; but it also constraints and frames what emerges from within it. Cities can sometimes consolidate to the point of sclerosis, and this is when it becomes essential to perform conservative surgery within the city's fabric, which unleashes new spatial or civic potentials without weakening vital urban functions.

Geddes believed that cities were 'the very incarnation of the evolutionary process', but he was not a determinist.[9] He did not see evolution as a given. Cities can improve over time and provide better environments for their inhabitants, but they can also sink into gloom or follow a downward spiral. Just like organisms, cities can decay. Policy and planning are tools to promote the health of cities and the well-being of their residents. Citizens and civic institutions play a major role in the improvement of their city. Geddes believed in education in civics and town planning, not just for a specialized audience but for the public at large.

Throughout his life, Geddes endeavoured to share his passion and understanding of the functioning of cities from technical and spatial standpoints, as well as from historical, cultural, and environmental perspectives. In 1892 he built the closest thing to our present-day Google Earth: the Outlook Tower in Edinburgh. It was equipped with an optical system – a camera obscura – which allowed the public to look at a reflection of their city. The instrument was a genial inversion of the biologist's microscope. The building also hosted an exhibition on various aspects of the city, including its botanical diversity.[10]

Geddes was interested in urban metabolism, yet he did not believe that cities should be reduced to their physical expression. Cities are the outcome of many intangible economic, social, and cultural dynamics. More than anything, it is the interplay between the spatial and the cultural that makes human habitat a tool of evolution. Built spaces act as memory banks and processors for the knowledge that humans produce. Cities are communication systems. Inspired by the biologist Jean-Baptiste Lamark's theory of the inheritance of acquired characteristics, Geddes believed that cities were a 'specialized organ of social transmission' of knowledge across generations:

> It is the vehicle of acquired inheritance. It accumulates and embodies the cultural heritage of a region and combines it … with the cultural heritage of larger units, national, racial, religious, and human. It stamps the resultant product upon each passing generation of its citizens … The city receives the experience of each passing generation and adds the record

on to the next ... It is the instrument primarily of regional memory, but serves also as the memory of larger groups.[11]

Because they are organs of transmission playing an important role in human evolution, neighbourhoods need to be treated with care and consideration, especially when they have been built over generations. Our collective memory is stored in libraries, museums, financial institutions, and server farms – but also in civic institutions, workplaces, schools, communal houses, cafés and restaurants, markets, and public squares. Street art and architecture convey meaning as well. But the city is primarily home to immaterial forms of transmission – language, habits, norms, values, regulations, and festivals.

Geddes insisted that the city does not simply belong to those who inhabit it today but also to future generations. Conceiving a neighbourhood in purely spatial terms and reducing it to discrete homes and surfaces of activity is a mistake. Incrementally developed neighbourhoods in particular – built over many years thanks to the investment of successive generations of inhabitants – cannot be redeveloped without destroying at the same time the cultural, social, and economic relationships embedded in their fabric. Once it is destroyed, the knowledge embedded in the fabric is lost to the world. Neighbourhoods are urban milieus, hosting active eco-cultural systems that can go extinct like dialects or species of plant or animal. The evolutionist approach is not necessarily preservationist. Built spaces do not need to be preserved for their own sake, because of a romantic attachment to the old ways. They matter only so far as the knowledge embedded in the built form is relevant to the well-being of communities that live in them.

Homegrown neighbourhoods are metabolic urban ecologies, able to evolve over time. The active agents of this evolution are the inhabitants, their knowledge of the place, the institutions they built, the time and money they have invested in their homes, the local builders and their skills, the material and biological elements that compose it. The impulse driving local efforts to build and consolidate neighbourhoods can be found all over the world, in celebrated cities from Rome to Shanghai, from Mumbai to Santiago de Chile, and in many other big and small cities and villages in Europe, Asia, Africa, and Latin America.

International agencies aiming to catch the attention of decision makers and the civil society often present shocking statistics about the number of people living in slums worldwide. According to the UN in 2020, about 1 billion people around the world lived in slums, and this number is set to double in the next thirty years. As explained in previous chapters, what exactly gets defined as a slum is debatable and sometimes politically instrumentalized. But our definition of the homegrown neighbourhood encompasses far more than slums (which can be organically developed or master-planned); it includes a wide diversity of habitats generated by local communities to respond to their needs.

Homegrown urbanism is a global phenomenon. It exists everywhere in different forms, sometimes appearing as a neighbourhood such as Dharavi, built entirely from within. Sometimes the impulse to build or reshape existing habitats is tightly controlled and repressed, as in an American suburb – but even there, we see constructions happening discretely within homes, garages, and backyards. One of the primary characteristics of homegrown neighbourhoods is that they develop incrementally. Unlike large real estate projects led by corporations, homegrown development relies on local resources. Such settlements are not built all at once, but are consolidated over time, by the users themselves or their neighbours.

Some of the liveliest and most diverse neighbourhoods in the world were developed incrementally – sometimes across the span of a few decades, sometimes over centuries. Varanasi, Jerusalem, and Venice are homegrown; any old European city, including Madrid, Napoli, and Belgrade, is partly homegrown. Even hypermodern cities, such as Tokyo, Hong Kong, or Taipei, are homegrown to various degrees. Pretty much every large city has some history of incremental development. Some cities have managed to control incremental development better than others, at least on the surface. Many homegrown settlements existed in the US until the twentieth century but they have since been cleared up, and this partly explains why many US cities lack the kind of urban vibrancy that can be found in cities that have a layered history of urban development and higher levels of density.

Almost every old European town consolidated and densified over time. The old quarters that were preserved have become destinations of choice for tourists and locals alike. New uses, infrastructures, and technologies have been retrofitted into well-preserved historical neighbourhoods. These cities have been carved out over centuries, and they continue to be improved. Wandering through the old town of Basel, Genoa, or Ljubljana, for instance, is a journey through time, full of surprises and hidden corners. Small open spaces and squares, meandering streets that rise and descend following the topography, trees growing out of stone walls, forgotten monuments, shortcuts and longcuts …

Old towns are often blamed for being dense, cramped, and dark, producing impossible proximity between buildings and allowing neighbours to see into one another's houses. They are far from perfect, but they also have many things going for them. They are usually comprised of beautiful, pedestrian, mixed-use streets, where daily needs can be met within walking distance. Many have become urban museums where buildings are preserved as monuments, making change and adaptation almost impossible. Some cities, such as Paris, allow modifications only inside the buildings, while the façade is preserved, making them unauthentic according to some critics. We observe that in the case of Paris, it is the blend of preservation and modernization, homegrown densification and high-level planning, that has made the city highly attractive.

Homegrown neighbourhoods emerge out of need. In cities such as Mumbai and Tokyo they are so numerous that their intrinsic qualities are overlooked. Newish low-rise, high-density settlements, built incrementally in the space of a few decades, are morphologically comparable to old towns. The main difference is that these newer neighbourhoods are changing much faster. Small houses are demolished to make space for slightly bigger ones. Floors are added onto existing structures. Infrastructure pushes its way in. Homegrown neighbourhoods, whether old or new, have in common the fact that they have developed outside of the planning framework. In a best-case scenario, such as in Tokyo (which we describe in detail in Chapter 7), urban planners have made improvements within the existing urban fabric without destroying it. In other cases, homegrown neighbourhoods are being cleared to make space for standard mass housing, as in Shenzhen, where until a few years ago half of the population lived in urban villages.

Vernacular and affordable

Homegrown neighbourhoods emerge in response to the need for shelter when urban planning and control is soft, weak, or absent. Many cities have sought to respond to the need for affordable housing through large development schemes. While some of these have been relatively successful thanks to the provision of qualitative amenities, many have been social and architectural failures. This is particularly true of mass housing built with low-cost materials and bad design, which makes them overly expensive to fix.

Many US post-war housing projects became insalubrious and

dangerous. Some of them, such as the Robert Taylor Homes in Chicago, have been demolished because they were considered broken beyond repair. France has produced suburban ghettos with abysmal living standards, famous for periodically bursting into flames. Brazil built millions of square metres of sordid and remote *viviendas* through schemes blighted by corruption. Slum rehabs in Mumbai are hyperdense, and built so cheaply that they fall apart after just a few years of use. Massive residential towers developed by conglomerates have become a defining feature of urban life in South Korea and China.

Once these habitats have been built they cannot be wished away, no matter how wasteful or dysfunctional. When they become too difficult to live in and maintain, their only future is demolition; until then they are the everyday reality that people have to face. This is why it is urgent for municipal governments to consider homegrown alternatives to mass housing.

Homegrown neighbourhoods can be insalubrious too, but they have an enormous advantage over mass housing – they can improve over time. Incremental development works through the efforts of successive generations. Houses are spontaneously improved and rebuilt by their inhabitants, usually with the help of a skilled artisan who lives in the same neighbourhood. With some help from the municipal authorities, even civic infrastructure can be retrofitted. This has been done even in the densest of built environments. Laying down pipes and electric cables along existing pathways, no matter how narrow, is not rocket science. Services can also be provided pretty much anywhere, especially with the support of local residents who are already mobilized on issues of water provision, garbage collection, and schooling, for instance.

Having worked closely with local builders in various cities, and having studied local construction process in homegrown neighbourhoods, we can attest to the fact that many houses built in the past five to ten years – in the so-called slums of Mumbai and New Delhi, in the barrios of Bogotá and Cali, in the favelas of São Paulo and Rio – are of decent quality. If anything, they are often over-engineered, as clients and contractors are obsessed with making the house *pakka* – meaning baked or solid in Hindi, as opposed to *kacha*, or raw, which is used to describe shacks made of fragile and temporary material. The relationships between contractors and clients are intimately connected to the social life of the neighbourhood. Contractors are themselves local residents. They are typically well-known people in the neighbourhood; they share the same local social network as their clients and are either direct acquaintances or friends of friends. Since contractors build mostly within their own community, their work is highly visible to potential clients, who can easily judge its quality by looking at past constructions and talking to neighbours. There is thus fairly little scope for the contractor to cheat clients or leave work unfinished. Obviously things go wrong from time to time, as with every artisan-client relationship, but for the most part it works.

Homegrown neighbourhoods usually have a well-functioning domestic construction industry. The word *industry* may seem a strong one, since construction is based on practical craftsmanship and artisanship skills; but it is industrial as far as the scale of production is concerned. The construction materials and techniques involved are often industrial too.

In order to illustrate the scale of the homegrown construction industry in Mumbai, we can use the example of Shivaji Nagar in Govandi, which is approximately 135 hectares (encompassing other neighbourhoods such as Baiganwadi, Gajanand Colony, and Lotus Nagar). There are about 50,000 structures, including houses, shops, temples, and schools. In this area alone, we estimate that 2,900 houses are built or rebuilt *every year – by local construction workers.* The houses typically have a footprint of 10 by 15 feet (3 by 4.6 metres), with a two-storey house costing anything between INR 4 lakhs and 12 lakhs (US$5,000–14,000) to build. A simple calculation tells us that if we use a low INR 6 lakh (US$7,000) per-house figure and multiply it by 2,900 houses, the construction market represents over INR 174 crores or US$20 million annually in Shivaji Nagar alone, which is only one of many homegrown neighbourhoods of Mumbai. Clearly, the municipal authorities know about the market since there is a standard 10 per cent informal tax on any new construction to be paid in the form of a bribe to municipal officers. Out of the total calculated, about US$2 million is lost in bribes. If this informal payment to municipal authorities were levied as actual tax, the money could be used to develop the neighbourhood's infrastructure and increase the salary of municipal officers.

While it is difficult to evaluate what the construction industry represents as a share of Shivaji Nagar's economy, which may be home to well over 200,000 people, we can be sure that it is a highly significant source of income and employment. In India the real estate sector is one of the largest providers of jobs.[12] It is unfortunate therefore that the authorities do not recognize the positive aspects of homegrown development. The local construction economy, which helps the poorest people, is destroyed each time a homegrown neighbourhood gets replaced by mass housing.

The benefit of local construction extends far beyond homegrown neighbourhoods. While houses are locally built, the materials used for the construction are not locally produced. Bricks, cement, and steel are all industrial materials produced by major corporations and distributed via well-established regional and national networks. Industrial construction material suppliers, including multinational corporations, have taken notice of the market represented by homegrown neighbourhoods throughout the city and are enthusiastically tapping into the proverbial base of the pyramid.

Besides their economic value, homegrown neighbourhoods are also an expression of the city's contemporary vernacular architecture. According to the art and architecture historian Pierre Frey, anything made through the optimal use of freely available or low-cost resources and materials, including labour, is vernacular. The architect Patrick Bouchain points out that the term *vernacular* comes from the Latin *vernaculus*, which means 'indigenous, domestic'; *verna* is 'the slave born in the house'.[13] The relationship to the home and the neighbourhood is thus integral to the definition of vernacular.

According to Ivan Illich, vernacular spaces are produced through use. In Roman times, he explains, the word *vernacular* designated 'the opposite of a merchandise. Vernacular was everything that was crafted, woven, raised at home and destined, not to be sold but to be used at home.'[14] From the time of construction onwards, a house is not simply an object (a product) made of bricks and mortar. The relationship between the builder and the family who lives in the house is embedded in interpersonal networks and usages. Once it is built, the house is continuously shaped by the movement of people and goods in and out. It is a porous entity open to the neighbourhood, affected by the same problems as the other houses on the street, and it benefits from the same access to local markets, institutions, and transportation networks. Each house is part of a process of constant improvement at the neighbourhood scale.

There is no doubt that homegrown neighbourhoods need planning and management. Civic infrastructure and amenities such as water pipes, schools or parks must be implemented at the neighbourhood scale, in consultation with the population. Yet, like John F. C. Turner, we believe that decision-making and initiatives on housing-related issues are better made at the local level.[15] In homegrown neighbourhoods, the proximity between homeowners and builders makes the former into agents of urban development. This reinforces their sense of belonging and attachment to the neighbourhood. It also keeps precious resources within the community, distributing jobs and salaries locally. Moreover, it reduces the cost and increases the quality of housing as compared to mass-housing schemes. While we strongly believe that the state should support the provision of social housing, we think that the construction of such housing would be much better delivered by artisan builders at the neighbourhood level than by large developers, who have no accountability towards the end users.

From New York to Mumbai, Bogotá to Paris, the provision of affordable housing is a major concern. The prevailing wisdom is that mass production reduces costs through economies of scale. This type of urban development has been mastered to such a high technical and financial level that we seem unable to produce alternatives.

The alternative, however, is already around us, everywhere. It needs only to be recognized, supported, and protected from speculative takeover. Allowing housing to be produced locally is hugely empowering to local communities. It helps to develop skills and institutions; it generates a sense of pride and identity; and it allows for the emergence of locally relevant and climate-sensitive solutions – among many other direct and indirect benefits.

Practitioners with first-hand experience of grassroots urban-development processes in different parts of the world have consistently acknowledged the usefulness of this model. Academics, architects, and urbanists have for decades been advocating loud and clear for this so-called alternative. Paolo Freire, Charles Correa, Turner, and Alexander among many others have not only written about it but also successfully experimented with incremental urban development. They have shown how a kind of development long seen as marginal, inadequate, hazardous, and informal could instead become a mainstream solution to the housing crisis, not only in so-called developing countries but also in the rich world. They have demonstrated how architectural practice could support the growth and consolidation of homegrown settlements.

Our own practice at urbz is nothing more than a continuation of this approach. We have been actively co-designing homes and community buildings in Mumbai and Bogotá for over twelve years. We have learned a great deal about the skills embedded in local communities in many parts of the world. We highlight in particular the case of Tokyo, as it demonstrates that there are other ways for cities to develop than the destruction of homegrown neighbourhoods and the production of mass housing by an industry that has no interest in creating viable habitats.

Figure 4.1. Construction site in Dharavi (photo: Julien Gregorio).

Instead, inhabitants and homemakers remain captive consumers of real estate goods, produced by an industry disconnected from local life and economy. What's truly difficult to understand is that there is no pushing back from civil society and democratically elected governments. Everything is as if we had accepted that there was no alternative.

Recognizing the homegrown city

Along with *homegrown*, the notion of *recognition* should also find its way into mainstream urban planning and design. Here, we want to emphasize the kind of attention to place that comes without preconceptions, the process that allows the emergence of new forms, and the necessity of accepting even what cannot quite be defined and recognized. Philosopher Judith Butler argues that not everyone has equal access to social and political recognition.[16] People with identities that don't fit into dominant tropes can easily be disenfranchised, especially when labels are imposed and fixated rather than emergent. According to Butler, we should recognize others based on the shared precariousness of our human condition rather than on fixed qualities or status.

She invites us to acknowledge the expression of complex and dynamic identities. Just because we cannot quite comprehend what something is does not mean that it is irrelevant or does not deserve to exist. Likewise, we often find it difficult to talk about habitats that don't fit the urban normative. Neighbourhoods such as Paraisópolis in São Paulo, Cazuca in Bogotá, Siloé in Cali, and Dharavi in Mumbai are identified as favelas, *barrios populares*, or slums, which traps them in the categories seen as problematic, as discussed in the previous chapter.

While the label of *slum* reinforces reductive stereotypes, the term homegrown settlements has a positive connotation – nowadays, every-one values what's local and organic. We are not arguing, however, that everything that is homegrown is necessarily good or desirable. It depends on the context. Mould on the kitchen wall is local, organic, and home-grown, yet not something we would universally want. Garden vegetables, worms, and mosquitoes are all homegrown entities too.

Neighbourhoods such as Paraisópolis and Dharavi are homegrown because their inhabitants built them from within, drawing on their own resources and skills. We use the term to put the emphasis on user partic-ipation in improving their own habitats, which we see as a strength. But the lack of recognition for this process makes homegrown neighbour-hoods particularly vulnerable. They don't fit into urban norms, and what does not fit in is usually seen with suspicion.

The stigmatization of homegrown neighbourhoods extends to the people who live in them. Residents are *framed*, as Butler would say, as slum dwellers – a modern term evoking disenfranchisement at best, and illegality at worst. Slum dwellers can at any point be dispossessed of the houses they have built. Even if their right of occupancy is protected in some cities, they have no rights to continue developing the slum. Any improvement of their existing conditions – such as connecting their house to the water system – is illegal. The result is a form of arrested development, a status quo imposed from above.

In India, unlike Japan, slums are prevented from evolving into neighbourhoods. If they were recognized and normalized, they could confidently pursue their processes of improvement, absorbing new tech-nologies and infrastructure along the way. In such efforts, they should of course get all the help they can. We strongly believe that it is the role of policymakers, urban planners, designers, and architects to engage with homegrown neighbourhoods and contribute to the inhabitants' efforts to improve their condition. Instead such experts usually contribute to the destruction of what has been built over generations, demolishing what they find and constructing something else altogether – something that usually benefits people other than the ones they found there.

The first step towards the recognition of homegrown urban habitats is for planners and policymakers to question their own professional frame of reference. What is considered a legitimate urban form and why? What does it take for marginalized neighbourhoods to enter the urban norm? How can the norm be adapted to other forms of urbanization? Can homegrown neighbourhoods be tolerated on the basis of what they mean to those who inhabit them? Recognizing is different from accepting, in the sense that it is dynamic and dialogical: it's about engaging with diversity and enlarging our frame of reference. What creates the slum is our way of integrating or othering it. Considering a slum as a legitimate part of the city and giving it formal recognition allows it to improve and turn into a pleasant neighbourhood, with its own history and morphology. Seen as a problem that must be addressed through erasure and redevelopment, the slum is victimized, pinned down by a paternalistic approach depriving its inhabitants from any form of agency.

Recognizing existing forms and integrating them into urban planning and policy requires the combined skills of ethnographers and urbanists. It also demands the capacity to establish links between parallel universes, connecting, for instance, the neighbourhood to the municipal administration. It involves fieldwork, interaction with local people, reporting, analysis, understanding of construction techniques and materials, land and space use ... It demands a particular attention to the relationship between spatial forms and social processes.

By recognizing existing urban forms, we should not fall into a formalist trap. What matters most is the intensive processes at work in their creation, not the forms themselves. The styles of the informal should not be fetishized and preserved or reproduced for their own sake. At their best, homegrown neighbourhoods are places of potential that foster the emergence of new forms in response to the needs, means, and aspirations of their users.

The level of inhabitants' involvement in the making of their neighbourhoods varies greatly from country to country. Japanese neighbourhoods are often relatively malleable, in the sense that users can easily rebuild their houses, decorate the street, or temporarily occupy public spaces. The attachment that residents develop for their neighbourhoods is related to their capacity to appropriate and shape them through use. It is an intensely cultural process which shapes the identity of a locality. At the same time, it is a universal impulse. We see people engaging with their surroundings in so many different ways. In the US this can take the form of a block party; in Switzerland it might be through the creation of housing cooperatives, participatory planning projects, or cultural events. In India we can find it in a festival or a street market.

In most cases appropriation is not a luxury but a necessity. Without direct involvement there is no local development. Most people in Mumbai live in neighbourhoods that were built by their peers and continue to be consolidated from within: homes, streets, religious sites, schools, toilets, and infrastructure. Dharavi was not easy to develop, and incomers struggled with the environment, the authorities, local strongmen, and economic limitations; but whatever forms they have managed to produce within these many constraints are constantly being improved and reshaped.

Urban forms do not emerge from nowhere. People involved in building homes in Mumbai have often brought skills from their villages. Religious monuments have their own frames of reference. New structures are built upon existing ones, sometimes re-using materials or extending where possible. The climate and topology of the terrain also dictate what can be built and where. Existing entry points and pathways are used and altered.

Parts of the city that were never planned or designed often acquire a strong identity over time, marked by the evolution and mutation of local economic and cultural practices. These practices of daily life, to paraphrase Michel de Certeau, shape space and produce context.[17] Space becomes the malleable receptacle of local practices. As use shapes space, space gains value for its users. Space becomes not only supportive of but also conducive to certain uses and practices. This process is at work in homegrown neighbourhoods, with different levels of intensity and various degrees of autonomy from the larger context of the city. Use connects space to a familiar past and an immediate future.

Focusing on the relationship between economic, social, and cultural patterns and the formation of habitats in planned and unplanned neighbourhoods would bring us closer to addressing some of humanity's most important challenges. Examining and learning from patterns of use across geographies and histories, as well as engaging with local people and recognizing their agency in the process of building their habitat, are some of the most exciting and urgent challenges faced by urban designers, planners, and policymakers today.

It is important to start with the understanding that citizens are agents of urban development: it is above all the efforts of those who struggle to improve their own habitats that must be recognized. This implies communication between local inhabitants and municipal authorities. Local involvement and the establishment of communication channels are the pillar of a planning approach based on recognition.

Recognizing unidentified urban forms and the dynamics that drive their emergence is a task that urbanists must embrace. Homegrown neighbourhoods have grown through the unit of the home as a collective entity rooted in a place. They cannot be planned or managed from above, but they need all the help they can to continue improving and consolidating.

5
Form Follows Process

Neat functions, messy processes

At one level, the phrase *form follows process* simply reflects our bias for process over form. It is a reductionist statement aimed at countering the even more reductionist assertion that *form follows function*. In both cases forms are produced not for their own sake but in service of something else. Process, as we understand it, is not linear and is difficult to control, especially at the level of the city. The urban process is like a river fed by many streams. Its complexity is such that it renders meaningless some of the most timeless architectural wisdoms, such as *form follows function* or *less is more*. In fact, the notion that a neighbourhood (or a city, for that matter) can be designed once and for all is fundamentally problematic. It holds urban forms to a single vision and restricts timely responses to emerging needs and uses. What may be wise at the architectural scale can be destructive at the urban scale.

We take no issue with the idea that built form should indeed be designed to fulfil specific functions. But there is more to form than function. Form gets shaped through use and contact with the elements, and as a result it has the potential to embody history and identity. At best, it can become better with time: more adapted to its users, more resilient to shocks, better integrated into the landscape. And while it should not try to freeze the identity of urban spaces in time, such identities can also become a means of transmission. There is always a danger in architecture of overloading form with meaning, so functional minimalism is probably good advice for designers. Users should, however, be able to leave their imprints on their space and shape it to their needs. At the very least, they should be able to determine what functions they require at different points in time. That's a process.

What could go wrong when architects pretend to know what a neighbourhood needs and to be capable of fulfilling these needs through urban design? This attitude fails to recognize that what makes a habitat resilient is its ability to evolve. A beautiful building can be maintained, maybe retrofitted with new technology, but its evolutionary potential is limited. A neighbourhood, on the other hand, changes all the time. Old buildings are transformed, replaced, or adapted to new uses; new technologies and infrastructure are retrofitted into existing structures; new modes of transportation change our relationship to the street; our sensitivity to vegetation also evolves over time, as do the ways we work and trade, our cultural habits, and demographic make-up. All these dynamics contribute to producing the neighbourhood as a site of constant transformation. The urban process is not just a river, but a torrent fed by many streams. It is a messy thing. What helps urbanists draft a good programme at the neighbourhood scale is serious attention to these many streams: how they have shaped the context up to now, and where they might be leading it. For this we need to focus on what is there already, rather than imagining that we are designing something from scratch.

Urban formations include buildings and streets, but also gardens and neighbourhoods, bridges and natural landscapes. As dynamic and interactive ensembles they are more than the sum of their parts: they derive their meaning, functions, and aesthetics from their relationship to one another and their shared context. Architecture theorist André Corboz said that what makes the quality of a building or a bridge is its relationship 'with the architectonic or landscape elements that surround it'. In turn, what makes the quality of an urban formation cannot be judged by the quality of the various architectural elements that compose it. 'It may be the case,' argues Corboz, 'that a group of elements form a "monument" and deserve to be preserved in spite of the absence of a major architectural work.'[1]

Many old urban ensembles seem to come together just right without ever having been designed. Think of an Italian square with no straight angles, surrounded by buildings from various epochs – some falling apart, some restored, some new; perhaps a fountain or a sculpture, not quite at the centre of the square; a mix of pedestrians, bikes, terraces, benches, and street vendors; an old tree flanked with pigeons. No one could have designed all these features, yet it seems perfect. The church that stands on one side of the piazza may be a specific site of interest to the preservationist, but its architectural quality should be considered in relation to its context.

It is easy to imagine how such quality can be generated over centuries of use, care, and craftsmanship in a European context. Heritage cities such as Porto, Arles, or Florence rely on tourism. But there is much more to the story than conservation; as André Corboz argues, there is often no object to be preserved at all – only a set of relationships.

Now picture a busy narrow street – people walking up and down, motorbikes and utility vehicles honking, electric wires and fibre cables hanging across, sometimes entangled to the point that it would be faster to lay a new line than sort existing ones. These cables serve as resting spots for birds and highways for small quadrupeds. On both sides of the street are buildings of three or four storeys: a mix of residential units, shops, tea stalls, temples, and clinics. These functions are not only adjacent but also piled up on top of each other; sometimes two structures merge to generate a larger space for a textile workshop, a banquet hall, or a temple. Often it is the other way around: several functions coexist in a single space. At the street level, political posters compete with ads and shop signs, some of which are hand drawn, others heavily photoshopped with colours saturated enough to stand out in this effervescent environment. There are people everywhere: kids in school uniform, construction workers carrying a pipe, colourfully dressed men and women on their way to work, a fish vendor carrying a basket with the catch of the day on her head, three ladies chatting with a fourth who's selling herbs and spices …

There are more functions in this scene than could ever be drawn into a plan. Dharavi is hyperfunctional in that sense, like a thousand other homegrown places that have been shaped through use and share a kinship with historic European towns – except that Dharavi and its counterparts in Asia, Africa, and Latin America are not glorified. On the contrary, they are seen as ugly, dysfunctional, and good only for demolition.

The majority of neighbourhoods around the world stand somewhere on a spectrum between two extremes. It is the constellation of relationships, uses, meanings, and sometimes aesthetic considerations that should guide any form of urban intervention. The spatial vitality of such neighbourhoods should be neither preserved at the cost of turning them into a museum nor dismissed to the point of destruction. The point is to work with it and contribute to its evolution from within.

Taken together, all the elements that compose a piazza in Genoa or a street in Mumbai form an urban ensemble that must be assessed and respected in its complexity and messiness. Any intervention must recognize existing dynamics. It is not enough to say that the street would be cleaner and quieter without motorbikes and utility vehicles. What if workshops can no longer deliver their products, or service providers cannot reach their clients? Kids would be safer on their way to school, but parents may be out of jobs. Traffic can and must be addressed; but there is a need to rethink the standard makeover approach that typically throws out the baby with the bathwater.

Ignoring or dismissing processes at work may destroy meaningful urban formations. For an urbanist, architect, or craftsman to intervene without breaking a neighbourhood apart is an art that requires a capacity to recognize the qualities of a space as well as the invisible human dynamics that generate them. This is why urbanists need as much help as they can get from anthropologists, ethnographers, economists, climatologists – and of course the inhabitants themselves.

Forms in movement

When the phrase *form follows function* was first coined by Chicago architect Louis Sullivan and then endorsed as a motto by the likes of the architect Ludwig Mies van der Rohe, it was a progressive statement meant to liberate architecture from the canon inherited from past generations.[2] The intention was not to produce a minimalist aesthetic, but rather to allow the emergence of architectural designs that belonged to their time and were not stuck in old motifs that had lost all meaning.

Modernism emerges in various places in various forms – it is by no means a European monopoly. In fact, the values we now see as definitive markers of modern architecture were already present in Greek and Roman antiquity, in Buddhist thought, and in Islamic art. According to Plato, good civic life was a matter of proportion and measure. The notion that good city form and a just society are two sides of the same coin, the idea that there is an alignment between what is beautiful and what is right, the realization that civic infrastructure is essential to physical and mental fitness, the capacity to generate wholesome spaces through an economy of means, the rejection of iconography in favour of abstraction – these central tenets of Modernism existed long before modern times.

While the values and principles embodied in modern architecture are nothing new, they were reasserted forcefully in late-nineteenth-century

Europe, which was torn between its belief in social progress and technological innovation, and its value systems rooted in aristocratic traditions.
Nowhere did this play out more dramatically than in Vienna, capital
of the Austro-Hungarian Empire, which at the turn of the nineteenth
century was at once a vibrant centre for intellectual and artistic life and
a city resolutely attached to its imperial grandeur.

Some intellectuals, artists, and architects believed that Vienna had to
move away from reproducing an aesthetic grounded in values that were
out of sync with the times. The architect Adolf Loos is often presented as
a precursor who fought the establishment and managed to open the way
for generations of architects who followed him. Yet he did not identify
as a functionalist or a minimalist; instead, he thought that architecture
should reflect modern values. In his writings he denounced the use of
ornamentation on the façades of buildings or in the design of furniture
as artificial because it reproduced the old codes in twentieth-century
middle-class housing. He insisted that such motifs were out of place and
anachronistic.

Loos reacted to the new buildings around him in Vienna, many of
which were simple concrete structures designed to mimic Baroque
stonework. Architects had become master decorators, able to reproduce
any style but unable to find an expression reflecting their time. This was
part of a wider crisis of culture, where applied arts seemed stuck the
past while technology, construction materials, philosophy, and art had
moved ahead.

The 1912 Loos house at Michaelerplatz, Vienna created uproar in a
city that was more accustomed to Gothic and Baroque styles.[3] To this
day, it is hard for non-architects (that includes us) to understand what is
so significant about this building's appearance except that it looks rather
bare, surrounded as it is by lush architecture and convoluted façades.
Responding to his many critics, Loos stated that while the Michaelerplatz
house's beauty was up for debate, one thing that no one could dispute is
that it was urban.[4] In this sense it belonged to its time and context.

At some level, Loos was saying that architects working outside their
context, without a sense of the circumstances, can never produce something that really fits in, nor can they create something that stands out. On
a plan, the architectural object seems static and self-contained, but on
site it interacts with everything around it. It is part of a dynamic urban
ensemble.

Loos described the process of building a rural home as follows: 'While
the mason lays brick upon brick, stone upon stone, the carpenter is

setting up nearby ... He is making a roof. What kind of roof? A beautiful one or an ugly one? He does not know. The roof.' The house is materially, functionally, and formally rooted in the landscape. This makes it at once beautiful and unremarkable: 'Is the house beautiful? Yes, it is beautiful, just as the rose or the thistle, the horse or the cow are beautiful.'[5] The object belongs to the context, the context is shaped by the object, and what connects them both are the processes that generate them.

At the urban scale, functions are multiple, interconnected, and changing. When the boundaries between one house and the next are not so clearly defined – when walls are shared and space is negotiated, when social norms rather than statewide regulations structure space – the forms that emerge are less self-contained, more connected and embedded in socio-economic structures. Even when contexts are more settled and defined by plot boundaries, the form of a house is determined by a series of internal and external factors, which are not so easy to delineate: the needs and means of the owners, the climate, available materials, technology, aesthetic sensibilities, cultural influence, relationships with neighbours, norms and regulations, and so on. The neighbourhood in fact embodies all the complexities of construction.

Nowadays, master-planning and urban design are dominated by an architectural imagination that mechanically adds up the individual elements and denies the interaction with time and space. The plan is treated like a larger version of an architectural drawing, where a big object – a neighbourhood or a city – fulfils a limited set of functions: living (housing), working (economic activity), leisure (public space), and a few civic functions (schools, museums, hospitals, police stations).

The social production of locality

Urbanism can't be reduced to its spatial dimension. Space should be neither the starting point nor the end goal of an urban plan; rather, it should be considered as a moment in a process. Urbanism is concerned with uses, which change over time as people adapt to their environment, adopt new technologies, and follow or initiate new cultural practices. From this perspective, paraphrasing Geddes, form and function are no longer considered in stasis, but in movement and in interaction. Both are open and evolutive instead of definitive and static: an open form – or, as Umberto Eco called it, an 'open work'.[6] We could even say that the best way to define the urban realm is as a permanent 'work in progress'.

Geddes brought his biological knowledge to the urban realm, seeing natural and human habitats as fundamentally enmeshed. He saw cities as entities powered by their inhabitants, as able to adapt to new circumstances and improve over time. He was deeply interested in how social processes and material conditions shaped human habitats. What people are building for themselves is usually a good clue to what works in any given context. This approach is not necessarily preservationist but rather a prerequisite to intervention. The focus is not on the form but on the forces that shape it – the processes at work.

Geddes believed that collective agency and communication between people and planning authorities were key to improving cities. Inhabitants are organically connected to their urban and natural habitat and as such they are conduit for information that's essential to good decision making, planning, and design.

> How very different from the present state of affairs would be a city in which such active co-operation could arise spontaneously between the citizens and their town council! In such a city real sanitary and economic improvements would be freed from harsh and wasteful clearances and from the sullen resistance of the people.[7]

The phrase *form follows process* thus pays tribute to Geddes's sociobiological understanding of cities and calls for participatory urban action. Everywhere people have developed their habitats in response to immediate needs, means, and conditions using available resources. In this respect, urban form is processed locally. However, material resources and skills are sometimes brought from far away. Construction techniques can be transmitted across generations but also over vast distances as people migrate from rural regions to cities, and from one part of the world to another. Techniques and technologies evolve over time, in situ, on a trial-and-error basis, but also in contact with new knowledge. They spread through trade and migration. The material production of a locality is therefore embedded in a wide web of interactions stretching far beyond the neighbourhood.

Homegrown urbanism is a universal context-generating process driven by collective agency. Indeed, according to Arjun Appadurai, locality is not a passive expression of context, nor is it purely spatial or fixed. Ethnographers are not merely recording the local life that has been created once and for all; rather they observe a transformative process where material and abstract realities converge and diverge.

Communities develop a sense of self which is linked to specific places, and which they transpose into new contexts. Space is a conduit for the generation and consolidation of social bounds. Yet locality extends beyond space and shapes it through cultural expression, such as rituals or construction practices: 'Materiality is sometimes mistaken for the terminus of such work, thus obscuring the most abstract effect of this work on the production of locality as a structure of feeling.'[8] The production of locality involves shared emotions and stories, social relationships, crisscrossing biographies, and economic specializations, which get projected onto the material reality of neighbourhoods that are in this sense 'social formations'. These formations, in turn, shape the interactions happening within them:

> Neighbourhoods provide the frame or setting within which various kinds of human action (productive, reproductive, interpretive, performative) can be initiated and conducted meaningfully. Because meaningful life-worlds require legible and reproducible patterns of action, they are text-like and thus require one or many contexts. It is in this sense that neighbourhoods are contexts, and contexts are neighbourhoods.[9]

Neighbourhoods emerge at the intersection of homegrown and external dynamics (such as national institutions, global politics, or the climate). They are both context-driven and context-generative.

The larger contexts that shape neighbourhoods are well out of reach, but how this is dealt with at the local level can greatly vary. The nation-state provides a political framework, which might be stable or insecure – it could for instance throw the country and all its inhabitants into a war with another nation. The environment can provide seasonal regularity, which farmers rely upon and which structures social life; or it can be erratic and changing, depriving farmers of the predictability they rely on.

The construction of neighbourhoods and the local context is precisely about sheltering them from unpredictability. It is through a shared sense of purpose, linked to an actual or ideal locality, that the community gets created as a bubble of solidarity in the face of a hostile world. Developing a *structure of feeling* – bonding people to a locality that is often more abstract than experienced – is an essential aspect of dealing with adversity. The structure of feeling is kept alive through local knowledge, including, for instance, construction techniques and aesthetic expression. As Appadurai puts it: 'Much of what has been considered local knowledge is actually knowledge of how to produce and reproduce locality.'[10]

The production of locality is not an end in itself. Rather, it is a way of mitigating and relating to the larger context in which it is embedded. Neighbourhoods are constructed at the intersection of internal and external forces, which are themselves enmeshed into one another. The development of local specialization can generate opportunities extending far beyond the neighbourhood – such as global trade. When it comes to the environmental crisis, we have learned that we must act locally – by recycling, growing indigenous species, and encouraging biodiversity. And as local communities we must also find ways to cope with what is coming to us.

The encounter between the local and the global can offer opportunities, but it often comes in the form of an imposition from the global onto the local. In *The Nutmeg's Curse*, anthropologist, novelist, and essayist Amitav Ghosh shows the devastating effect of colonialism on indigenous populations and local ecosystems.[11] Colonization does not only subjugate locals; it also breaks locality apart. Ghosh describes how the population inhabiting the Banda Islands in Indonesia, which were blessed with a unique ecosystem and a great variety of local species, did not think of nature as inert or even external to them. Over centuries these people have understood themselves as being part of a living ecosystem with which they interacted intensely. The trees and nutmeg were active agents and had to be reckoned with. Treating them as mere inert objects disrupted the possibility of relating to them as agents in an ecosystem that also included humans.

A community bound together by a shared sense of locality, whether actual or abstract, is often seen as a threat by the powers that be. Minorities are often viewed with suspicion as subversive agents who may not fully buy into national, religious, or ethnic discourses. They ultimately represent the universal threat of larger social units breaking into smaller ones, claiming territories and autonomy over their rulers.

The tension between the local and global is a constant feature of human existence. People's capacity of cohabiting within a given space and cooperating economically and otherwise determines their capacity to exist collectively and individually. Nowadays we insist on the importance of local governance, which creates communication channels at various levels. To exist, localities need to institutionalize their relationship with the wider world through politics, trade, and environmentalism. Urban planning and design too, rather than being a mere instrument of administrative control, should provide an interface between the locality and the context within which it evolves.

Often, however, urban planning imposes itself on a neighbourhood in such a way as to destroy all sense of locality. Just like the colonial takeover of Banda, it breaks the community apart, and people are left with a collective memory of a locality that they can no longer materially produce or transform. Sometimes, it is inhabitants who decide to leave their neighbourhood for good, driven by their needs or aspirations. Appadurai points out how increased mobility at a global scale allows groups of people to transport their localities with them from one part of the world to another, by creating virtual enclaves and social imaginaries that recreate a sense of belonging despite geographic dislocation.[12] Migrant groups from rural to urban territories bring skills, memories, traditions, and lifestyles to their new neighbourhoods. When the same people return to their villages they carry a certain urban imagination into their rural contexts.

In a study on rural–urban connections (described in Chapter 9), we show how this exchange of contexts linked to the constant production of locality shaped both neighbourhoods in Mumbai where migrant communities settled and the villages from which migrant communities had arrived, creating a loop of interrelated contexts that influenced the form of habitats in both places.

What this tells us is that inhabitants are active presences in their contexts; they have a propensity to shape and sculpt their surroundings. Appadurai demonstrates how this happens in a more universal sense – through a reading of the sociocultural processes of context formation. This helps us to appreciate the harnessing of these dynamics as a conscious tool by an urbanist such as Geddes, who very much relies on such spontaneous acts and intentions by inhabitants and makes them the starting point of his urban interventions. What both Appadurai and Geddes evoke is a kind of inter-referencing that exists in all places between form making, relationships, collective action, and feelings.

Working with processes

With the help of Geddes and Appadurai, we see the possibilities that the idea of collective agency generates in the context of form. Both thinkers indicate that the forces generating urban forms are internal to the specific habitats and spaces that constitute them. When Appadurai describes neighbourhoods as the context as well as the process that produces the context, he acknowledges that an element of collective agency is at work through which the structures of everyday life are produced at a fundamental level. When Geddes directs his attention to the relationships that are embedded in spaces, he engages with the physical structures they produce and refers to the very same collective agency.

Yet this sense of the collective is not one that evokes the mobilization of people *en masse* towards a particular kind of urban intervention; rather, it suggests an ongoing process in which agency is embedded in everyday contexts and is performed through a set of relationships in which clients, service providers, residents, masons, and traders all work together in the production of their habitat. These relationships shape neighbourhoods and are the constituent parts of collective agency at the local level. They are the visible, though not always acknowledged, expressions of participation that urban experts tend to ignore, and they are not usually acknowledged as such even by those involved.

A neighbourhood plan generated through a participatory process will not resemble a plan drawn from an architectural studio. It may look more like an unplanned, incrementally built neighbourhood. It will demand an illustration that reflects the multiple perspectives and experiences of its users – a view from within. A participatory process generates a rich programme, made of stories, affects, and aspirations brought together through dialogue. It may be difficult to fit such an outcome into the regulatory framework, because there is nothing standard about it. It is specific, embedded, and idiosyncratic. It is true to the spirit of a place and connects with ongoing dynamics. A plan in which form follows process may very well be one that reveals itself through collective action – in other words, a plan that follows action rather than one that leads it. Such an approach requires a fundamental change in architecture, urban design, urban planning, and policymaking. And it may be much more pragmatic than plans designed without participation.

Architects are trained to conceive of a plan that will land on an empty surface, and at most may have to connect to whatever is around. In real life, there are no empty plots. The land on which an architect is projecting something is inhabited already – if not by people then other forms of life. It has a history, topology, climate, ecology, and perhaps neighbours and users as well. So the story does not start from scratch. *Nothing is nothing*; there is always something, and even if we are unable or unwilling to see, that doesn't mean it isn't there. Recognition is always the starting point. This is not necessarily the work of the architect, but the architect cannot start working without a brief that describes not only the intentions for a new construction but also what is already there.

Good architects spend time creating this brief for themselves so they can design something that makes sense. In reality, this crucial part of the planning process is often dismissed by clients, architects, and planning authorities alike.

According to the philosopher Yehuda Safran, *good design requires talent, but a good programme requires genius.* We believe that this genius can only find expression in the context of a participatory process.

At urbz, we have developed a practice that puts social processes and participation at the heart of urban design. For years in Dharavi we've been concerned with urban form as an expression of economic needs and means in a specific environmental, cultural, and political context: the house doubling up as a workspace; the street used as a marketspace in the morning, a platform for political expression in the afternoon, and a festive space in the evening; the temple used as a space of worship and social gathering point. These observations serve as starting points for the recognition of patterns of use. Discussions with the users themselves bring to light invisible arrangements which structure space as solidly as bricks and mortar: the street-cart pusher who pays rent to the shop owner to set his cart in front of her shop; the vendor sitting on the same bridge every day who sells only one type of item (books or vegetables) because he is registered with the police for these sales; the weekly use of the street for Friday afternoon prayer, which means that all traffic stops for an hour or so. Recognition of these local arrangements is the first step towards any action plan.

In Dharavi Koliwada, we have been actively engaged with the local community for over a decade, contributing to the design of many buildings. We are currently working on a participatory plan for the entire neighbourhood of Koliwada: reconnecting it to the shore, making space for a garden of festivities, restoring historical structures, putting street lights into dark lanes, conceiving a new water sewage system, imagining the revamping of the old fish market. There is nothing easy about this process, especially since we are getting very little recognition and support from the municipal authorities, which would prefer to see this historical fishing neighbourhood demolished and redeveloped along with the rest of Dharavi.

When we work in a new neighbourhood, we always start by engaging with residents and recognizing their ongoing initiatives, whether they are involved in construction, culture, social work, or economic activities. We were recently tasked by the urban planning department in Geneva, Switzerland, to lead a participatory process in a municipality called Versoix on the outskirts of the city. The aim was to densify a 14,000-square-metre plot accommodating a few houses built in the 1960s. The urban planning department had previously tried to densify the same site, but the project was rejected by the population at a referendum. The citizens did not want massive buildings in a quiet residential area of mostly middle-class villas with small gardens.

We followed a radically participatory approach, which started with the involvement of neighbours in and around the site and expanded to include anyone from the town who was interested in the project. We organized workshops mixing local people with students and young professionals from other cities who had no previous knowledge of the site. Our first move was to establish a base in a house on the site itself. We fixed up the house and used it to host neighbours and visitors, exhibiting our work in progress and organizing brunches and discussions. Every week we were gathering more knowledge about the place, ideas for its transformation, and feedback from existing residents. The network of people who were aware of the project kept growing, along with interest from neighbours.

We had no plan to show for the first three months, but a shared vision emerged out of the material generated through the process. It was structured around a few principles and value statements. On this basis, taking into account many of the site's constraints, we produced a detailed programme, which was communicated to the public in the form of a narrative that people could engage with and contribute to. The feedback we were getting was constantly integrated into the story, making its engagement with the community rock solid. We had a good explanation for every choice, based on previous conversations. Telling the story of the project over and over again, it really took shape in our minds and we could start visualizing it clearly. The programme was illustrated from the users' point of view – from within the neighbourhood, rather than a bird's-eye view. It was presented to the public on multiple occasions at different stages of development. Once the concept was largely accepted we continued drawing the plan, marking every topographic curve, listing every type of tree, analysing sunlight, the acoustic qualities of the site, and so on.

Work on the form itself followed a process of integrating the reality of the terrain and its technical constraints (such as a railway line running along the site). What emerged was not a typical urban plan, but something that looked more like an incrementally developed neighbourhood, where space had been carved out by users over the years. Every part of the plan had its story, expressing its current stage and its potential, as well as its connections to all the other parts.

For example, a house set to be demolished was owned by a ninety-four-year-old man, who had built a workshop in the basement. He had created some very special inventions, such as the 'tack', a tool that allowed anyone to plant a nail at the push of a button. He wasn't against something new being built on his land; he had himself made plans for a small building years before. His only request was that he wanted to finish his life in the house, so nothing should be built before his death. We therefore planned the project in such a way that some plots could be built first and others later, so every homeowner could develop their land on their own timeline.

During discussions with this inventor and many other people from the neighbourhood, we discovered that Versoix had once been a neighbourhood of artisans. There were still a few left, but by and large the town had become a dormitory suburb of Geneva, and did not have much life during the day. People wanted to see activity and young professionals in Versoix again. So on the land owned by the inventor, we proposed a residence for young artisans who were just starting their careers. A foundation was looking for a place to develop just that kind of project, and this was much needed in Geneva. On the ground floor we proposed a makerspace, where anyone from the neighbourhood could use tools to fix or build all kinds of things. This activity usually brings people from all walks of life and generations. This proposal, one of many such ideas that had emerged out of the process, struck a deep chord among residents. All other parts of the plan were the result of such interactions: some existing buildings were preserved, and new ones were proposed.

According to Loos: 'What characterizes a construction that has been authentically felt, is that on the plan it produces no effect.'[13] This was the case for every building we put on the plan. None of them stood out because they were simply the product of a process embedded in the context.

The urban planning department loved the process, but not the plan. The officer overseeing the project told us that a plan should look like a logo; we should be able to read the neighbourhood immediately when we see it on a plan. Our plan, which was very contextual – based on topography, history, relationships, a shared vision, and a narrative – was conceived from the point of view of the users, not of the architect-planner. Space was the expression of a programme, which itself had been generated by an interactive process, involving hundreds of discussions with a wide range of people.

It was a disruptive process that produced a plan that looked like the result of an incremental development process rather than a typical master plan. The project was welcomed by the local population who had been involved at every step, but it was ultimately rejected by the authorities on the basis that it did not comply with the regulations. Yet we had made sure we it did; it was also financially viable, and we had even found people willing to invest to develop the vision. This happened in a context of acute housing shortage in the city, with very little land left to be developed.

At this point, we realized that even though participation was demanded by the authorities, it wasn't so easy for them to accept its outcome, when it challenged the prevailing planning culture. Since then, we've worked with other clients and partners and have been able to realize projects in Switzerland, France, Colombia, and India following our methodology, which puts process before form and users before the master-planner.

From Europe to Asia, master plans are at once a reduction of function to quantifiable surfaces and an expression of the architectural grammar expanded to the scale of a neighbourhood. This does not do justice to the dynamics of localities. From their conception onwards, master-planned neighbourhoods are fundamentally rigid, imposing themselves on the present and constraining the future. They coerce movement, activities, and ways of living. They deprive inhabitants of agency and of the power to shape their environment. Public activities are reduced to square metres attributed and subsidies provided; street cultures struggle and contest the imposed spatial framework. Eventually life spills out and subversion becomes the norm. The wall becomes a canvas for graffiti, the bench becomes a railslide, the parking lot becomes a social spot for teenagers, the square becomes a shelter.

This mostly happens because form and function were reductively conceived to start with. In reality, functions are neither discrete nor finite: they follow processes, merge into one another, and evolve over time. That is why it's more useful to think of processes and flows which are dynamic, adaptable, sometimes weak but always present. These are not fantasies but living histories. Struggling favelas in Brazil, occupied spaces in Kenya, marginalized settlements in Mumbai, and homegrown neighbourhoods in Tokyo are all examples of this process-oriented urban development, which needs planning of a different kind.

They emerge through processes that weave the urban fabric, agents of development working from their homes and streets, making do with the help they can provide each other, improving their habitats against all odds. Homes are grown by their inhabitants, who rely on available skills and materials, deal with multiple constraints, and in the process design meaningful patterns, which are there for us to recognize, respect, and nurture. They are the plan in action. They are localities being produced.

Incremental development is a well-known notion in urban studies, but it is usually dismissed in planning and architectural practice. Planning for incremental development seems to contradict the common-sense notion of the professional execution of a project – which is supposed to go from plan to execution. But this is largely an illusion, as an urban or architectural project that has not yet been appropriated by end users is necessarily unfinished. This appropriation often implies a transformation of the project initially framed by the architect, the planner, the client, or the regulator.

In existing neighbourhoods, it means accepting that users will continue to alter and adapt their habitats in all kinds of ways, as they have always done. How a project evolves over time is unpredictable, and planning for such unpredictability is probably the toughest challenge facing cities and planners. Far from meeting this challenge, however, municipal authorities routinely deprive users of the right to intervene in their environment. In Dharavi, for instance, residents are banned from rebuilding their homes, as the area awaits a large-scale redevelopment project that has been in the works for decades.

6

The Design Comes as We Build

Embedded knowledge

Construction activities often spill out from institutionalized professional boundaries. They go beyond the metropolitan architectural projects, urban infrastructure or real estate developments that rely on large-scale mobilization of capital, usually sourced in speculative financial markets. These spillovers are typically found where inhabitants raise small amounts of capital from their community networks to finance a local economy of incrementally growing construction projects, building houses, shops, and even infrastructure. Such incremental processes have always been at work, and have been instrumental in the development of habitats, not only in villages but in some of the largest cities in the world, including Mumbai, São Paulo, Seoul, and Tokyo.

In Mumbai's homegrown neighbourhoods, contractors (local builders) are hired by a family wanting to rebuild their house. The family selects the builders on the merits of their previous work and common acquaintances. Both the contractor and client typically live close to each other, and often belong to the same community. They discuss their plans, agree on a schedule and budget, and start work. No formal plans or contracts are signed, with trust and reputation being the cornerstones of the process. Design is organically co-created, with users giving input through the process and the contractor autonomously adding flourishes and harnessing skills. The unexpected and the unforeseen become rooted in the structure since the design is linked to the process.

While houses are locally built, the materials used for their construction are not locally produced. One hardly ever sees mud houses or bamboo roofs in Mumbai – at least not in homegrown neighbourhoods. Not only are these noble materials often locally unavailable, but they may be more costly to process and distribute. Most importantly, they are not aspirational. Industrial materials are seen as solid, desirable, and contemporary by homeowners and builders alike.

Neighbourhoods developing outside administrative control or under a lax planning regime tend to generate a variety of forms because they do not necessarily follow urban development codes, such as height limits or functional segregation in different zones of activity. Consequently, what emerges are urban forms that tend to match the means and needs of their users closely. From this perspective, such neighbourhoods become living laboratories for the emergence (and design) of diverse forms of social and urban organization.

These forms are not devoid of logic. On the contrary, they embody processes that must be understood by planners interested in developing locally sensitive approaches. They reflect a multifaceted context as well as the best efforts of local communities to respond to it. Far from curtailing the designers' creative freedom, they provide the most potent source of inspiration. In other words, these homegrown settlements follow their own adhocratic logic.

In our years of collaboration with local builders in Mumbai, and through observations about similar processes elsewhere, we have witnessed how their work expresses a contextualized intelligence and a resourcefulness born out of adversity. Local skills and resources fuel construction practices in neighbourhoods that fall outside the planned regimes of urban habitats. Self-organized masons, labourers, and artisans produce habitats, and transmit skills and knowledge to the next generation of local builders. The result is a global vernacular urbanism that is systematically overlooked or dismissed as informal.

In India craftsmen and artisans are often considered to be of lower status because of their proximity to materials such as leather, earth, and waste products, based on the cultural notions of purity and pollution. This framework also maps onto hierarchies related to habitats, with slums placed at the very bottom. However, these so-called slums are also teeming with talent and skills connected to a multitude of crafts that are a valuable resource in the world of construction and placemaking. It is this talent that in the past contributed to the construction of celebrated Indian architectural monuments. The artisanal communities who built these monuments were historically marginalized and pushed to the edges, their neighbourhoods seen as low-caste enclaves, similar to contemporary slums.

Yet the skills and talents of these communities continue to sustain and nourish their habitats. Such skilled artisans work in the shadows of social hierarchies that undermine their contributions. Most artisans of homegrown neighbourhoods in India are undervalued due to prejudices linked to caste. Dharavi has several artisanal home-based industries, including leather, pottery, carpentry, and weaving. These activities create the typology of the tool-house, which we describe in detail in Chapter 8. Tool-houses belong to the same category as the shophouse or home factory, that exist in different parts of the world and are connected to combined live–work conditions. These are familiar structures that local contractors and artisans in Dharavi tend to reproduce in response to local demand.

Our engagement with these structures works at several levels. First, it recognizes the skills and craftsmanship of all the undervalued artisanal communities that make up a large part of the urban poor and sees them as a major resource in the world of architecture, urban planning, and construction of built forms. Second, it validates and recognizes the typologies created by them for their neighbourhoods. We have been collaborating with residents and contractors on the design and construction of many houses in Dharavi and other homegrown neighbourhoods in Mumbai.

The construction of homes by local artisans, with practical skills and no academic training in architecture or engineering, continues to happen throughout the world, even as, or perhaps because, the industry of construction is becoming increasingly expensive and hyper-professionalized. The surplus talent that exists outside the industrial building sector can and does get utilized whenever opportunities arise beyond the spaces of planned projects. We believe that it is the role of architects and urbanists to engage with the local processes at work – contributing without imposing our own preconceptions.

Homegrown construction is carried out by a web of local owners, contractors, labourers, carpenters, electricians, plumbers, and material providers. Their structures are built in a vernacular style, but using industrial products such as bricks, corrugated sheets, cement, steel pipes, and I-beams. These products are bought at market prices from hardware and material stores located in the neighbourhood itself. As any middle-class homeowner would, homeowners and contractors in these

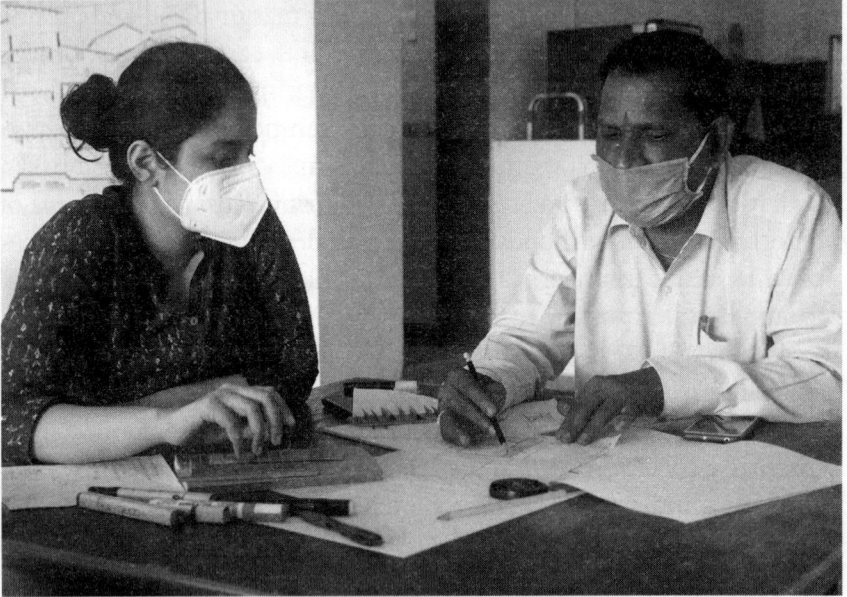

Figure 6.1. Collaborator working on a project with contractor Giriraj Sherekhan (photo: Partha Shrungarpure / urbz).

neighbourhoods choose high-quality materials over low-cost ones whenever they can afford it. An investment in quality is justified if it means enhanced use value in the form of higher living standards or improving the income-generating capacity of the structure.

The project described in this chapter is a tribute to the local contractors and artisans in Dharavi, Mumbai. It spotlights the self-taught process through which residents and contractors in high-density, mixed-use settlements create and maintain their neighbourhoods. We attempt to validate the architectural typology embedded in this process, and to recognize and honour the role of local agents (often blamed by civic authorities for operating illegally) in the production of habitats. We see them as the anonymous heroes of an epic story about building neighbourhoods out of nothing, transforming meagre local resources into functional mixed-use habitats.

Recognition is not condescension. We see talent being expressed within a context of hardship. We believe that engaging with the local economy is the most pragmatic thing we can do as professionals. We also believe that all the technical knowledge we have acquired as architects, engineers, or urbanists is worth nothing if applying it comes at the cost of dismissing the knowledge embedded in localities. Knowledge only becomes practical if it can connect with the reality on the ground.

Architecture as applied ethnography

The Design Comes as We Build project self-consciously uses an ethnographic lens but specifically works with the language of architecture to look at how houses are built and imagined by artisans, who, day after day, build thousands of tiny houses accommodating multitudes of low-wage workers to sustain the city's service and manufacturing sectors.

We initiated this project to reveal the hidden logic in the way Dharavi houses are built, to turn the faceless artisans of construction into designers and model makers – in effect turning a building type often dismissed as informal into a form that is not only perfectly rational, but also beautiful in its simplicity and ingenuity.

In this project, the urbz team helped contractors realize their ideas into architectural plans and then design templates for the artisans. As the contractors saw their designs brought to life by the artisans working on their models, they spotted design flaws and corrected them on the spot, asking the artisan to make changes accordingly. Sometimes the artisans offered their own suggestions. This exchange reflected the on-site, adaptive, and evolving manner in which the contractors worked.

Throughout, the project documented and collaborated on models built by skilled labourers in Dharavi out of the materials they specialize in – typically steel, clay, wood, glass, and recycled plastic.

To translate the practical expertise of local builders into drawings that architects could read, our team asked several builders from the neighbourhood to think of the best possible design for a typical Dharavi house of 12 by 15 feet, which should also accommodate some form of economic activity, as most households use their home as a tool of production. We turned these visions into three-dimensional drawings. We did not intervene in the designs but encouraged the builders to be ambitious and think of the best-possible small home for Dharavi. Some of them described new ways of optimizing space and the use of materials, using spiral staircases, creating semi-open spaces on the rooftop for social gatherings, or making provisions for a family's future growth. Others imagined multiple ways in which the house could be used to generate income, providing space not only for retail on the ground floor, but also rental units that could function independently from the rest of the house. Some projects included innovative systems to protect inhabitants from sunlight or ventilate the house.

Once the drawings were done, we asked the artisans to build models using the materials they specialized in. The builders and craftsmen sat together and modified the design as it took form. This resulted in a series of models, videos, and photos that show how people manage to create habitats that are full of life, even in the most difficult conditions.

The inaugural series of models from the Design Comes as We Build project were exhibited at our office in Dharavi, and then at the Bhau Daji Lad Museum, Mumbai's city museum which has been chronicling the everyday life of its residents, especially through the lens of decorative and industrial arts, since its inception in 1855. It permanently displays ethnographic models representing the different castes of Mumbai, which date from colonial times. It was the perfect context for our models. Our intention was to show the contribution of local builders and their continuation of the city's artisanal-industrial legacy, but also to produce a counter-colonial narrative through objects that represent the skills and knowledge embedded in communities that have been historically marginalized.

It is this active legacy that we wish to recognize and value, as we believe it is the key to improving the living conditions of the majority of Mumbaikars who live in so-called slums. This potential should be integrated into the government's urban development strategies. The models represent not only the kind of housing typology that exists in Dharavi but also the capacity of local artisans to imagine and produce a better version of their existing habitat. The models have since been exhibited at the MAXXI Museum in Rome and at an Arc en Rêve exhibition in Lille; three of the models were acquired by the M+ Museum in Hong Kong for its permanent Asian design collection.[1]

Figures 6.2, 6.3, and 6.4: Three models designed by contractors and created by artisans (photo: Bharat Gangurde / urbz).

From artisanship to design

One of the first houses was designed by Joseph Koli, a contractor from Dharavi Koliwada, Mumbai. It was a four-storey structure (Figure 6.2) with a grocery shop on the ground floor, two residential units on the second and third floors, and a roofed terrace as a multipurpose space. The second-floor residential unit was to be used by the shop owner's family and the first-floor unit would be rented out, with each unit having a separate kitchen and toilet. Joseph wanted the house to engage with the street, and designed balconies for every floor. These balconies could be used for a variety of purposes ranging from socializing to drying laundry. An artisan who specializes in clay, Ashwin Narshi Bhai Wadher, made this model. He was born in Mumbai, but his family hails from Lodhva village, Gujarat. He is part of the Kumbhar (Potters) community that has settled in Kumbharwada (Potters Hamlet) Dharavi. For the construction of the model, each part was designed to be easily dismantled, as Joseph strongly believes in recycling building components once the structure has served its purpose.

Another model house (Figure 6.3) was designed by S. Murugan, a contractor from Tamil Nadu and resident of Kamla Nehru Nagar, Dharavi. The structure was a four-storey tool-house, with the ground floor to be used as a shop by the homeowner, who would live on the first floor. The first floor has a living space, a kitchen, and a toilet, as well as a balcony. This balcony became the access point for the steps leading to the second floor, which was an open terrace-like space that he called his 'Sunday room', with a space for family dinners and recreation. Adjoining this on the same floor was a separate kitchen and washing area.

He made the third floor an enclosed residential unit, including a kitchen, toilet, and living space, which he planned to let. The roof was sloping to accommodate a mezzanine level that would serve as a sleeping area. The staircases and balconies on all floors functioned as an interconnected system through which the tenants could access the third floor without entering the private family spaces. This model was made by Manoj Viswakarma, a carpenter who was born in Uttar Pradesh and has lived and worked in Dharavi since 1996.

A third model house (Figure 6.4) was designed by Mallappa Kotam, who hails from the state of Telangana and has been working as a local builder in Dharavi for over a decade. His design attempts to realize some of the aspirations of local Dharavi residents. The entire structure is three storeys instead of the usual four; this allows for higher ceilings, resulting

Figure 6.5. Models of houses designed by builders and artisans from Dharavi, exhibited at the Bhau Daji Lad Museum in Mumbai.

in better light and ventilation, and extra floor space in the form of mezzanines, to be used for sleeping or storage. The ground floor accommodates a workshop, including a workspace, a cabin for the workshop manager, and a loft for storage. The first floor is designed for a family of eight, with the sleeping area on the mezzanine, an independent kitchen and toilet, and a balcony. The terrace is roofed and can be used by all the residents. It also has space for a water tank. The remarkable feature of this house is the spiral staircase, which optimizes space and provides independent access to each floor. The artisan who produced this model was steel fabricator Rehman Abdulah Khan, who has a workshop in Kamathipura (a neighbourhood in South Mumbai with its own artisanal–industrial legacy) that fabricates steel components for roofs and metal staircases.

A Homegrown Street

The Design Comes as We Build project morphed into a new phase called Homegrown Street, where we attempted to finance the upgrading of an entire street by selling the models of each house. We chose a street in Dharavi, Mumbai – Sangam Gully, which translates from Hindi as literally a street of confluence or convergence. It is a street we have been documenting for over fifteen years, and we have seen it consolidate over time.

We invited design proposals and models for twenty houses and shops on either side of the road. The brief for each house is based on existing and projected uses, formed using a participatory process involving discussions with each family and shopkeeper on the street. We asked the residents and traders to imagine what the house could be in five to ten years' time. We then invited local builders to design these houses led by the briefs. We sat with the contractors as they described how the house should be built, translating their vision into three-dimensional drawings. Again, we avoided intervening in their designs and simply encouraged them to express their ideas very freely and to the best of their ability. Once the drawings were done, we asked local artisans to build models using the materials they specialize in.

We have produced models representing about half of the street so far, and these have already been exhibited in our office. The model makers and designers came with their families and friends and were intensely proud to see their work exhibited as art pieces. One of them told us that it gave him goosebumps and made him realize how beautifully he could design a house. Local builders, who are known as contractors in Mumbai, are usually portrayed by the media, public administrations, and professional architects as unreliable at best, and crooks at worst. Our intention was to showcase their contribution to the city and the potential they represent for a city that has proved unable to provide quality mass housing for its enormous population.

Urban practice beyond form

Our practice combines urban planning with anthropology, disciplines that complement each other well. Both tend to focus on locality from different perspectives – spatial and cultural. Both deal with the relationship between humans and the material world. Both carry embedded weaknesses, notably regarding the question of the subject: urban planners look at the city as experts; they can only plan by distorting the lived experience of places – quantifying, imposing metrics, translating places into charts and plans, and flattening their dynamic and evolutive nature. Likewise, anthropology has long been expressed only in terms of an outsider's gaze, objectifying and theorizing the other, and in the process imposing the worldviews of the observer onto the observed.

Figure 6.6. Plan of Sangam Gully in Dharavi (illustration: urbz).

01- JAYA NADAR
02- BHARATI PASWAR
03- ASGAR ALI
04- BINDU PATTRA

05- MEEMOHAMED DOMRID
06- HAJI RASHEED
07- RAVINDRA SINGH
08- MOHAMMED

09- KANTILAL VERSHI
10- JOSE ULOCH TAILOR
11- CHANDRIKANT SONI
12- SANTOSH GUPTA

13- SABOUR HUSSAIN
14- IBRAHIM ANSARI
15- EJAZ KHAN
15a- NOOR AHMED KHAN

17- KOCHITELI
18- FAROKH ANSARI
19- SAJID ANSARI
21- ANIL HINGORJA

Anthropology was notoriously used by colonial powers to understand and rule local populations, yet it produced tools and methods that have generated an archive – however distorted – that provides detailed portraits of localities. As Arjun Appadurai explains, these ethnographies become valuable when seen not as portraits of fixed cultures but as descriptions of processes that are self-produced by the inhabitants of each place. The tools communities engage to describe and analyse these processes are invaluable: they help us have patience with the granularities of places and encourage us to see them as conjoined with human agency. It is this faith in the process and its inhabitants – the commitment to engaging way beyond the typical period of designated fieldwork and the creative desire to participate in co-creation – that gave us the tools for our practice.

We propose an approach to localities based on a deep and meaningful engagement. It comes from the acknowledgement that while we may know a lot about what is common to urban contexts around the world, we have very little understanding about the particularity of any actual place. It considers the inhabitants, or users, as knowledge bearers – resources that are central to any form of intervention. Ultimately, it is they who will build and consolidate their neighbourhoods.

Our approach relies on collective intelligence: the idea that we become smarter when we can see a question from multiple points of view. We do not situate ourselves outside of the locality we work with, but firmly inside. We see ourselves as participants who have a specific background and knowledge, which we share with others from an equal standpoint. When we share our knowledge, we necessarily put ourselves into the story, as actors whose presence and actions in the local context have an impact. It is this impact that we analyse in relationship to the context.

Engaging with any context brings together a universe of skills and learnings – the professional, the institutionally trained, the self-taught, local expertise, and a whole lot of collective skills that are rooted in diverse community lives that coexist in that space.

The moment we turn our attention to that context, a specific locality, we see how it nourishes and shapes all the worlds that emerge there – built, natural, and cultural. And what almost every formally trained professional acknowledges at some tacit level is that she or he must eventually depend on the knowledge that is embedded in that locality to fulfil the project – be it architectural, social, civic, or environmental. Not only is the local's expertise an objective asset; her involvement or lack of it can make or break the project.

What the Design Comes as We Build and Homegrown Street projects suggest is that each locality is a point of convergence – and that there is a special place for local inhabitants – in this case the home builders and their intimate knowledge of context. Importantly, these participants are professional in their aspirations, and this needs to be recognized.

Our own interventions become part of a joint process enriched by the dialogue between the trained urbanist and the self-taught builder. Both are aware that recognition of their learning and processes means an exchange of skills and knowledge across professional boundaries with an openness to different styles and attitudes.

7

Mess Is More

Homegrown Tokyo

The phrase *mess is more*, which plays on Mies van der Rohe's famous *less is more*, is our gateway to understanding important urban experiences that are often overlooked. We focus on Tokyo as a unique city that can transform our gaze and help us to appreciate ways of being urban that defy the dominant twentieth-century global model. Following anthropologist Mary Douglas, who argued that dirt is nothing more than matter out of place, we see Tokyo's many contrary dimensions from a perspective of relativity that seeks to engage with, rather than dismiss, their apparent messiness.[1]

We advocate for the story of Tokyo to appear in every urban planning and design syllabus. Long dismissed as an urban mess, a complex by-product of Japan's economic 'miracle', Tokyo is now gaining attention as a model of urban management.[2] There are lessons to be learned from Tokyo for other cities around the world.

Many writers, photographers, and cinematographers, Japanese and foreign, have marvelled at the village-like atmosphere of Tokyo. Donald Richie was one of the most eloquent admirers of Tokyo's meandering streets and human-scale neighbourhoods. He explored Tokyo in 1947 as a young soldier during the US occupation and quickly fell in love with it. Richie depicts Tokyo as an atemporal organism generated over time by its residents – one which can only be grasped through immersion. He saw Tokyo as a city unfazed by its own destruction, the DNA of its neighbourhoods forever that of the villages that once bordered its historical self, Edo:

Compared to the European medieval city, the sixteenth-century Japanese capital was eventually a congeries of little towns, each with some degree of self-sufficiency, each formed so naturally from the common needs that the whole was enriched ... Such an urban pattern was perhaps once worldwide, but it is now no longer found in Western cities, where units are welded together to create residential areas, business areas and so on. In Japan, only modernized in the last century, these units remain independent; hence the feeling of proceeding through village after village each with its own main street: a bank, a supermarket, a flower shop, a pinball parlour, all without street names or numbers because villagers don't need them.[3]

Donald Richie describes how Tokyo blends the micro and macro dimensions of urban space. It is not a monstrous, inhumane, incomprehensible city but rather a constellation of many small places, each with its own internal logic, all of them interconnected to form a complex yet functioning whole. Richie's Tokyo resonates with Kevin Lynch's description of the organic city:

It does have differentiated parts, but these parts are in close contact with each other and may not be sharply bounded. They work together and influence each other in subtle ways. Form and function are indissolubly linked, and the function of the whole is complex, not to be understood simply by knowing the nature of the parts since parts working together are quite different from the mere collection of them. The whole organism is dynamic, but it is a homeostatic dynamism ... So it is self-regulating. It is also self-organizing ... Emotional feelings of wonder and affection accompany our observation of these entities.[4]

Kevin Lynch acknowledges the power of the organic city metaphor, but eventually finds it too literal. According to him: 'Incorporating purpose and culture, and especially the ability to learn and change, might provide us a far more coherent and defensible model of a city.'[5] Lynch prefers to think of cities as evolving learning ecologies. Indeed, what we call a city, especially if that city happens to be the largest in the world, is the product of internal dynamics along with larger environmental, economic, and political forces – such as war, trade, earthquakes, and climate change.

Architects and urban designers have often tried to replicate the look and feel of organicity, while ignoring the social, economic, and environmental processes that generate organic forms in the first place. New-urbanism schemes, for instance, aim to reproduce the low rise and pedestrian typology of incremental habitats, evoking idealized and domesticated versions of the village and the natural environment. Other token green buildings and eco neighbourhoods fit in the same category: all form, no process.

Some experts, such as spatial anthropologist Hidenobu Jinnai, believe that Tokyo's urban fabric is the result of cultural specificities. He argues that the city's success depends on its capacity to nurture its special brand of urbanism instead of copying best practices from the West:

> A glance at the history of modern Japan makes it obvious that transplant-
> ing the European notions of artfully arranged squares and tree-lined
> streets directly onto Japanese soil has failed to create a space that is both
> interesting and full of energy. Rather, it is only in disorderly, thriving, and
> appropriately small spaces, where human feelings and not an expanding
> vista take charge, that one can find a proper Japanese urban life.[6]

Architect Kisho Kurokawa agrees. According to him, it is the Japanese ability to accept that mess and order are inseparable that explains the

Figure 7.1. Mess Is More in Shibuya, Tokyo – incremental, dense, and high-tech.

city's morphology. A city, he says, 'is composed of complex and multi-layered relations between an organised structure and the multivalent, heterogeneous elements that can be called noise. The city is always changing dynamically as it continuously incorporates new elements.'[7] Yet, this dynamic, metabolic vision of the city was notoriously difficult to translate into architectural practice. Kurokawa was a prominent contributor to the Metabolist Movement, which produced heroic structures in the 1960s. These were supposed to integrate biological principles but were sterile in evolutionary terms. Kurokawa's iconic Nakagin Capsule Tower is a case in point.

What makes Tokyo a dynamic ecology is its multitude of anonymous participants – architects and planners, contractors, artisans, shopkeepers, and residents – who operate in each neighbourhood and have built the city, house by house, street by street. Such local d/evolution of urban development strengthens construction capacity at the local level.

Figure 7.2. Yanaka, a historical homegrown neighbourhood in Tokyo, in 2007.

The politics of incremental urban development

Cultural factors may help understand Japan's tolerance for urban forms that seem unsound by modern Western standards. Yet one must look beyond cultural specificity to realize Tokyo's relevance for urban planning and design practice in other parts of the world. Tokyo's morphology was shaped by local economic life, combined with a tolerant planning framework and relatively supportive urban management systems.

The so-called Tokyo paradox, observed from the late 1960s onwards, is the coming together of first-class infrastructure with an urban typology supposedly reminiscent of Asian slums. This form puzzled some commentators, notably those from the West. Figure 7.3 is a photograph shot in 1987 by US journalists to illustrate the problem of housing in Tokyo.

More than the image itself, which shows a cityscape familiar to anyone who knows Tokyo, the accompanying comment reveals a prejudiced gaze. It mentions that the city's houses are sometimes called 'rabbit hutches' and wonders how these cramped wooden houses can subsist amid the surging wealth of Japan. What the commentator missed is that

Figure 7.3. 'Rabbit Hutches': photo and comment published in the *Morning Call*, a US newspaper, in 1987.

behind this apparent mess there were organizing forces at work. Ryue Nishizawa, principal of Sanaa, an architectural firm, describes a city that is developing 'without a master plan, in a natural way', and which may look chaotic but is well managed:

> Tokyo appears to be very disorganized, but it is a city that works. There is no train delay. Every morning huge crowds are moved in a very orderly way from one point to the other. Very few crimes are committed in Tokyo. It is very orderly, even if the landscape looks disorderly. Some Westerners come to Tokyo and say this is chaos! It may be true, but people manage it very well.[8]

Tokyo provides a powerful alternative to the clearance and redevelopment of unplanned neighbourhoods in cities such as Mumbai, where a majority of the population is said to be living in slums. We have written about the capacity of local actors in unplanned neighbourhoods such as Dharavi in Mumbai to improve their habitat over time through home-based economic activities and local construction practices. Likewise, Tokyo's entrepreneurs, service providers, and artisans were responsible for the reconstruction of Tokyo from the 1950s onwards. The city's residential neighbourhoods are largely homegrown, meaning that they were initially built locally with almost no help from the government, which focused its resources on the development of infrastructure and industry.

Local economic development

After World War II, most businesses were small-scale, family-run, and rooted in traditional social structures. Micro-enterprises provided the bulk of employment. Small shops, artisans' workshops, micro-industries, and businesses shaped Tokyo's neighbourhoods. While the government employed a large number of people in big infrastructure projects, many more were working as independent masons and contractors building Tokyo's millions of tiny homes, one at a time.

While the Japanese economy completely transformed in the post-war period, one thing remained constant right to the end of the twentieth century: the vast majority of workers were employed in small businesses of less than twenty people, many of them family-owned. According to economist Hirohisa Kohama, the share of the working population employed in small and medium enterprises remained stable between 1955 and 1998, at around 70 per cent.[9]

Many houses were rebuilt following the template of traditional Japanese houses, which provides highly flexible usage. Residential units were typically used to run small retail businesses and home factories. Conversely, working spaces laid with tatami mats could easily be converted into sleeping rooms or dormitories at night, as was common in villages. As late as 1981 in Japan: 'Some 30.6 per cent of the total labour force work in minuscule units ... Some three-fifths of small businesses, and four-fifths of retail stores, are "home businesses" in which owners and families constitute more than half the labour force.'[10] It is worth noting that, according to Hugh Patrick and Thomas Rohlen, who studied small businesses in post-war Japan, the modus operandi of these units was not competition so much as networking, cooperation, and functional integration. Thus throughout the post-war period tiny factories spread all over Tokyo, making parts that were then assembled into industrial goods – and contributing to the legendary economic development of the city and the country. This allowed the incremental emergence of a middle class that would re-invest part of its earnings into home improvements, thus contributing to the overall development of the city.

Figure 7.4. A home factory in Tokyo, 1949.

Whatever was not immediately spent or reinvested was saved in banks and postal accounts, helping to build Japan's financial might and allowing banks to lend to the government and corporations, big and small. The government used these savings to finance large-scale urban infrastructure projects connecting neighbourhoods through state-of-the-art transportation infrastructures, which helped to turn Tokyo into an incredibly efficient urban system.

From failed master-planning to successful urban management

According to historian André Sorensen, in the immediate aftermath of the Pacific War, the city's modernist planners dreamed of rebuilding Tokyo as an urban system made of many small cities, divided by generous parks, forests, and agricultural land. Instead, Tokyo became a huge, dense, and contiguous urban landmass without much green space. Planners initially wanted to force all landowners to contribute 15 per cent of their land for greenbelts and public spaces; they also tried to impose new building codes and strict zoning between residential and industrial areas. None of that happened.[11]

Japan was bankrupt after the war, and US occupation forces did not consider urban planning to be a priority. The government had neither the authority nor the financial means to enforce any of its ambitious schemes. Instead the city was rebuilt on the footprint it had inherited from the high-growth Meiji period. Land once planned as protected green spaces soon turned brown and grey, as hundreds of thousands of survivors built shelters and workshops. Planners were unable to control the city, so residents took charge of its development. This level of local autonomy and organization was not new in Japan; it was rooted in the cooperative ethos that prevailed in rural areas.

As a result, there was no real post-war shift in Tokyo's pattern of development, but rather an acceleration of the developmental process that had started decades ago, and which implied the merging of rural and urban landscape in an apparently haphazard process. In the Meiji period, Tokyo was already a world-class city, according to anthropologist Theodore Bestor.[12] The subdivision and conversion of agricultural land continued, and urbanization typically preceded the implementation of civic infrastructure. But the urban chaos that ensued was mitigated by the capacity of newcomers to establish collective management systems inspired by the places they had come from.

Sometimes it was the absence of planning that provided the biggest push for local initiatives. According to economist Yoshitsugu Kanemoto, plots smaller than 1,000 square metres did not need construction permits and were not required to follow the guidelines for residential development.[13] It is in part thanks to such lenient policies that small owners and contractors became the largest producers of housing in Tokyo, right into the 1990s.

According to data from the Tokyo metropolitan government, from 1957 to 1996, non-incorporated individual landowners have built more floor space than large-scale corporate developers and the government combined. Families who invested in their own homes and local contractors were the main agents of urban development at the neighbourhood level. Thousands of local, non-incorporated builders and artisans specialized in small-scale construction.

Affordable housing through local construction practices

This practice kept construction costs low and contributed to generating a hugely diversified housing stock in terms of style and quality.[14] This diversity is still apparent in low-rise residential parts of Tokyo today. It was not until the 1990s that the government revised the Building Standard Law and essentially killed the hugely dynamic market for the construction of small houses.[15] This was done in the name of safety in the context of Tokyo's seismic vulnerability. Local construction practices were not without their shortcomings, but they did manage to produce a massive amount of affordable housing in one of the most expensive cities in the world.

According to Ann Waswo, this form of laissez-faire was not simply the result of an incapacity to plan but was also an integral part of the government's post-war housing strategy. The 'myriad small building companies and a few large, industrialized construction firms' constituted 'the vital 'fourth pillar' of housing policy':

Smaller companies tended to specialise in the building of traditional wooden single-family dwellings in both urban and rural areas of the country, the re-building of traditional dwellings that had been destroyed in natural disasters or merely come to the end of their normal lifespan and the building of wooden apartment houses in or near cities, to take advantage of the market for fairly inexpensive rental accommodation among urban newcomers and newly formed urban families.[16]

Individual contractors and artisans hired by small homeowners were responsible for developing most of Tokyo's urban fabric from the Meiji period right up to the end of the twentieth century. Far from being a fading memory, this aspect of Tokyo's post-war development is still very much visible in the city. Small contractors were not merely building traditional homes but also adapted their techniques and adopted new materials. In this respect, the construction sector mirrored the evolution of the manufacturing sector in Japan, which managed to remain relevant throughout the twentieth century by constantly upgrading its skills and technologies. According to economist Takeshi Hayashi: 'Technological transformation in Japan took one of the following two paths: (1) modernizing traditional technology, (2) making modern technology traditional.'[17]

From the government's perspective, the development of small rental units on a large scale reduced the need for public housing. Small houses responded to the need of single occupants and young couples, and were also a last-resort option for families looking for affordable housing. The tax regime favoured the construction of new homes over the restoration of older ones. This helps explain why homes in Tokyo were typically built to last for about a generation and why neighbourhoods are, to date, always bustling with construction-related activities.

Standardization versus confusion

Loose zoning regulations allowed the spontaneous merging of residential and economic activities. Tokyo's neighbourhoods were teeming with industrial and commercial activities throughout the last part of the twentieth century. Everything merged and mixed in ways that responded to users' immediate needs. This generated serious environmental concerns, and zoning was used to segregate polluting industries from residential areas.[18] It was never used to reorganize existing urban space along functionalist lines, however, as happened in Europe and the US. The 1978 Standard Building Code recognized mixed land use as a reality of urban development and adopted a rather pragmatic stance towards it:

Of course, from the point of view of standardization or purification of land use or land use districts this is not a favorable phenomenon but, for example when part of the production process of textiles takes place in the home as a cottage industry, and thus one part of a residential home is used for this purpose, which is not uncommon, it is thus possible to give authorizations recognizing that, limited to a particular model, construction of this sort may be allowed in residential districts.[19]

The use of words such as *standardization* and *purification* to qualify a well-zoned city reflects a bias against mixed-use of urban land. The prevailing idea at the time, in Japan as in Western countries, was that zoning urban spaces along functional lines would increase efficiency and quality of life. According to the authors of the code, zoning would also make the city more 'peaceful and easy to navigate'. The absence of zoning would

Figure 7.5. The Tokyo–Mumbai homegrown continuum: collage showing Ikebukuro, Tokyo on the left and Dharavi, Mumbai on the right. Collage by Matias Echanove.

result in a confused city.[20] As we have seen, however, confusion may not be such a bad thing – it literally means *with fusion*. This confused state allowed the emergence of the mixed-use and human-scale morphology that makes Tokyo such a liveable and lovable city today.

While many neighbourhoods in Tokyo were (and still are) destroyed to give way to large-scale infrastructure projects, which have always been seen as a national cause in Japan, the approach to hyper-dense, low-quality, haphazard settlements has generally been integrative, with an emphasis on retrofitting and allowing them to improve over time. This is why we can see high-tech, well-managed, attractive versions of the same neighbourhoods that were once shanties.

Unfortunately, even in Tokyo, homegrown neighbourhoods are under constant threat. Hidenobu laments the disappearance of what he calls Tokyo's 'neo-alleys' in some of the city's central areas:

> the modern city continues to grow relentlessly, thriving on one 'cruel' remodelling plan after another. Whole city blocks are often covered by one huge building, leaving neither interstices nor space to the rear. The word *town* once connoted streets defined by houses with storefronts, which created a confused – but nevertheless unified – space. In the process of urban rebuilding, these houses were replaced first by commercial structures, then by elegant office buildings. No longer is there room for the vulgar elements of the city – shops, restaurants, and other 'immoral' businesses – except underground ... Such a development is no doubt the symptom of an urban civilization distorted by the incessant pursuit of functionality and efficiency, most clearly embodied in the principle of 'all yield to the automobile' that now governs our lives. It symbolizes the defeat of the human elements of the city.[21]

The concept that neighbourhood life needs all kinds of services to exist in close proximity, with a dose of improvisation guaranteeing diversity of form and function, became mainstream only in the last decades of the twentieth century. For a good part of the twentieth century, planning was dominated by a modernist discourse holding that visual order, efficiency, and quality of life could be achieved only through masterplanning. Alternatives were popularized by the likes of Jane Jacobs, who echoed the voices of Patrick Geddes and others before her. In Tokyo, much of the homegrown fabric survived, thanks to its embeddedness with local economic activities as well as cultural sensitivities and local management systems.

8

The Tool-House

Recognizing a familiar typology

The tool-house is an urban typology that can be found all over the world in different avatars. It played a central role in the development of post-war Tokyo, and it is now helping countless families to sustain themselves in Mumbai's homegrown neighbourhoods. In its simplest form, the tool-house is a home that doubles up as a tool of production. It is built locally, and is convivial, in the sense of Ivan Illich's *Tools for Conviviality*. According to Illich, a convivial tool is one that does not need a user's manual; it can be understood by everyone through familiarity and affordances – for instance, a spinning wheel, a kitchen, or a bicycle. It puts productive power into the hands of the common people and draws control over the means of production away from experts. Its operating system is simple enough that if it is broken it can be repaired by the user.[1]

The tool-house typology also echoes Le Corbusier's 'machine for living' to the extent that it is designed to fulfil specific functions, with users in mind.[2] The houses of Dharavi are basic tools that perform residential and income-generating functions for a family. Every tool-house is also a component of a more complex live–work machine – an urban compound or neighbourhood.

Even though they are man-made, there is an organic quality to streets lined with tool-houses. This is because every house is embedded in its surroundings, connected to a network of other tool-houses where each performs specific tasks, contributing to the economy of the neighbourhood. No tool-house is fully self-contained. It derives its productive energy from the presence of other tool-houses and people that move from one to another. A family unit receives a pile of freshly cut shirts on which they sew some motifs. They buy needle and thread at their neighbours' shop down the street. They bring the finished products to another place to be packaged, before they are stored and displayed at a wholesale shop on the main street.

The tool-house economy is a cooperative, networked economy, where the whole is larger than the sum of the parts. It rarely occurs as a singular phenomenon. It derives a lot of support from multiple versions of itself, allowing for a sharing of resources and the development of collective strength in numbers. It also allows for a massive diversity, decentralization, and multiplication of economic functions all over the neighbourhood. Since it is small in scale and easy to set up, emerging from a fundamental need for sheltering, it is found on a large scale with a wide variety of skills, services, goods, and activities. This is why it is possible to find diverse services in any section of Dharavi. The tool-house in its singular and multiple forms makes a significant contribution to the locality's fabric as dense, but also functional, productive, and liveable.

A tool-house connects the city to a layer of economic activities on which a large number of people depend. It is an answer to the scarcity of land, emerging from an inability to own the land, along with a lack of insurance that anything that is built will be allowed to remain. This means that its value cannot be generated speculatively; it must be produced through use.

A tool-house can be an elaborate structure with many activities happening in its different parts, or just one corner of a room might be used in multiple ways. It can be a family home with a shop on the ground floor. It can be a room used to sleep in at night, which doubles up as a tiny assembly unit during the day. It can be a restaurant with a bedroom for the employees, or where tables and chairs are pushed to the side at night and sleeping mats are rolled out on the floor. It can be a dormitory-workshop, where a group of men work during the day and stay at night for a few weeks or a few months.

In Mumbai, even an upper-middle-class apartment provides income and receives services every day from a range of service providers: cooks, cleaners, gardeners, or garbage collectors. In the meantime, a family member might run a consultancy from her laptop. Every home becomes an economic unit and a gateway to economic activities.

As a growing scholarship indicates, structures similar to the tool-house can be found across cultures and socio-economic backgrounds. Like Howard Davis, Frances Holliss, and the large community of academics and practitioners who recognize the persistence and relevance of live–work conditions, we consider this to be one of the most enduring artefacts of pre-industrial society.[3]

Yet as a structure epitomizing dual use, the tool-house does not have the legitimacy it deserves. In fact, in many places, thanks to strict zoning laws and rigid conceptions of urban order, it is considered outdated, or worse, an illegitimate urban form. Any regulation that rules out the possibility of mixing functions within a single space necessarily attacks the logic of the tool-houses. With the universalizing principles of the industrial revolution becoming mainstream, homes and workspaces have been decisively cut off from each other.

The modern city emerged through a division of functions which have long cohabitated in space and time. As working and living became spatially segregated, they also became increasingly regimented along temporal lines. When the self-employed artisan became a factory worker he splintered his workshop-home and his days: he had to commute to a separate place and compartmentalize his time in strict schedules demarcated as work and leisure. Ever since, the practice of separating residences from places of manufacture has shaped the way we think of cities, work, and time. In particular, the organizing of space according to these principles has become the main purpose of urban planning.

In practice, however, tool-houses exist everywhere and always will. They are perhaps the most predominant urban typologies that ever existed. No matter how much they are repressed by planners, they sprout back to life. The reason for their resilience is basic economics. In a context where self-employment is ubiquitous and urban development keeps pushing up the price of space, the home needs to double up as a productive site.

The search for alternatives to the industrial city is sparking interest in live–work typologies in academic and architectural circles. A growing body of economic commentaries describe the return of the home-based workspace (in the US this is supposed to be an antidote to outsourcing) and the re-emergence of the post-industrial artisan. The contemporary world of industry and commerce is proving to be a live exhibition space for the display of different eras and epochs.

According to Frances Holliss:

The Covid-19 pandemic triggered an experiment in enforced home-working across the globe … An unarguable outcome is that WFH (work from home) during Covid has been more prevalent, persistent

Figure 8.1. Tool-house in Dharavi (photo: Ishan Tankha for urbz).

Figure 8.2. Tool-house in Dharavi (photo: Niccolo Gandolfi for Domus).

and popular than predicted – and this has major social, economic and environmental implications, globally.[4]

Still, the evolution in people's habits has not been reflected in the way neighbourhoods and buildings are conceived. The narrative arc based on the movement from home to factory, however arcane and incongruous today, continues to shape urban planning projects focused on commutes and separating living and working conditions.

An economic unit

The fact of the matter is that the logic of the tool-house is intimately linked to the larger economic context of informality, decentralized production, and the subsidizing of costs by using space in complex and layered ways. It is organically connected to the unit of the family and the home, the community, and the persistence of the village form in the modern metropolis.

The home is many things – a shelter, a unit of production, and a node in the community that becomes a valuable resource in the economic life of the neighbourhood. The etymology of *economy* evokes the idea of managing the home. Homes loom even larger in settlements that are self-reliant and identified as outside the urban norm. Just as the local is the foundation of spatial logic across scale – even the most global of all activities and abstractions is rooted in a locality – the productive home is the foundation of neighbourhoods, particularly homegrown ones.

In cities such as Mumbai, more than half the population lives in homegrown neighbourhoods, creating a commuting statistic that is the envy of the developed world. According to the Urban Age Mumbai research on transport conducted by Philip Rode, more than 55 per cent of the city's population walks to work and an overwhelming majority of this demographic comes from these neighbourhoods.[5] Instead of building on this arrangement, the city is continuing to invest in destroying these spaces, spreading the population to far-flung areas and ensuring that more and more people use cars or a poorly equipped, struggling public transport system.

The fact that this typology is already overwhelmingly prevalent should be seen as an opportunity. It is connected to a layer of economic activity on which many people depend. It economizes space and allows for a densification of people and activity. This is a viable alternative to vertical growth, which is otherwise the only, rather expensive, direction in which urban space is venturing – one that densifies buildings and creates speculative space more than anything else.

What would an alternative space-time arrangement look like, if the artisanal tool-house was fully accepted? The streets of Tokyo's older low-rise, high-density areas, provide us with a glimpse of such a possibility. Tokyo's ability to retrofit infrastructure and make use of railway networks to allow for the co-existence of commuting and local-scale economic activities is a source of inspiration. But this is only one possibility among many.

There is potential for different urban typologies to develop functional relationships with each other in creative ways. In São Paulo, for example, modern complexes with their own economic and residential zones sit close to favelas, which are enmeshed in the developed neighbourhoods through services rendered. At the same time, many of these areas have their own economies running from each home.

Similarly in Mumbai, middle-class neighbourhoods often are in proximity to so-called slums so there is minimal travel time for their service providers. Here too, service providers are part of households whose members perform economic activities from their own homes. This proximity between middle-class homes and service providers is a form of subsidy which propels an upward mobility that energizes the whole economy of the city. This combination of factors helps make employment more available and accessible for a large number of people.

It is already recognized in some planning practices that urban space-time can become more flexible if it is allowed to escape from the zoned residential, economic, and recreational divisions. However, mixed-use spaces are not simply about juxtaposing these purposes; they emerge from the basic unit of combining roles and functions within each dwelling, and this facilitates economic activities, increasing savings and productivity. Such spaces emerge when we start to conceive of all homes – whether in the favela or in a high-rise apartment – as being tool-houses to varying degrees, as this allows for a diversity of built forms and economic activities to coexist within an urban fabric, no matter how messy and uneven its appearance. This changes the nature of the everyday commute, which despite great advances in transport technology never solves the problem of growing populations who continue to move *en masse* from one point to another at fixed points in the working day.

Instead of focusing on increasing speed to get people from one point to another for work, many transport specialists have advocated policies that encourage the proximity of places of work and residence. Yet this is rarely translated into practice because of the obstacles of economic exigencies, real estate value, and the practical realities of existing urban arrangements. Such a goal can only be met if we approach the problem not from the point of view of a physical rearrangement but as one that takes into account the basic units that build an urban fabric. If that unit is conceived as a split entity, it will unfold as one, divided into zoned spaces that extend across distances. If it is conceived as a holistic one – both domestic and economic at the same time – then it is easily translatable into a form in which proximity between work and residence is the norm.

For us, the tool-house is a concept that epitomizes the antithesis of the split, which became the foundation of a widespread vision in urban planning in developed economies. Cities grew and became connected through transport systems, but distances kept growing regardless of how efficient such systems were. Real estate speculation kept pace with these distances, measuring each square inch in terms of proximity to some valued destination. Centres and peripheries became the defining principle of urban space, and time became as valued a commodity as space.

Helicopters zooming in and out of the terraces of tall buildings in large cities have become powerful symbols of the unsustainable nature of this logic, which more and more cities continue to rush.

If instead the tool-house principle becomes the organizing logic – something which advances in communication technologies have already made a reality for people across the class spectrum – then a different city emerges: a city that affords different modes of travel and commutes, from walking to helicopter rides, without privileging one over the other, its enmeshing of economic, residential, and recreational activities creates streets and neighbourhoods that are culturally dynamic and economically mixed.

If the city of the future is to be anywhere close to the fifteen-minutes city that experts are advocating, then we must look more closely and carefully at neighbourhoods that already epitomize these principles. They exist in the most unexpected of places – already functioning and functional, from villages in Mumbai to favelas in São Paulo.

The home-factory, the shop-house, and the loft are typologies that exist all over the world – in the small alleyways of Tokyo, the colonial precincts of Singapore, the designers' studios of Berlin and New York. These typologies are making a big comeback. News reports and studies keep popping up to show how, thanks to new technologies, working from home is becoming the norm for great cohorts of people. For millions all over the world, the choice or compulsion to work from home has become a reality. Working from home – whether as an artisan making objects, a professional providing services, or a homeowner converting a portion of the house for rent – has shaped cities throughout history.

Modern urban planning saw mixed-use dwellings as promiscuous and hazardous, and tried to segregate cities along functionalist lines throughout the twentieth century. Whenever planning norms were weakly enforced or deliberately relaxed, however, the industrious home thrived.

The overwhelming presence of live–work conditions in Indian cities is striking, from Bareilly to Agra, from Coimbatore to Surat – let alone the enormous manufacturing and processing hubs in Delhi and Mumbai.

The synergy between economic life, family, and community is particularly strong in India. This shapes the economy as well as cities, because production here is still a local community affair. Many eatable and wearable goods consumed in cities, for instance, are made by a myriad of small producers rather than large-scale factories. For governments, this tends to be a problem: while they talk of the value and importance of informal industries, the official parameters of economic development have no place for the intricacies of small-scale arrangements – especially when they become distractions in the context of ambitious city makeovers. Neighbourhoods where this kind of production happens don't look modern enough in the eyes of policymakers – they are typically low-rise, high-density, and unplanned.

But a closer look at such arrangements reveals that this attitude may mean that governments are missing an opportunity to unleash India's highly advanced local economy. Economist Smita Srinivas has thought through the way Indian economic practices are embedded in urban and social contexts.[6] What happens in Indian neighbourhoods is an intricate, detailed scale of production that works flexibly and simultaneously for local, regional, national, and global markets. In all this, the local economy acts as a foundation – a bedrock – drawing deeply from familial and community resources.

Local needs can be specific and peculiar, ranging from implements and raw materials needed for community rituals, to jewellery made in a particular regional or ethnic fashion, or specialized household items that are not always found in the regular market. This reflects the layers of traditional practices and needs that have become integrated into new chains of production and exchange. It makes it easier here than elsewhere to customize the production of any good, object, or service – thanks to the presence of high-quality but affordable skills that are constantly testing and experimenting at the local neighbourhood level. This is as true for constructing homes as it is for adapting tailoring skills or servicing industrial needs. People live in clusters that allow families and communities to develop networks of co-dependence.

While most developing countries are trying to make their cities look modern by eradicating what many consider backward lifestyles and livelihoods, some cities are focusing on creating new forms of craftsmanship, merging manual skills with new technologies. It is precisely this combination that has propelled Shenzhen to the very top of the global electronic and robotic industry. It is also what is preserving the relevance of West European craftsmanship in Germany, Switzerland, France, and Italy. Everywhere, cities are reinventing themselves by combining craft, creativity, design, and technology, tailored to niche markets both locally and globally. Mixed-use neighbourhoods are key in this process. Many cities are actively promoting them – arguing that producing locally and consuming locally, while participating in a global network – is not only smart but also good for the environment.

India is ripe for this new economy. It has industrious neighbourhoods at the core of its cities, and the internet has penetrated deep into all socio-economic strata and sectors of activity. What's more, a high proportion of urban youth who come from families engaged in artisanship have been to college and know enough about media, law, and accounting to reinvent their family businesses. The same youth who suffer from discrimination when they hunt for white-collar jobs in large corporations should be given incentives to start the creative enterprises of tomorrow. Tool-houses in Agra are already producing high-end goods for designer studios in Milan – the know-how is there. It must be harnessed. India has no shortage of creativity and an increasingly large consumer market.

What needs to change is not the scale of production but the scale of support for existing practices. Crafts must be promoted, transmitted, and reinvented. Vocational training must be developed at all costs, but not only in new institutions with no connection with the local economy – it should be rooted in productive neighbourhoods. This also means resolutely accepting and legalizing homegrown, mixed-use neighbourhoods all over Indian cities, allowing their residents to invest in their homes and businesses and making every effort to improve civic infrastructure. This can become an opportunity for simultaneously improving the working and living conditions of millions of people. This is especially important for the millions of women for whom working from home is a daily reality. Working at home must become less of a trap and more of a tool for economic and social emancipation. Encouraging its upgrade will transform the whole urban context and strengthen the economy at the same time.

Three tool-houses in Dharavi

The three case studies produced between 2012 and 2015 illustrate live–work arrangements typical of Dharavi.[7] They show how the use value of space is maximized by the overlaying of various functions. The live–work conditions described here are far from being aspirational, but they accurately represent how such arrangements allow people to cope in a context of poverty and marginalization, and how flexible use of space can, to a certain extent, favour upward mobility. Since these studies were made, most of these houses have been rebuilt or improved. Some names have been changed.

1. Shalimar restaurant and Faizal Mohammad's stitching workshop

The Shalimar restaurant owners, the Lalwanis, have been running their establishment since the 1960s.[8] They rent the first floor to Faizal Mohammad, a twenty-five-year-old entrepreneur who runs three stitching workshops in the area. In addition, they rent a tiny extension of the house to a needle vendor. Many of the workers sleep in the house at night.

The Lalwanis' tool-house is located in Dharavi's Sangam Gully, a four-metre-wide street, that has been gradually expanded into by establishments on both sides. Sangam Gully is a diverse and busy street. Next to Shalimar one can find a mosque, several wood shops, tea stalls, cell phone shops, sandal stores, and so on. The word *Sangam* means 'coming together'.

Virtually every structure on both sides of the street is a tool-house. While the ground floor is usually used for retailing activities, or activities that merge retailing with production (such as the wood shops), the upper floors are often used for productive activities during the day and as sleeping spaces at night.

The multiplicity of economic activities is notable for a high degree of specialization. The area where Shalimar is located is particularly well known for its embroidery workshops, often run by specific Muslim communities who have specialized in this trade for centuries.

The combination of clustering similar activities and multiple, varied specializations creates a business-friendly environment, as everything one may need is available within a five-minute walking radius. It is not only space that is optimized but also time. The proximity of diverse but complementary activities facilitates the production of complex goods such as suitcases or furniture that require an range of skills and products.

The transportation of goods from one place to the other is often shared among different businesses. This is one of the most striking aspects of the working environment of the neighbourhood. Such moments of coming together, and the sharing of space, time, and mechanisms of mobility, indicate the collective energy of the tool-house, present in its multiple forms.

The space is optimized through intensive use involving numerous functions and layered activities. In addition, the restaurant is a hub where all kinds of people meet and conduct business. Anuj Lalwani, who runs the restaurant with his five brothers, also uses it to conduct other types of business. For instance, it often serves as a meeting space to handle administrative matters. Anuj acts as a middleman, drawing on his vast network, which includes municipal officers, policemen, politicians, and businessmen. He lives in a house just minutes away from the restaurant.

The restaurant used to be open twenty-four/seven until a new law forced all public establishments to shut at 1:30 a.m. at the latest. It opens at 7:00 a.m. and serves breakfast, lunch, dinner, and snacks from different cuisines, including Indian and Chinese. The income generated by the restaurant is divided among the five brothers. They receive additional income from the workshop upstairs. Faizal Mohammad, who runs the workshop, could find cheaper rent in other parts of the city, but he decided to set up in this area, as it is conveniently located to transport goods and people. The workshop operates from 10:00 a.m. to 8:30 p.m., and at peak time employs about twenty people.

After a long, busy day the house serves as a three-level dormitory. At the time of the study, about fourteen people slept there, all of them employed either at the restaurant or the workshop. Usually more people sleep in the workshop, but many had gone to their villages for the summer holiday (which runs from May to July in Mumbai).

Figure 8.3. Stitching workshop in Sangam Gully, Dharavi, Mumbai (photo: urbz).

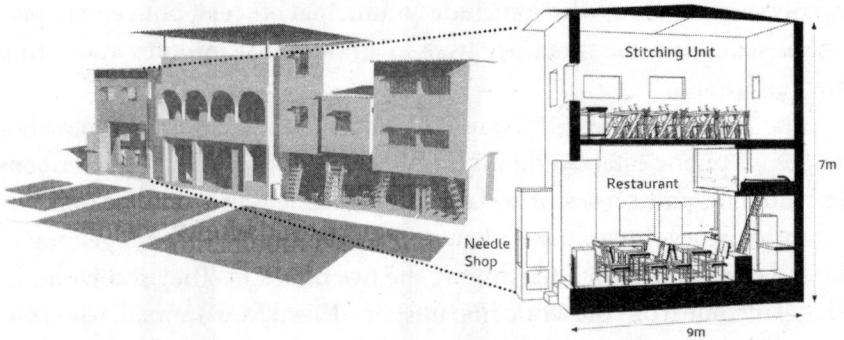

Figure 8.4. An illustration showing the different uses in the Shalimar restaurant structure (illustration: urbz).

2. The Hussain family's tool-house complex

Javed Hussain and his brothers inherited their father's business and social good will in the community, along with the workshops that make King Camp shirts and those for other local brands. The family business operates three workshops, one of which they own; the others are nearby but owned by other people, to whom the Hussains outsource part of their production. Javed's family (including his mother and three siblings) live in the space above the godown (warehouse or wholesale store) from which they operate. Their workshop is one plot away from the shop.

Altogether, the Hussains' workshops produce around 5,000–6,000 garments every month, from which around 4,000 are exported to Goa (which is 587 kilometres away). The brothers own a shop in Ponda, Goa, which is managed by a maternal uncle. The remaining shirts are sent to shops in Mumbai, mainly in Dadar West (5 kilometres away) and Khar East (7 kilometres). The Hussains' own shop in Dharavi is around twelve years old, and they have been in this business since 1987.

Javed's workshop is part of a multimillion-dollar cloth-manufacturing industry, which is segmented into different grades of products. He sees himself as part of the medium-quality sector; his goods are not sold to global brands or retailers but to small shops aimed at the domestic lower-middle-class and middle-class market. The workshop is located in a neighbourhood where there are several other businesses like his, but they do not see each other as competitors because they focus on specific segments and types of demand. Cloth producers in Dharavi actively cooperate and use each other as subcontractors; this allows great flexibility in output and delivery time.

Javed's premises are best described as a tool-house complex, as it consists of several structures in close proximity, off 90 Feet Road, the major arterial street in Dharavi. The main tool-house consists of a storage area stocked with shirts along the walls on the ground floor, which functions as a showroom. The living premises are on the first floor and include a living room, bathroom, toilet, kitchen, and bedroom. Just a couple of shops away, Javed has an establishment on the first floor where workers both live and work, the space functioning as a dormitory and manufacturing space.

The tool-house complex does not have access to the main road and does not need it, since its products are sold elsewhere. As a workspace, it is secluded and workers are undisturbed. It is strategically located within a cluster of embroidering and stitching units and near wholesalers – all within walking distance and belonging to the same social network. The family is an intrinsic part of the business activity and participates through supervising, coordinating with buyers, and managing the transportation of finished goods.

Over time, the tool-house complex has continuously developed. In Javed's father's time there was just a small room. As the business expanded

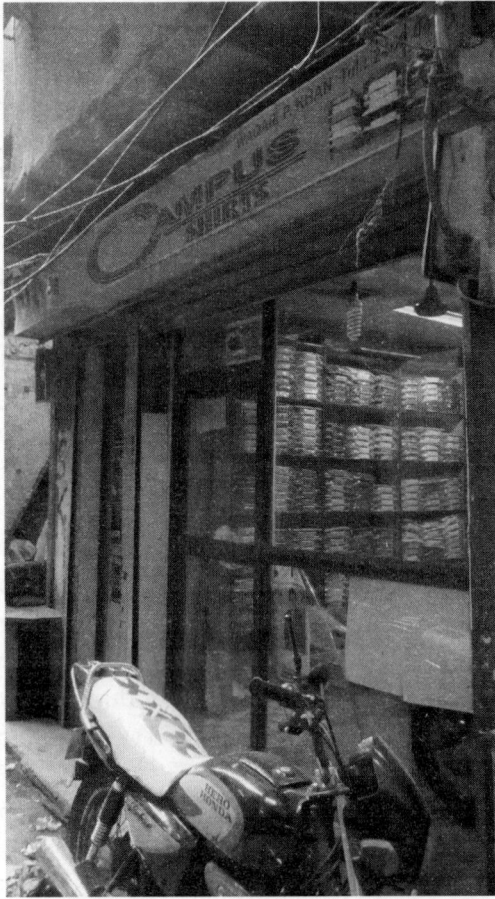

Figure 8.5. The Hussain family's showroom in Dharavi (photo: urbz).

Figure 8.6. The Hussain family's workshop (photo: urbz).

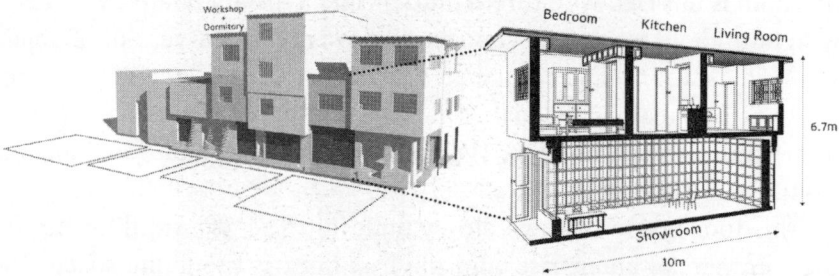

Figure 8.7. The Hussain tool-house complex comprising a unit with a showroom on the ground floor and an apartment on the top floor, as well as a workshop down the road. (illustration: urbz).

and revenues grew, Javed's father built another storey to make room for his growing family, and subsequently bought another space. Today, there is a decent-sized living space for all the household members – one that includes most of the amenities of a middle-class home.

3. The Koravars' tool-house

The Koravar family belongs to one of the most vulnerable communities of Mumbai in terms of its social history. This community was officially referred to by the inaccurate, unfortunate, and misguided label of 'habitually criminal tribe', and subsequently 'denotified tribe' – both categories that a colonial-minded administration used for rebellious nomadic groups (now officially classified as the scheduled tribes) in the erstwhile state of Bombay. The present city of Mumbai was one nodal hub of that state, functioning as its main coastal port. Bombay state included towns, villages, cities, mountains, and forests, once covering a territory that spanned Karachi in modern-day Pakistan to Goa in the south and reaching the borders of the old Hyderabad state in the east. The city has always been a destination for a variety of communities, rich, poor, and vulnerable, from all over the state.

Today, the family lives in their tool-house that generates revenue through a matching centre, where women come to buy matching coloured blouses, duppattas (scarves), bangles, imitation jewellery, cosmetics, T-shirts for kids, and other assorted items. The household's income is supported by the patriarch, Appa (a driver), supplemented by the earnings of family members. The nine members in the household comprise the oldest couple, Appa and Sunita, their two sons, one of whom is married with three children, and a distant relative who helps with household work. The younger son, twenty-seven-year-old Ranjan, works in data entry and earns a monthly salary. He also plays in his company's cricket team in his spare time. The household's women work from home and manage the shop. The household receives additional income from renting part of its space.

This tool-house is a two-storey building. The ground floor houses the commercial enterprise, and the first floor is the living space. The commercial section comprises an adequately furnished showroom with proper display tables and racks for clothes and jewellery. The space is equipped with efficient lighting.

The first floor consists of a living room, two bedrooms, kitchen, and bathroom. Each room has a television set, as well as an air conditioner and a matching bed-and-wardrobe set. The structure has an adjacent space on the ground floor, which is rented out as a tea stall.

The tool-house grew incrementally, and features were added as the household revenue increased over the years. The spatial organization of the tool-house relies extensively on its ability to increase the density of use and thus enhance its spatial capacity.

This implies making space available for different kinds of use on a temporal basis. The shop occupies pride of place, also serving as a living room where people come to meet the family. Its function as a shop is of prime importance, but at night it can easily be used as a space for sleeping by family members as well. There is always a need for more sleeping space, especially when relatives visit the family. In the morning, all traces of night use are erased and the space is made ready for commercial use again. The formal residential space is private, especially during the day – a place to cook, eat and function as a family.

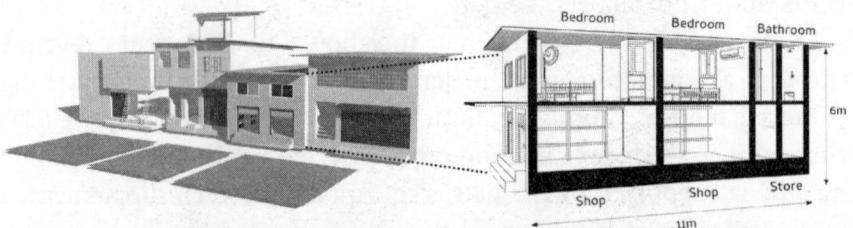

Figure 8.8. The Koravars' tool-house (illustration: urbz).

Figure 8.9. The Koravar house viewed from the street (photo: urbz).

Figure 8.10. Inside the Koravar house (photo: urbz).

Tool-houses in the twenty-first century

Cities such as Mumbai refuse to integrate the tool-house into urban plans because it is seen as a misfit in controlled, formalized, and regulated systems. Tool-houses are seen to be part of a disorganized, uncontrolled urbanism in which all official regulations are transgressed. In Mumbai and many other cities in Asia, Latin America, and Africa, entire urban populations are segregated on the basis of their settlements' image. If their homes and neighbourhoods are not constructed by large conglomerates or the structures do not conform to zoned, functionally divided spaces, they are likely to be classified as slums, favelas, and other similar discredited categories.

Lack of recognition of the homegrown and tool-house typologies means invalidation, and subsequently erasure and replacement with generic mass housing. In the name of improvement, the authorities often wipe out these habitats, resulting in losses of livelihoods and economic dynamism at the local level; this primarily impacts those who are already vulnerable or marginalized but eventually prices out even the middle classes.

In addition, such rehabilitation projects disperse urban populations into larger areas, increasing their dependence on expensive modes of transport to take them to jobs with little scope for growth. What gets lost when tool-house neighbourhoods are bulldozed is not only what people have invested in them, but also the activities they run from them, and the opportunity for their owners and tenants to be entrepreneurs.

The reason why tool-houses need to be factored into the contemporary urban planning regime is that they help make explicit the relationship between production, livelihood, and space. The inability to see these dimensions as active principles in the lives of millions of urban residents all over the world reveals a dire lack of imagination and aborts the complex and organic evolution of more effective and inclusive urban forms that are especially needed in a context of scarce resources and ecological fragility.

Tool-house landscapes indicate the need for a sharp restructuring of the way in which labour, work, and capital are understood, or should be understood, in contemporary times. They help us visualize a future in which the dated dichotomy of the formal and the informal organization of production and services can be transcended – where the new spatial-temporal order that internet-based and mobile-communication technologies have introduced in our lives can be acknowledged, and the complex dialectic between the artisanal, organic, decentralized, and industrial mass-based products in the contemporary economy become validated.

Where urban development is left to local people, we observe the (re-)emergence of live–work spaces that are less dehumanizing than the housing block and its twin, the office tower, which are promoted across the ideological spectrum – including real estate investors and NGOs, and the government – as the only acceptable path.

It is time to acknowledge that for all the lack of infrastructure and presence of overcrowding, several so-called informal settlements demonstrate a trend that can be beneficially integrated into a post-industrial landscape. They can be seen as a highly successful model of grounded development, with the tool-house at the core.

Providing legal tenure and incentives to improve the civic infrastructure of low- and moderate-income houses is the surest way to address the global shortfall in affordable housing. Instead of relying on the state or the market, communities need to be seen as the most reliable resource that can produce homes – provided, of course, that they are understood not just as homes but also as places that generate income. Unfortunately, the land on which they are located is perennially competing for real estate value, and this creates obstacles to acceptance.

To counteract this, the tool-house needs to be recognized as a vital dynamic presence with its own transformative power. It is an economic foundation for millions of marginalized families, communities, and neighbourhoods, while simultaneously embedding them in larger regional, national, and global flows of value. It creates a strong, resilient, and dynamic base from which other scales and contexts can be accessed and engaged with. It helps regulate the systems in which we operate through what economic anthropologist Keith Hart refers to as the *human economy*: 'The object of a human economy is the reproduction of human beings and of whatever sustains life in general. Such an economy would express human variety in its local particulars as well as the interests of all humanity.'[9] The tool-house in particular and working homes in general are powerful symbols of such a human economy and can act as an instrument of transformation.

Today, cities continue to violate the principles of human scale; they exist in systems where distances keep growing ever wider. Where the house and the workspace are forcibly divided, the city will grow in that vein: zoned, divided, and dispersed. If it is conceived as a holistic one, something different will emerge.

The tool-house is a living example of such holism, and it symbolizes urbanism on a human scale, either by default, accident, or intention. It needs to be recognized and validated to become a pathway towards creating a better urban horizon for all.

9

Beyond the City

The rural–urban connection

Conceptualizing Mumbai simply as a megacity is inadequate. Rather, it is a hub in a larger urban system with deep, overlapping, and persistent ties to rural India. These ties are stronger and deeper when seen through the lives of families who live in homegrown neighbourhoods, but they are by no means absent in the lives of many middle-class and even some upper-class families. Family ties, livelihoods, and even political affiliations stretch across the subcontinent.

Although India is still far from the level of urbanization seen in China or Europe, according to recent projections over 600 million Indians are living in urban areas.[1] However, a simple urban-to-rural ratio hides an important fact: rural–urban migrants, including those established in cities for generations, have a relationship with their villages that, as Ashis Nandy points out, is not only historical, spiritual, and psychological, but also practical.[2] This relationship is sustained through frequent family visits, financial investments, and institutional linkages.

These dynamics keep shaping new habitats that continue to transform villages into small towns all over the country. These urbanized networks are more smoothly woven into their rural hinterlands. Sometimes, if they are well connected, these networked regions may even make it easier for people to avoid migrating to a big city and instead travel more selectively for specific commercial and personal reasons.

The logic of frozen categories such as rural and urban does not do justice to the complexity of India. The subcontinent is not made up of one-way channels between bifurcated rural and urban sectors, but functions through a circulatory system of movement and exchange, in which the railway plays a powerful role, as do road and electronic communication networks. This movement is validated through the vast statistical data produced on seasonal migration, quantified in the invest- ments being made by returning urban migrants to their villages, and observed in the multiple ways through which households divide the roles of individual members across a range of sectors.

Until recently, most policymakers tended to refer to India as a country with relatively low levels of urbanization. The 2011 census showed that India was less than 30 per cent urban, with slowing rates of growth in larger urban agglomerations.[3] According to some estimates, India will be 60 per cent urban in 2061.[4] Yet the census indicates growth in small towns and a significant increase in non-farming economic activities in traditionally agrarian regions, including manufacturing, processing of agrarian products, construction, and other services. Significant rural– rural migration also hints at dynamism in formerly agrarian regions, which are now generating income through both farming and non- farming activities. Even on a very small scale, a family may have members dispersed across the country involved in a range of economic activities. Different economic sectors thus contribute to the family's income and provide them with social security.

The census points to increased rural expenditure, due in part to urban migrants sending money home on a regular basis. These migrants are often from poor homegrown neighbourhoods in cities such as Mumbai; they are increasingly vulnerable to instability as real estate specula- tion reaches new heights and the government–developer nexus pushes poorer populations to the city's periphery while grabbing the land they live on. Even if they are provided a spot to live in after displacement, it often comes stripped of the web of economic and livelihood opportu- nities they had woven around themselves in their previous settlement. Under these circumstances the connection to villages becomes a lifeline. Urbanization was never a one-way street for such migrants.

These observations do not indicate any pathology in the Indian urban story; rather they reflect a need to revisit the narrow lens through which urbanization is typically viewed everywhere. Anthropologists such as Anthony Leeds have provided a more comprehensive and inclusive narrative of urbanization that fits the Indian reality much better.[5]

According to Leeds, the rural and the urban are not necessarily dis- tinct entities. The rural can be viewed as a subcategory of the urban, but not in a way that undermines the village as a habitat. This structure may allow for a perspective that expands rural life. Farming can be seen as an urban activity, in a sense, as farmers are economically, technologically, and institutionally connected to urban power centres, primarily through market networks. Large agrarian regions have historically been connected to urban industrial centres through tax regimes, trading activities, and political-legal systems. Narratives which oppose a modern, industrialized, and networked urban world to one of traditional villages evolving in relative economic and cultural isolation don't reflect the reality of many regions in India, where circular migration – a phenomenon that describes a to-and-fro movement between villages and cities thanks to dual-household family structures with one foot in each realm – is the norm.

From a related perspective, by linking the miner, the lumberjack, the farmer, the artisan, and the fisher as participants within local, professional, technical, institutional, and social systems, Leeds disrupts the neat division of regional territories into urban and rural. His conceptual framework questions the notion that cities are economic engines that must necessarily grow outward, swallowing the towns and villages on their peripheries. His framework suggests that different scales of habitats can be, and often are, integrated and interdependent.

This framework can better be understood when seen through the example of Mumbai and its immediate southern hinterland, which

Figure 9.1. Participatory installation created by urbz showing rural–urban linkages at the Bhau Daji Lad Museum in 2017. Visitors were asked to pin a thread connecting their neighbourhoods in Mumbai to their villages in any part of India.

illustrates such a complex rural–urban formation. Like most cities embedded in their regional networks, Mumbai has special connections to its nearby coastal region. The Konkan is a cultural-geographic name that refers to India's west coast along the Arabian sea, stretching from the metropolis and covering three states all the way to Karnataka. Mumbai was the dominant urban node for the movements of people from this region in the nineteenth and early-twentieth century. These migrants significantly shaped the city's growth. A spotlight on this dimension of the city's history is useful to understand how connected urban and rural systems remain in India, and the consequent impact of these connections on the way we view cities, evolve urban policy, and consider urbanization processes.

From the village to the city and back

Just as it is vital not to categorize habitats rigidly by identity (such as tribal, rural, or urban) or to set these terms in fixed narratives of belonging, it is equally important not to measure habitats in terms of distance and proximity that are perpetually locked into notions of centre and periphery. Instead, a more fluid and integrated understanding of these concepts is needed.

The peculiar way in which connections across habitats (at large distances from each other) keep replaying themselves in new contexts is crucial to such an understanding. Existing definitions of the city are highly unsatisfactory because they do not give an account of one of the most fundamental aspects of urban life: the interaction between the multiplicity of contexts and people.

That the rural is embedded in the urban became particularly apparent to us in our study of patterns of mobility and commuting along Mumbai's Konkan coast between 2012 and 2013.[6]

In the course of our research, we learned that most of the travellers or commuters in our sample on the Mumbai–Konkan railway network – we focused on six stations on roughly 700 kilometres of track – had varied commuting and mobility patterns. Most were not moving back and forth on a daily basis: many took the train only a few times each month – or year – for social or business reasons. Others organized their physical and personal spaces along professional and familial lines in their own idiosyncratic rhythms. Workers could live in a shared room in Mumbai for most months of the year (always on the phone for a few minutes every day with their village relatives), along with spending almost an equivalent amount of time in their rural homes, hundreds of kilometres away.

Many who were unable to afford a middle-class lifestyle in the city reproduced it in their village, bringing their urban imaginary to a space where it could be realized.

According to Leeds, economic specialization, institutional linkages, and technological penetration are all indicators of the degree to which a village may already be urbanized. It is equally true that its relationship to the city may well be part of its survival strategy as a village. This is not so much because the village must define itself for or against the city but rather because it must function alongside it. It is nearly impossible to find a village that has not historically been part of some larger social, political, and economic dynamic, even if it meant a single strand of exchange – trading just one commodity, supplying seasonal labour, or sending an annual remittance. It would be a real challenge to find a village on the Konkan coast where none of the villagers travelled for work to some other part of the region or beyond (if not to Mumbai).

During the period of our study, the train on the Konkan railway was used mostly by passengers to travel on a monthly or yearly basis. Fewer than 10 per cent of the people interviewed used the train for their daily or weekly commutes. Some 40 per cent used it frequently – at least five times a year, but less than once a week. The remaining half used the train only occasionally (one to four times a year).

The rural–urban migration narrative, which is often used to explain the demographic explosion of Indian megacities and second-tier cities in the past decades, has obfuscated this narrative: that of the regular, long-distance traveller who never severs ties with their village, keeping active relationships with family and community. They go back often for personal reasons, to perform religious rituals, or to attend weddings. They can be investors in their villages, contributing to the agricultural modernization or the gradual urbanization of their habitat.

Sociologist Dipankar Gupta points out that the census fails to account for the multiplicity of roles that any one individual might assume. He argues that categorizing individuals in set roles and socio-professional identities invisibilizes the level of economic diversification and urbanization in rural India. It systematically represents the rural economy as dominated by farming when the reality is much more diverse. He gives the example of small machines that allow manufacturing to happen almost anywhere. These and a range of other non-agrarian activities, services, and technologies are transforming the countryside, seamlessly but fundamentally.[7]

The linkages between the village and the city established by family and community networks add another layer to this complex story. A measure of the ability of families and communities to have one foot in the city and the other in the village – and of the way these economies come together through the bilateral transfer of skills and knowledge – may help us understand more deeply the resilience of the rural sector in India.

Circulatory rural–urban–rural movements are part of a larger, accelerating exchange of ideas and images that redefines the sense of space and location in rural India. François Ascher writes about multiple belonging, expressing the fact that people often define themselves in more than one social space at once, and using the notion of the 'hypertext' to convey the idea that people can move from one space to another instantaneously.[8] Thanks in part to the development of communication technologies, including of course the railway, the aeroplane, and the internet, people occupy an 'n-dimensional' space.[9]

Along with going from here to there and 'switching' from one 'code' to the other, as Ascher puts it, people are also increasingly occupying multiple spaces at once. Yes, they go back and forth, but they never fully leave one space for the other.

The village remains a real presence in the life and mind of a migrant worker in Mumbai who may have left his family behind. Even while in the city, he remains in the village through his social networks, his professional skills, and his frequent exchanges with family back home. It is only because he has never left the village that he can endure the harshness of his city life.

At the same time, he takes the city and its dreams back to the village with him. The middle-class home that he helped build in Mumbai, the streetscape he experienced in Dubai, and the shared aspirations of his neighbours all contribute to produce an urban imaginary that may eventually be expressed in the village when he builds a home there for his family. Even the architectural styles emerging in many small Indian towns and villages are part of a hybrid local–global vernacular that brings many influences together in the actualization of a dreamed object.

In a subsequent chapter of the same study (2014–16), we made detailed ethnographic portraits of four families (and a religious sect) with deep ties to their neighbourhood in Mumbai and their village in a district on

Figure 9.2. The rural, a subcategory of the urban (Chiplun) (photo: Ishan Tankha for the Mobile Lives Forum and urbz).

Figure 9.3. An urban home in the village, 2017 (photo: Ishan Tankha for the Mobile Lives Forum and urbz).

Figure 9.4. An urban home in the village, 2017 (photo: Marius Helten for urbz).

the Konkan. Here we present the story of one such family, which had one home in a homegrown settlement in the neighbourhood of Bhandup and another in a village of the Konkan district of Ratnagiri.

Family portrait

Some parts of the neighbourhood of Bhandup in the north-east of Mumbai, with its hills embedded with homegrown settlements, are reminiscent of Brazilian favelas. They are populated by tight-knit community structures, with families who constantly navigate between their villages and their Mumbai homes.

With no help from the government, most of them started life in those neighbourhoods by physically building their own houses, then religious shrines, followed by other civic amenities including community halls. They continue to organize festivals and ceremonies perpetuating ancestral rituals and traditions, and belong to a world that merges characteristics of their rural and urban homes.

In their settlement in Mumbai, hens and chicks can be seen grazing along narrow pedestrian pathways. Small colourful houses decorated with tropical plants around modest piazzas with freshwater wells give the neighbourhood a distinct rural feel, though with a much higher level of density. Even amid the jostle of many houses, we see a few coconut trees rising above a sea of sloped roofs, many of which have the Mangalore tiles typical of Konkan buildings all along the west coast.

The Kule family lives in a small brick house on a hillside in this neighbourhood.[10] The Kules belong to a farmers' caste from the Konkan. Parshuram Kule, the patriarch, came to Mumbai over fifty years ago to finish his primary education, leaving behind his ancestral village near Chiplun, 250 kilometres south of Mumbai, where he has now returned to his farming roots.

He proudly says he never lost touch with the village and made sure his children developed strong bonds with it. These bonds are apparent in the way his family continues to navigate the city and the village. With savings from Mumbai, they purchased new farmland, which they started to cultivate in addition to their older plots. They also opened a shop on the roadside and built two houses where Parshuram resides with two of his four children.

When Parshuram first left this village, then only a tiny roadside hamlet, for Mumbai, he stayed with relatives, moving out only when he secured a job as a mechanic in a factory. As soon as he could afford it, he bought a plot of forested land from a farmer near his factory, in Bhandup itself. In those days the land in the neighbourhood was even more heterogeneous in terms of activities, with farming happening alongside small workshops and manufacturing units. The fabric changed dramatically when the textile factories of Mumbai city started shutting down in the 1980s and workers began to move out.

Parshuram and other natives from his region were among the first settlers on what was then a forested hill. They used skills acquired in the village to build small mud-and-straw huts. They levelled the ground and built wells and pathways, with some of those wells still active even today. When Parshuram first moved in, the area, unbelievably, looked very much like the region he came from – a jungle dense with wildlife, including snakes, monkeys, and even panthers.

Parshuram's small mud house was first rebuilt in the late 1980s, and again in the 2000s. It is now a two-storey brick-and-cement structure measuring 15 by 20 feet that opens to a courtyard with a functioning well and a coop for chickens and ducks. Since it was built on a slope, he made sure that the foundations were strong.

Parshuram had become well known in his neighbourhood for his ability to make monsoon-resistant structures, with which he was very familiar; after all, his ancestral village and his home in Mumbai shared the same geography across the couple of hundred kilometres that separated them. The furious Mumbai rains could easily wash away houses built on shaky ground, just as the southern winds of the same monsoons lashed his village home. He recounts the tale of how a particular resident from a different part of the country, having resolutely declined to follow Parshuram's step-layered style of construction, had his house destroyed twice over.

The Kules' Mumbai house is now occupied by Parshuram's son and daughter-in-law, along with their son, his wife, and their young daughter. Parshuram spends most of his time in a grand house he has built and improved near his native village, with his second son and one of his three daughters – both of whom were born in Mumbai but chose to move to their ancestral village.

The relatives in Mumbai manage the daily operations of a spice business that Parshuram had started with his son years ago in the city. Other members of the family, both the rural and the urban, travel regularly between the city and the village, maintaining strong familial and business bonds. Their life reflects the hybrid nature of their belonging, just like their habitats on both sides of the spectrum.

The Kule family does not operate alone. They are part of kinship and community networks that neighbour them on both sides. Bhandup's many neighbourhoods continue to resonate with the collective rural memories of its inhabitants through vivid religious celebrations and festivities. These memories are also reflected in shared economic activities that involve processing and sales of agricultural produce that are regularly brought from the village. Interestingly the residents are politically active in the city's local and national elections and carry over their affiliations to the village. They have a strong voice in municipal or village elections as they vote along communitarian lines with family members, making sure their endorsements matter on both sides.

At the same time, the demographic of the neighbourhood also reflects the cosmopolitanism of Mumbai. While the state language Marathi with its many regional accents is spoken widely in its streets, one can also get by with Konkani, Hindi, English, and other regional languages.

The families we interviewed acknowledge that Mumbai provides the kind of educational and professional opportunities that cannot be found in the village. Many people have government jobs, run small businesses, or are employed in large corporations. Most families have reached middle-class status in terms of income and education levels; electricity rarely goes off, and most homes have running water and access to toilets.

Unfortunately, this does not mean that the threat of displacement does not constantly loom over them. There is a persistent lack of recognition that these are valid settlements. Expensive real estate in the city continues to recycle entire neighbourhoods in the name of redevelopment, and this has inevitably become part and parcel of local aspirations.

Many early settlers in the neighbourhood, including the Kules, are eligible for slum rehabilitation schemes, though eligibility is not guaranteed to all slum dwellers. Even those who are eligible may not want to live in a tiny flat from which they cannot run a business. The threat of redevelopment may explain why most families continue to invest their savings in their ancestral villages; and while many foresee their future in the village, especially as it keeps improving and developing, they want to keep one foot in the city as well.

The fact that two of Parshuram's Mumbai-born children, a son and a daughter, have chosen to live in their ancestral village long before their retirement years reflects the discontinuities of the rural–urban dynamics that make up their lives. As the main reason for their choice they cite 'a better quality of life', especially cleaner air and proximity to nature. Yet having a toehold back in the city remains equally important.

Figure 9.5. A Konkan family's home in the city, Bandhup, Mumbai (photo: Ishan Tankha for the Mobile Lives Forum and urbz).

Figure 9.6. Bhandup, Mumbai (photo: Ishan Tankha for the Mobile Lives Forum and urbz).

Circulating across generations

This dual belonging is not rare; it is important to acknowledge that the best of both worlds is a real choice for many families such as the Kules. Our study reveals that even third- or fourth-generation migrants value contact with nature and village life while also wanting urban comfort and opportunities, especially brick houses with modern kitchens and Western-style toilets.

Paradoxically, the urban lifestyle that is mostly out of reach in the city can to some extent be realized in the villages.

Konkan villages receive significant financial flows from the city – not only from Mumbai but also from other Indian cities and even from abroad, including the United Arab Emirates, where there is a large Indian workforce. Money is primarily invested in land and homes, but also in water systems, religious shrines, and schools. Sometimes, it is used to help deserving children pursue their studies away from the village. Many also invest in farming tools, vehicles, or help their relatives start a business.

These circular migrants are perhaps the most significant players in India's urbanization story on both sides, in cities as well as villages. User-driven development is an equally important part of cities, but they tend to be trapped in perceptions that make it difficult to value.

Homegrown settlements around Bhandup are the first sight the city offers to visitors who land in Mumbai by air. At first glance they appear dystopian, a symbol of the city's failure to modernize. Little attention is paid to their economies, and the way their residents contribute to improving the neighbourhood from within – especially that they manage to do this without disrupting older forms. But this unfortunately contributes further to negative perceptions, appearing as further proof that these neighbourhoods are urban failures.

Similarly, user-generated forms of urbanization generated by circular migration tend to be undermined in rural India too, because they are small scale, scattered all over the country and without a narrative that recognizes them. Even when distinctly urban forms appear in the countryside, credit is rarely given to the urban–rural migration that residents between cities and villages navigate, carrying with them resources, aspirations, and investments enriched by both experiences.

The story of the Kule family is emblematic of the rarely told story of a user-generated urbanization that eludes statistics. Officially, India lags behind China as far as urbanization rates are concerned. This preoccupies the Indian government, which endorses the orthodox view that it is only by increasing the narrowly defined urban demographic that the country can achieve first-world standards. Such a mantra of development through urbanization, however, rests upon assumptions that are being increasingly challenged by a new generation of researchers.

Urban theorist and geographer Neil Brenner, with sociologist Christian Schmid, questions the notion of the urban as derived from a clearly defined city boundary. For him, the urban is a forcefield that cannot be so easily quantified and conventionally mapped. Brenner argues against those who consider urbanization as a demographic shift from a rural to an urban context:

It is misleading to equate the urban with any singular, bounded spatial unit (city, agglomeration, metropolitan region or otherwise); nor can its territorial contours be coherently delineated relative to some postulated nonurban 'outside' (suburban, rural, natural, wilderness or otherwise). Conceptualizations of the urban as a bounded spatial unit must thus be superseded by approaches that investigate how urban configurations are churned and remade across the uneven landscapes of worldwide capitalist development.[11]

Brenner and Schmid explain the necessity of viewing geographies in a way that transcend pre-fabricated categories and to avoid seeing movements across terrains as if they are unidirectional and always a marker of urbanization.

> With the deconstruction of monodimensional, city-centric epistemologies, urbanization can no longer be considered synonymous with such commonly invoked developments as: rural-to-urban migration; expanding population levels in big cities; the concentration of investments and economic capacities within dense population centers; the diffusion of urbanism as a sociocultural form into small- and medium-sized towns and villages; or the spreading of similar, 'city-like' services, amenities, technologies, infrastructures or built environments across the territory.[12]

The mapping of such complexities in cartographic studies and visualizations by Brenner and his team can potentially help many regions around the world revisit their official concepts and policies in relation to the urban.[13] They provide a new understanding of regions, tracing the flows of people, resources, and energy with fresh eyes, through the lens of critical geography, unconstrained by assumptions about the categories of urban and rural.

They encourage us to ask more questions: How do the specific movements of people forging pathways across territories shape larger political realities? When people refuse to relinquish their connections to the village even as they settle down in cities, what does it mean for the accepted notion of urbanization as a supposedly inevitable process of transformation that is designed to erase or diminish the rural?

The reality is that rural and urban lives are simultaneous and complementary for many people. This relationship, and the fact that there is movement in both directions, explains not only why the Indian village is undergoing a kind of urbanization that statistics cannot quite grasp but also why it continues to play an important role in the life of a majority of urbanites in cities like Mumbai. The village is often part of one's identity and lifelong journey – even for those who were born in the city. Strategic decisions made every day by ordinary people in the city are constantly affecting village life. A natural event or a dispute in the village can dramatically impact family life in the city.

For millions of Indians, the village and city are not separate spaces but a continuum of relationships and choices. Two realities are embedded in one another, providing access to complementary sets of opportunities and contexts. The movement from one to the other is not experienced as a constraint so much as a means to improve one's life. The movement from one to the other generates social and economic mobility.

The imprint that the village leaves on the city – and vice versa – defines the nature of urban life in India. This relationship is not easily trapped in categories or labels, and embodies several dimensions.

One can live and work in the city for five or ten years without physically returning to the village but at the same time never really being away from it. A relative who carries news and rice from the village; the remittance he brings back with him; the discussions with co-workers from the same region; rituals performed here (the city) just as there (the village); the money earned in the city and invested in a well or a new house that will change everyone's life in the village – all these are part of unified life for many Indians.

Of course, such perspectives still use the categories *rural* and *urban*; they rest on the ideas of village and city that Brenner and Schmid question. We hope it will soon be possible to describe the complexities of contemporary lives with better concepts and categories. For the moment, we must make do by infusing our framework with the steely critique that these theorists provide, even while continuing to use the standard lexicon of urban studies and practices.

Their critiques expose neoliberal economic interests as the dominant strand in the choices made by most governments – local and national – who use habitats and national territory as ideological constructs to push their agendas. Such interests focus on concentrating and managing resources and populations in a capital-friendly way, and view less-urbanized spaces within cities with suspicion. If the residents do not belong to the official workforce – if they are not part of the private-property sector as owners of real estate, if they generate their own capital and resources rather than relying on the organized frameworks that are controlled by the state – then they are to be erased, demolished, disappeared.

Urbanizing villages

During our explorations of the Konkan region, we observed tangible transformations in the home architectures of emerging villages. Families have shifted from building houses in stone, bamboo, hay, mud, and cow dung to building with bricks, concrete, steel, and tiles. At the same time, we came across a keener awareness of the limitations of industrial materials, with some going back to traditional materials while making design innovations.

An increasing number of families have built modern kitchens and toilets in their houses, which has required the development of related water infrastructure. This effort typically extends beyond single families and involves several houses, whose inhabitants all contribute through labour or investment to transform the environment gradually into a version of its urban counterpart.

The same people who are restricted in terms of their city home's appearance, because of limited space and the risk of demolition, can freely express themselves in the design of their village homes. This results in an explosion of colours and building styles in many parts of rural India. Indian villages are becoming living laboratories for contemporary vernacular architecture. Every community takes inspiration from specific sources – such as a Buddhist temple that merges Nepalese and Japanese elements with Vastu-style colour systems. In Muslim enclaves, houses are often ornamented with domes and glass façades reminiscent of Dubai, where so many villagers have travelled for work.

A quintessential architectural typology from Mumbai, the chawl, has also made deep inroads into villages throughout the Konkan. Chawls comprise rows of rooms lining corridors with shared washrooms on every floor; they were modelled on army barracks and first imported to India by British colonialists. They were subsequently adopted by industrial mill owners to accommodate workers, many of whom came from the Konkan region. Chawls are emblematic of the city's temporary-accommodation infrastructure.

Interestingly, we have seen this typology reproduced and reinvented in various villages, either to accommodate migrant labourers from other parts of India or to house extended families with members living in the city but keen to keep a rural toehold in the village with a room in this familiar structure.

This, more than anything else, summarized for us the narrative of India's complex urbanism with its deep ties to a dynamic, changing, and distinctly circular rural world.

10

Accommodation Versus Housing

Disentangling urban needs

Since the late 1990s, Mumbai has incentivized market-driven provision of affordable-housing, led by real estate developers. The slum rehabilitation scheme in Mumbai is an example of this approach: formerly occupied lands in officially designated slums are released by relocating residents in vertical structures, while providing valuable transferable building rights to developers.

In practice, slum rehabilitation schemes have not resulted in any visible reduction of so-called slums, which seem instead to spread and thrive in other areas. What such policies fail to acknowledge is that the slum is not just meeting the need for a house; it answers a cluster of economic, social, and political needs in which accommodation is also a variable. When the rehabilitation schemes cannot cover all this, populations who do not own property have to find accommodation elsewhere for their economic, social as well as needs for shelter.

There is no doubt that the needs for housing are staggering. According to the Ministry of Housing and Urban Poverty Alleviation, India had a total housing shortage of 18.78 million in 2012 and could not even provide a fraction of the amount.[1] This need was expected to reach 30 million units by 2030.[2] Even more shocking is the poor quality of the stock that is being produced today.

To address the growing need for housing, developers are purchasing cheap land wherever possible and targeting new buyers from the lower-middle-class sector, which has so far been unable to afford housing at market rates. This housing is made affordable by lowering construction costs, minimizing the footprint of individual units, and scaling up the size of housing projects.

This logic has led to all kinds of material malpractices reflected in poor-quality buildings. After a few years in existence affordable-housing blocks typically start crumbling, leading to rising maintenance costs, which ultimately decrease the value of the building. Very soon they look and function not much better than the slums they were meant to replace, and are ready to be redeveloped themselves.

Between 1997 and 2002, the government and construction industry built 500,000 houses in urban India as part of official housing projects; at the same time, local builders and inhabitants built 8.5 million unauthorized units in homegrown settlements. One of the reasons for referring to these settlements as slums is that they exist on contested land or have negotiated occupation rights that have to be constantly renewed. What is overlooked is that despite these instabilities, residents and local builders manage to produce massive volumes of structures that are used for work, residence, and temporary or long-term accommodation. Ignoring this potential is a major shortcoming in urban policy.

This only highlights the need for conceiving, producing, financing, and designing new strategies for affordable housing, so as to break the self-defeating logic into which affordable housing seems to be locked in today.[3]

Current policies tend to flatten out urban needs and ignore nuances linked to livelihoods, accommodation, community ties, and residence. In this chapter we focus on a much-overlooked aspect of Indian cities: the need for accommodation in a much longer cycle of rural–urban movements, of which housing is one component.

Accommodation and housing are related but distinct needs. Recognizing this – particularly in a context where migration tends to be connected to circular and seasonal movements of labour between villages and cities – will create more realistic planning and regulations for cities. In fact, a significant percentage of city dwellers all over the world do not intend to stay forever – they arrive for work, leisure, or learning and then move back to their provincial home or move on. This is as true in Mumbai or Berlin as in Seoul and Dhaka.

Not everyone seeks permanent residence status in Mumbai. The need for accommodation for various durations is met through a range of systems – ranging from individual home-based rentals to familial and community-based support systems, including home stays. These are tied to economic opportunities as well – since many workers and service providers live and work from the same space, with business premises doubling up as hostels and dormitories.

For a vast majority of such residents – most of whom are in Mumbai for a livelihood for fixed periods of time – homegrown settlements provide an important service in a city that is otherwise extremely expensive.

In cases of redevelopment or slum rehabilitation programmes this entire system of co-dependency collapses, as long-term residents are promised tiny new apartments in buildings, while the majority are moved out. These schemes tend to allow private developers to take over slum land by relocating the minority of qualified residents in the settlement into vertical structures on that spot, while most of the land is then developed as private real estate.

Because these new vertical structures provide a valid occupancy right for former slum dwellers, they offer an important transition for many residents. At the same time these people are wary of what is to come. Typically, the texture of the entire neighbourhood changes after such a move, leading to residents selling their properties and moving elsewhere.

This happens primarily because the conjoined economic and residential fabric that once existed there has now vanished.

The biggest casualties of this process are temporary residents with part-time accommodation needs, who are dependent on their livelihood being generated there as well as the cheap rental opportunities on offer. In most cases, they too move to another settlement that continues to respond to their needs, typically in a distant area, until such a time that the tentacles of the redevelopment project extend there.

After spending stretches of time in the city, these residents are often pulled into the speculative drama and political negotiation on occupancy rights and redevelopment schemes. They are vulnerable to this because there is almost no security of tenure for poorer migrants looking for non-permanent but secure affordable accommodation. There are few systemic mechanisms for this type of provision.

Because of this, it is important to break down debates about housing into a more nuanced conversation – one where the needs of *accommodation* – understood as temporary or seasonal, directly connected to livelihood issues – is distinguished from *housing* – which is required by most (but not all) residents of the city, but is imperfectly supplied by the market, and in cities such as Mumbai gets supplemented by homegrown settlements. The fact that half the population of the city lives in homegrown neighbourhoods means that such arrangements must be better understood and acted upon.

Workers' tenements as accommodation

The late nineteenth and early twentieth centuries saw a settling of the urban-industrial haze that had enveloped economic and political centres all over the world. During the preceding turbulent decades, cities were still shaping themselves vis-à-vis emerging modern industrial realities, primarily by increasing demographic concentration in dense neighbourhoods.

Tenements of various kinds were being created and developed to absorb working-class populations. New urban configurations needed workers but could not always accommodate them: workers often lived in cramped quarters, and the term *slum* was coined to describe specific conditions in Victorian England.

The working-class tenement has been a much studied and documented typology around the world. The classical working-class habitat is the 'barrack', as described by Friedrich Engels in *The Condition of the Working Class in England*. The production of this form of housing responds to the logic of optimization, where workers are given only the bare minimum to keep them active. The rationalization of the means of production accompanies the rationalization of space, in which the city becomes the prime locus of work.

In some contexts, the barracks and tenements made way for mass-housing projects. In Italian cities, for example, the *casa di ringhiera* – small rooms arranged along long corridors overlooking courtyards with shared toilets – emerged in the late nineteenth century. These were modelled on convents and other communal-living spaces from an older era. Similarly, the *cortiço*, a building of several rooms to house families, with shared toilet and other facilities – was common in Brazilian cities and catered to working-class populations for several hundred years.

The chawl in Mumbai is part of this history; its structure resembles these typologies but also shares as much in common with dormitories and hostels – including their overcrowded conditions. It emerged in the early twentieth century, typically as a three- to five-storey building with long corridors and rooms for families arranged in a linear mode, with common toilets at the end of each floor. This typology is considered representative of the form, but the colloquial term *chawl* has a much wider range of references. It can be used for various kinds of tenements and is most often deployed to distinguish it from neighbouring settlements, especially slums.

At one level, the chawl – often pronounced as 'chaal' in Mumbai – is a space serving as the urban home for a family that is split between the village and the city. As we saw in the previous chapter, dual-household families generate a dynamic exchange of time-and-space sharing, made possible by family support systems.

In such scenarios, there is one home in the village, often the permanent ancestral home, and another in the city. They are both part of a cyclical pattern of migration in which individual members of an extended family have different orbits of movement, ranging from short-term stays to annual visits. Adults might also spend their working life in the city before returning to the village, or there could be a permanent settling down in either location.

Such a bandwidth of possibilities is what characterizes rural–urban lives for a majority of urban working-class Indians. The story of the chawl is something that needs to be located within this narrative. For many with a dual sense of belonging, it has provided a reliable and secure source of urban accommodation through their life.

In cities such as Mumbai, which has held (and still holds) prejudice towards slum tenements, as well as allowing residents to move constantly between the village and the city, the chawl also represents an accessible

Figure 10.1. Jairam Shet Chawl in Dharavi in 2017. This chawl has since been rebuilt into a higher chawl, able to accommodate the original tenants as well as new ones (photo: Bharat Gangurde, urbz).

Figure 10.2. A new chawl, replacing the old Jairam Shet Chawl in Dharavi. The urbz team contributed to its design (photo: Bharat Gangurde, urbz).

way to climb the socio-economic ladder and become part of an emerging middle-class.

Within this narrative, the workers' tenement represents a stage in people's lives, marking rural–urban transitions in the sharpest way possible. In the best sense, it was about recognizing the industrial worker's rights as an urban citizen and treating this phase as a stepping stone towards a more settled family life that would come with the rationalization of time-and-space sharing.

What Engels described in Britain remains valid in certain contexts of Mumbai, with one crucial difference. As Cambridge historian and chronicler of the colonial working class of nineteenth-century Mumbai Rajnarayan Chandavarkar points out, the industrial proletariat here never fully gave up the pull of the village. So while it was true that the industrial workers settlement – the chawl – thrived and was used intensively by workers and their families, this crowding of rooms did not mean that workers had given up their village for good.[4]

In fact, it was not just families of workers who came to the city but sometimes entire villages – and yet, they were not fleeing the village permanently. This movement to and fro had been part of their lives for centuries. Even before Mumbai emerged on the horizon, many residents of Ratnagiri district were part of established circulatory-migration trajectories. In the past, employers were armies, artisanal workshops in adjacent kingdoms, construction sites, or agricultural enterprises. It was in such a pre-existing network of mobility that the newly industrializing city of Bombay became one more alternative. In the early years of the past century, the city's industrial establishment sent recruiters to invite labour from the Konkan coast, because they were reluctant to move to a place so far away and comparatively unknown.

It is in this context that the industrial workers' settlement in Mumbai, while showing a similar rationalization of space, time, rights, and political sensibility that Engels described, also did something more. It consolidated communities and village ties, making the presence of the rural family and community occupy urban space on its own terms and carving out a distinct political trajectory.

The community factor

Family, community, and village networks shaped contours in the city, and this was powerfully expressed in relation to caste identities. Mobilization among the Dalits opposed the caste system and resisted the continuation of caste in an urban context. Dalit writers such as Daya Pawar have narrated powerful memoirs which show the complex ways in which social transitions were happening. In his biography, he describes how important it was for his mother to define the boundaries of her home as a chawl to distinguish it from the slum outside, notwithstanding the near-identical and precarious quality of life in both spaces.[5] At the same time, he underscores the fact that the village to which the family belonged – caste atrocities and all – was never forgotten. The desire to return to the village, buy land, and reinvent community relationships remained strong.

The city equipped Dalits to emerge stronger and reinstate their identity on new terms back in the village. When fellow villagers came to share tiny sleeping spaces in the chawl when looking for jobs, and when its corridors were filled with community brothers and sisters, the ideal was not only to escape the oppression of the village but to consolidate forces in the city and return stronger to the village.

In our own experiences in Dharavi, we came across several communities from marginal caste histories, mostly from Tamil Nadu, a state with a strong social movement against caste discrimination. They often constructed shrines in the neighbourhood because they were prohibited from doing this back in their village. Dharavi gave them an opportunity to consolidate economically and socially, so that they could set up schools and open new establishments (typically schools and hospitals) back in the village.

In his study of twentieth-century industrial Bombay, Rajnarayan Chandavarkar points out that the majority of workers in the city were from Ratnagiri district. All through their lives as factory workers they kept returning – especially during monsoon season – to help in the labour-intensive paddy fields. They sometimes took leave for three to four months; while other family members or villagers would take their place in the factory in a circulatory relay of work obligations, often staying in the same room in the city chawl. So not only were these spaces not a marker of transition from rural to urban lives, but they were in fact the means of continuing active links between the two places.[6]

When the industrial houses and the city government limited the building of these chawls, especially after Indian independence, immigrant workers under political patronage continued to build rooms in the same form but used a different fabric – something more spontaneous and homegrown. A closer look at most homegrown settlements, urban villages, and slums in Mumbai shows that a version of the chawl typology persists, continually created and recreated.

On the other side of the migratory divide in the villages of Ratnagiri, we can even find an ex-Mumbaikar now based more permanently in the village who has designed his newly built house in a manner reminiscent of the chawl.

Mess in Dhaka

Scholar Shreyashi Dasgupta has described a new type of building in Dhaka, Bangladesh:

> Local builders there have created a stock of small rental apartments in
> mid-rise buildings that meet the demand of migrants on long cycles of

work away from their villages. These structures are modelled on student housing and derive their name from the common place where students would eat together – the 'mess' which is where the typology gets its name – 'Mess housing'.[7]

According to Dasgupta, mess housing is here to stay as part of Dhaka's urban fabric. Her study aims to formulate an academic framework based on comparing the low-income housing and everyday movements and experiences of workers in Dhaka and Mumbai.

The city of Dhaka has emerged as one of the world's fastest-growing megacities, with a population of nearly 15 million. The proliferation of urban settlements in Dhaka was largely unplanned, emerging from fault lines such as the scarcity of buildable land and lowlands around the city. Despite some of these crippling challenges, Dhaka's phenomenal industrial growth (especially ready-made-garment factories), cheap labour, and export of skilled and unskilled workers to foreign countries have significantly contributed to making it an economic hub. This growth had a direct impact on the demand and supply of rental housing in the city.

Dasgupta documents the emerging typology of private mess housing as a distinct urban form, drawing from the ethnography of low-income housing settlements in Dhaka. Private mess housing (also known as *mess bari* in Dhaka) can vary in form, with both horizontal (three-storey) and vertical (five-storey) structures. As the illustrations show, they are *pakka* housing built with concrete materials. They can be found anywhere in downtown Dhaka and are deeply embedded in the landscape of the city.

This typology developed near the work centres, close to small- and medium-scale industries and around affluent residential neighbourhoods. Its location gives cues about the entwined dependency of the workers, their housing, and their livelihood.

Broadly, mess housing can be further subdivided into three categories: accommodation for men, women, and family units. Some housing is also mixed, including all the above-mentioned categories. Each of these categories has a distinct mode of functioning, leading to different experiences and narratives for the occupants. Anecdotal evidence reveals that many working-class and lower-middle-class families have a strong preference for and aspiration towards private mess housing over slums. This expresses a larger societal phenomenon as the form reflects cultural representations of the formal city (low- to mid-rise mess buildings), but internally mess housing retains the social fabric of a classic slum (low- or mid-rise and high-density).

An interesting aspect of this typology is that it was specifically planned, designed, and built to accommodate workers. These settlements are built by landowners themselves or by subcontracted local masons and daily-wage labourers. An interview with Anwar Bhai, one of the local masons in Mirpur, revealed that it took him between eight months and a year to complete the mess building. The duration might vary depending on the finance available from the landowner. Some mess houses are temporary, both in form and use, while others are permanent.

Usually, the residents living in these housing settlements are involved in diverse sectors – drivers, domestic workers, garment workers, small-scale shop owners, entrepreneurs, students, and so on. Rent differs from unit to unit. On average, a room of 10 by 6 feet can accommodate around five people.

Semi-structured interviews with some of the residents gave a sense of their everyday movements and lived experiences. Mokshed Bhai, resident of a mess housing for men in Rayer Bazaar, said: 'I was born and brought up in Chengatia village in Barishal district of Bangladesh. I came to Dhaka for work and am now employed as a driver. I have been living in mess housing for the past few years. I have changed these accommodations as and when the location of my job changed. In between I even went back to my village and again came back for work. In this particular room, I have lived for two years. A friend from my village recommended this place to me. It is hard to find a good place which is closer to work, has access to water supply and charges affordable rent.'[8]

Like Mokshed, other interviewees also commented on the inextricable link between their community networks and native rural origins that helped them to find a place, get roommates, and travel back and forth to their villages during the holidays. Dhaka is almost shut during long holidays such as Eid, when workers retreat to their native homes, giving respite to chock-a-block traffic on Dhaka's congested streets.

Private mess housing is one of the classic examples of emerging urban forms in the cities of the global South. The vertical nature of these buildings has earned them some sort of credibility among varied stakeholders. Does that mean these structures are legally tenable? Yes and no, depending on whom you ask. Of course, to residents, landowners, caretakers, and local municipal authorities, these are legal housing settlements. Residents pay taxes to the municipal authorities and in return they receive water, electricity, and other basic services. But these structures are illegal in the view of the Capital Development Authority, a public agency responsible for coordinating urban development in Dhaka (known locally as RAJUK).[9] Most of the mess houses have not been approved by RAJUK; they lack a formal plan and have been built outside the purview of the building codes. Discussions with police officials in Wari echoed this position; they mentioned several recent cases in which criminals from 'these' housing typologies had been arrested.

The case of mess housing raises a series of intriguing and intricate processes in the context of urban housing and governance. One of the key aspects is to understand that people increasingly reside in more than one place or move back and forth to urban centres on a temporary basis. The Dhaka scenario is helpful in understanding the debates around housing's temporal dimension and is relevant to other cities in the global South. It is necessary to acknowledge these emerging typologies or forms

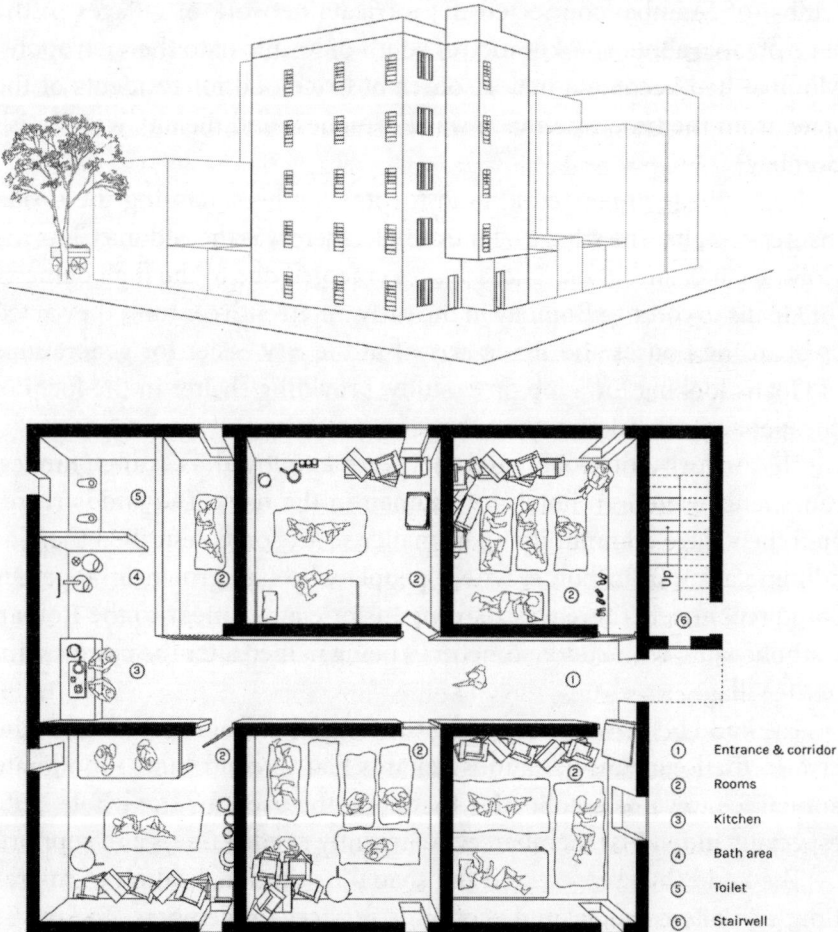

Figure 10.3. Mess housing in Dhaka (illustration: urbz, based on fieldwork by Shreyashi Dasgupta, 2016–17).

and go beyond traditional urban scholarship on slums and high-rises, formal and informal, legal and illegal, to look at the arrangement of habitats based on contemporary urban processes.

In fact, these typologies are not a mere response of the speculative urban capital but are deeply imbricated with historical understandings of the production of space. Dhaka's bustling urban habitat, built around the movement patterns of migrant workers, gives definitive cues to such emerging typologies.

The case of Mumbai's Goan kudds

In the late nineteenth and early twentieth centuries, the Goan kudds (clubs) of Mumbai connected the intricate network of villages in the state of Goa, about 560 kilometres south of Mumbai, to the metropolis. Mumbai had become a major source of livelihood for residents of the state, from the time when Goa was Portuguese and the city was British Bombay.[10]

Each village organized a kudd for its members, naming the urban institutions after the village – for example, there was the Aldona Club, the Colvale Club, and so on. These spaces emerged due to the high demand for Goans to come to Bombay in the early nineteenth century; they acted as boarding houses and made arrival in the city easier for generations of Goans looking for a job or to study, providing shelter in the form of cheaper accommodation than that of the market.

The majority of Goan migrants were employed as cooks, nurses, musicians, waiters in hotels, or seamen in the navy. The kudds recreated the village community on a smaller scale; some described them as a 'home away from home', where people who had grown up together could reconnect. There was a strong historic attachment to the Roman Catholic faith, with kudds sometimes being named after the patron saint of the village.

The kudd helped by subsidizing the migration from the village to the city. In the long run, the kudds' tenants had to contribute a moderate annual fee towards a collective that could be used for the whole club, especially individual members who urgently needed funds and support.

The kudd thus represented the spatial institutionalization of migration, and offered social and economic services to members. Today, the clubs are under threat for multiple reasons. First, they have become costly to maintain. Most of the places that the villages rent for the clubs fall under the Bombay Rent Control Act, which froze rents at 1947 levels and made selling much more economically viable for owners. Today, kudds are considerably less frequented than they used to be, mainly because most Goans go abroad for work rather than to the city. Goa itself has also grown economically and today attracts migrants from all over the country. The rise of worker tenements in villages in Goa – providing shelter and accommodation to poor workers from elsewhere – completes a dynamic circular movement in a different direction.

The fact that the early decades of urbanization in Mumbai saw several institutions and establishments that reflected the circulatory movements of people is an indication that the city once provided more avenues for diverse needs. There were hostels and dormitories for members of specific communities, villages, and regions from all along the Konkan coast and the hinterland. In colonial parts of the city you can still find hotels with signboards indicating that there were once separate dedicated rooms for businessmen or others coming from specific cities – Mangaluru or Udupi, for example – for just a few months every year.

Today, homegrown settlements continue to provide a complex and clustered service of both accommodation and housing for a significant demographic – but the narrative has been simplified. Now most workers and members of the labour force become entangled in the narrative of a permanent move, and all their needs are flattened into the need for 'housing'. That their lives are still enmeshed in villages through their joint families and communities is an inconvenient fact that authorities mostly ignore.

11

Back to the Future

The Geddesian way

In the early years of the twentieth century, the royal rulers of the central Indian city of Indore invited Patrick Geddes to visit when he was spending time in the country. They wanted his help to rid the city of plague and other diseases. Typically, the authorities blamed it on the bad habits of the poorest residents. According to scholar Indra Munshi, Geddes painstakingly pointed out that most residents in fact kept their homes and streets scrupulously clean, and it was the lack of civic management by the authorities which led to water-logging and accumulation of dirt in some neighbourhoods – not unlike the situation in many urban contexts today.[1]

Munshi illustrates Geddes's deep desire to engage with the city's holistic civic consciousness by detailing a particularly eccentric incident. To bring the whole city together to respond to the dangers of the plague, Geddes organized a huge carnivalesque procession during Diwali, one of the most popular festivals on the Indian subcontinent. The festival is characterized by a celebration of lights and fireworks, preceded by a huge home and neighbourhood cleaning ritual.

That year, thanks to Geddes's special engagement, the procession departed from the traditional Hindu and Muslim neighbourhood routes and instead went through the forgotten alleyways that had been most successfully spruced up. Thanks to this incentive, which publicly recognized residents' efforts, 6,000 loads of garbage were apparently removed and thousands of rats trapped. Priests took the lead in cleaning up the precincts of their temples. During the procession itself, after the usual cavalry parade led by the float of Laxmi, goddess of cleanliness and wealth, came an unusual performance. It included wails of despair accompanied by scenes of a broken city and models of huge rats. This was immediately followed by a series of floats in which the spotlessly attired city cleaners and workers marched in like warriors along with civic officials, the mayor, Geddes himself (in a maharaja costume), and a goddess – only just conjured for this special event – Indore City herself. The aim of the performance was to clearly locate the onus of cleanliness on the shoulders of the civic authorities and not on the residents or on the design or structure of their homes!

For Geddes, a city is not 'just a place in space, but also drama in time', and in his willingness to engage directly with both these dimensions he was far ahead of his time.[2] He knew that the spirit of urban planning lay in the spirit of the people and the ethos that infused their habitats. His ethnographic eye looked deep into the contours of the physicality of a city and immediately saw the inner arrangements that shaped it – whether cultural or economic.

The attention Geddes paid to economic dimensions was exemplary. He was deeply interested in the regions surrounding cities. When drafting plans for Indore, he pointed out the problems faced by cities that had created modern economies by converting their surrounding geographies into supply zones for specific raw materials. Mumbai, for example, required a lot of cotton. The metropolis was connected to its hinterland (then part of the Bombay presidency, presently the states of Gujarat and Maharashtra), on which it depended for the supply of cotton for its textile factories: large swaths of agricultural fields had been converted to the monocultural production of this non-edible cash crop. Bombay's growth and scale were a consequence of its large textile industries which fed a global market and were supplied by the cotton farms of the region. Geddes saw the civic problems facing the city as partly connected to the logic of the production and consumption of this cash crop. He wanted Indore to depart from the experience of colonial Bombay and similar English towns by looking critically and deeply at the nature of the cotton-based economy – especially the way it treated industrial workers and their living conditions. In Geddes's worldview, cities have a character, and this character is shaped by its materiality, right down to the stuff and substances that make it.

For him, the inner world of people's lives, their everyday acts of survival, and local modes of organizing were the units through which the spectacle of the city unfolded. Tinkering with only the physical form without paying attention to these interior elements would not have the desired effect. The planner could not afford to work in abstractions, locked up in an office. He had to be on the ground, operating within the fabric of the city's ordinary everyday existence.[3]

Above all, Geddes wanted to reveal connections and build bridges between people as well as link existing historical, cultural, and environmental contexts with modern methods and technologies. His 1925 plan for Tel Aviv, aimed to create 'a transitional place and a link between the over-crowded cities of Europe and the renewal of Agricultural Palestine'.[4] His plan connected the old city of Jaffa to the new development in the North, seeking to establish a link that was spatial and social as much as temporal and symbolic.

He acknowledged that change and intervention were an inevitable dimension of urban evolution. Socio-economic and political transformations were the living theatre that demanded constant response in the physical configurations of urban life. Cities evolved along with these changes.[5] The way in which he translated his learning into projects, agendas, and plans, always considering the present as the starting point, was what gave his projects so much appeal.

People-centred urban theorists and practitioners such as John F. C. Turner and Jane Jacobs are part of a legacy that traces back to Geddes, who produced a large body of practice and theory in India, including several urban planning reports between 1915 and 1922 in which he laid out his observations and analysis and suggested solutions and strategies.[6] Practice and commentary happened together, making praxis a spontaneous aspect of his methodology.

Geddes's methodology for civic and regional surveys was all about studying the 'place as it stands, seeking out how it has grown to be what it is, and recognizing alike its advantages, its difficulties and its defects'.[7] His approach strove to 'adapt itself to meet the wants and needs, the ideas and ideals of the place and persons concerned'.[8] Geddes went on to organize cities exhibitions, which travelled around the world. In India, he was appointed as chair of the Department of Sociology and Civics at the University of Bombay between 1919 and 1924.

He also contributed to creating the Shantiniketan Indian School with Nobel laureate Rabindranath Tagore near Kolkata, which was coupled with a village outpost, Sriniketan, conceived to interrogate and develop the linkages between the rural and the urban. These initiatives along with dozens of others demonstrated Geddes's strong belief that cities and regions had to be studied in their own right. He felt that through a better understanding of their functioning, experts and the general public could contribute not only to the improvement of the urban environment but also to the advancement of humanity as a whole.

He may have been trained as a biologist, and worked as a passionate sociologist and educator, but in terms of legacy Geddes is most revered as an urban planner. He synthesized a hyperactive and diverse trajectory of learning that included conversations with Charles Darwin and Thomas Huxley, earth sciences, botanics, gardening, engineering, and economics. He had a special ability to see a place as a simultaneous infusion of human presence, social relations, physical resources, and fantasy, and as a node in a larger network. He felt that experts tended to split apart such universal thinking. In his own words:

> Each of the various specialists remains too closely concentrated upon his single specialism, too little awake to those of the others. Each sees clearly and seizes firmly upon one petal of the six-lobed flower of life and tears it apart from the whole.[9]

Faced with the complexity of urban life – which pans in the multiple dimensions of the spatial, the cultural, the political, the economic, and the environmental, Geddes called for an approach to urban intervention that valued response in the most intricate and precise way possible. Just as interventions can be made in the body without tampering with the essential mechanisms that keep the body alive, the planner, according to Geddes, intervenes carefully in the living system of a settlement or neighbourhood. As explained by Karthik Rao-Cavale:

> Geddes' 'conservative surgery' involved only selective clearance of buildings – typically those which needed reconstruction anyways. Road-widening was not proposed unless absolutely necessary, nor was the essential layout of the neighbourhood tampered with. Geddes understood that strict separation of land-uses would, in the Indian context, be no solution at all.[10]

An eye for detail and interconnections helped Geddes detect the necessary intervention without destroying the whole system. Not only would this keep cities healthy, but it would also help to generate adaptive and evolving urban habitats. Imagine Indian cities in the twenty-first century following Geddes's vision to evolve, transform, and adapt to the ongoing theatre of political, economic, technological, and environmental change?

This is a vision where local community life with its repertoire of skills, many involving the construction of homes and infrastructure, would shape large parts of Indian cities.

What emerges is not unlike the vernacular urban landscape that pops up where the official urban imagination ends – in smaller towns, within homegrown settlements. The only difference is that it would be expressed on a larger scale and with exuberant confidence. More importantly, it would help tackle issues of hygiene, provide economic security nets, and move towards an even more inclusive community fabric than the one that exists today. There would be a completely different narrative with regards to slums.

All this does not mean a passive role for the planner. Far from it. Geddes had a clear head and a sharp eye that prevented him from confusing ideals with reality. There were many problematic neighbourhoods too – which lacked open space or air flow. It would not take much to guess that such settlements often belonged to marginal communities or lower castes. Geddes's strategies – which often included decongesting space and planting trees – would help in transforming the physical contours of the settlement in a manner that modernized them too.

Along with his surgical interventions, Geddes was an early advocate of citizen participation through a set of exercises that involved exhibitions and discussions. This meant that one had to include the inhabitants as well as their traditional modes of community life in the exchange of ideas. Some influential people in India were ambivalent about Geddes's faith in vernacular structures, especially since it inadvertently involved a strong role for communities and the strong possibilities of preserving caste-like structures that came with it. If there was a slow fading away of his influence, it can be partially attributed to this inclusive approach. However, considering him again from the vantage point of the early twenty-first century – where caste, community, and religion have barely budged from their structural locations (never mind the rhetoric) – we feel that had his approach been adhered to it would have made a more effective and concrete difference in material lives, locality by locality.

For Geddes, the city should be the path to eutopia, 'the good place' that lies in existent urban reality and is what we need to work towards – as opposed to Utopia, which is 'no place'.[11] Eutopia could be described as a better version of the existing situation. The work of the urbanist is to find the path from here to there. That which exists is always evolving (towards consolidation or degeneration), and therefore does not have to remain as it is. For Geddes, existing community configurations were the stepping stone to discarding its more undesirable aspects, even its fundamentals, without necessarily throwing away everything – just as contemporary impulses to erase the caste system must acknowledge that caste, as a form of discrimination, exists. This means working with the category as a perspective from which to destroy the oppressive structure of caste itself.

Likewise, we must acknowledge not only the existence of slums, but also their social construction through policies that deny their residents agency. Once we understand that habitats are dynamic realities and that they are boiling with internal forces for change, we can appreciate the path from slum to neighbourhood. One way we integrated Geddes's spirit and approach was by transforming our conception of space from one of fixed systems to processes, from a spatial to a temporal understanding of urbanism. The understanding that human habitats are 'learning, evolving ecologies' extends to all contexts, independent of wealth and culture.

Geddes left behind him universally relevant insights that the world has yet really to recognize and endorse. One of his most prominent disciples, the writer Lewis Mumford, did much to propagate Geddes's wisdom, and this clearly inspired a few post-war architects and urbanists. Today, Geddes is still a source of inspiration for devoted followers such as us and others in Europe and India. A group connected with the French National School of Architecture in Montpellier is working hard to keep his memory alive and preserve what is left of the school he created there: the Collège des Écossais (Scots College) was created to bring together nature and civilization, with a strong focus on botanical knowledge and gardening applied to human habitats.

Indian modernism

Urban experiments that took place in South America and India from the 1960s to the 1980s were very much in line with Geddes's thinking. Experiments such as the PREVI project in Lima and the Sites and Services Scheme in Mumbai were widely presented as failures. We believe that they were hugely successful. We are hopeful that in the near future such projects will not only be recognized as important, but that they will be studied in depth by architecture and urban planning departments, and that they will inform the policies of enlightened cities seeking homegrown alternatives to mass housing throughout the world.

In the 1980s, the World Bank encouraged the development of Sites and Services Schemes throughout India and other parts of the world. These were based partly on the pragmatic conclusion that state-produced housing was usually expensive, of poor quality, and disconnected from people's needs. State-led social housing was in crisis in developing countries and the West back then, as it is now. The World Bank, driven by a laissez-faire ideology, posited that the free market was the most efficient provider of all things, including affordable housing. Turner's observations in Latin America seemed to provide a path for development by the people, which was compatible with the World Bank liberal ethos.

Turner was actually interested in finding out how planners and architects could support the local production of habitat rather than impose their technocratic and context-insensitive solutions from outside. His observations, along with the contributions of many others, inspired innovative housing schemes in many parts of the world, including in Mumbai where the World Bank financed slum upgrading schemes. Over ten years, tens of thousands of people benefited from policies that encouraged them to build their own dwellings on land provided by the state and equipped with basic infrastructure. Others were encouraged to form cooperative societies that would be given leases to the land they occupied. This effectively converted their status from slum dwellers to homeowners without simply giving away the land or selling it to developers.

Other Sites and Services schemes in India, such as Aranya, were planned in the early 1980s by architect B. V. Doshi (a disciple of Le Corbusier and a Pritzker Prize winner) in Indore, Madhya Pradesh. Aranya provided low-income families with a plot served by basic infrastructure, as well as a few models of houses that they could build on.[12] Aranya had clearly been inspired by innovative projects and urban thinking taking place in Latin America from the 1960s onwards, such as the PREVI project in Lima, which was sponsored by the United Nations.[13] PREVI was an early attempt at exploring alternative models for partly self-built housing. In the late 1960s, twenty-six international and Peruvian architects built 1,500 dwelling units on the understanding that their residents would modify them over time. Today it is nearly impossible to see where the original houses were built because they are fully integrated in their surroundings thanks to the continuous work of residents to expand and improve them over time.

A few Sites and Services projects were implemented in the periphery of Mumbai. One of them, located in Charkop, is today a pleasant, middle-class neighbourhood where many houses double up as work-spaces (tool-houses).[14] People have continued to improve their homes over time, and the only thing remaining from the initial plan is the ground-level layout.

These projects were based on the idea that users were capable of managing the construction of their homes on their own. All they needed was good provision of infrastructure and a well-designed model, which served as a starting point for incremental development. Doshi's LIC Colony in Ahmedabad is another example of creative adaptation based on user needs and means.[15] Residents of the colony have extended their homes and launched business ventures inside them in ways that could not have been foreseen by anyone, creating what is now a successful dense and diverse settlement. Doshi's LIC project was conceived to allow users to expand their houses, and from the start it acknowledged the fact that the architect would not have the last word in the building's final forms. After an initial gesture, which gives a sense of direction to the project, the architecture continues its course as the lives of its inhabitants unfold. For Doshi, who was a disciple of Le Corbusier, this project was a way of acknowledging people's desire to appropriate space and make it their own. The LIC housing project conceived of its inhabitants as participants in the construction process.

The Artist Village in Belapur, New Mumbai (a twin city of Mumbai, today known as Navi Mumbai), which was designed by Charles Correa in the 1980s, provides another successful example of a planned neigh-bourhood that improves over time.[16] Correa focused on designing an intricate street layout with open spaces on different scales, ranging from very large and public to much smaller and intimate. He built a few different model houses on the site, all simple and inexpensive, with the idea that residents would adapt them to their needs. Today, only a few of the original houses remain unchanged. Most have been extended or rebuilt altogether; only the footprint and street layout have remained. This has produced architectural variety within the area, which contributes to its vibrancy. Residents were supposed to manage the public space in front of their houses collectively: some chose to transform their clusters into miniature gated communities; others have abandoned common spaces altogether. Others still have found cooperative ways to maintain these spaces. We talked to some of the residents, and whether they complain about the original design or praise Correa, most inhabitants feel strongly about the neighbourhood and are proud to live in one of the nicest parts of Navi Mumbai. We had the chance to converse with Correa about this neighbourhood, which is one of our favourite urban projects. He was thrilled with the way people had taken over the development of the neighbourhood and explained very clearly that this was his intention from the start. The transformation of the original structures by the residents is not a mark of failure but of success.

The works of Doshi and Correa demonstrate that there is no contradiction between planning and homegrown habitats. A settlement can be planned to develop over time, and, as Geddes advocated and demonstrated a hundred years ago, a homegrown settlement can also be planned over time through surgical interventions. Homegrown urbanism, vernacular architecture, and the craftsmanship of construction have been major sources of inspiration to these giants of modern Indian architecture and urbanism. The street-level layout of the plan in the Aranya and Artist Village project was inspired by the structure of traditional villages, with narrow streets and a multiplicity of shared and liminal spaces. This emphasis contributed to providing these neighbourhoods with a sense of identity that was strengthened by residents' interventions and incremental improvements.

Though Correa's Artist Village and Doshi's LIC Colony were not Sites and Services projects, they followed the same logic. Such schemes were gradually abandoned, as it was difficult to ensure that the plots would benefit the people they were intended for. Some people who were allotted a plot at affordable rates would soon resell it to better-off people at market rates (often illegally, as initial beneficiaries were required to keep them for a certain number of years before they could be sold). Nonetheless, Sites and Services schemes can be said to have succeeded in producing desirable and functional human-scale environments at a low cost to the state. The same cannot be said of the current mass-rehabilitation schemes in Mumbai, which are just as likely to be turned over and speculated upon by the beneficiaries.

Upgrading and self-help projects in Mumbai were left behind in the mid-1990s as the real estate market reached surreal heights. It kept rising throughout the 2000s and continues to boom to this day. Public land became too valuable to give it away to the poor. Officials refused to legitimize the situation of its slum dwellers, routinely referring to them as squatters even though most of them had purchased land from previous owners, or had built on land they themselves had reclaimed from marshes that were considered uninhabitable.[17] Mumbai thus turned away from the progressive policies of the 1980s and adopted public–private schemes that incentivized top-down, high-rise redevelopment projects like the ones Turner had fought against his whole life.

The redevelopment projects promoted by the authorities of today are just the same as the centrally administered mass-housing schemes and high-rise buildings that Turner and Jacobs denounced. It is sad that after all these years of experimenting with different models and approaches, we are back to square one.

We believe that it is time to treat citizens as stakeholders in the production of their habitats. Planning for incremental development, as Doshi and Correa have done in some of their projects, seems to contradict the logic of architectural plans, which are supposed to go from start to finish and deliver a product that is ready for use. What these projects have demonstrated is that we can give agency back to the end user, and that the end users have the ability and desire to participate in the making of their habitats. Today we witness the tremendous level of intelligence, creativity, and skills that have gone into the continuation of projects such as the Artist Village or LIC Colony that were planned for incremental development. We also witness, obviously, the resourcefulness of generations of slum dwellers that has turned slums into neighbourhoods, not just in India but in every part of the world.

Ivan Illich argues that nothing meaningful, sustainable, or economically viable can be done without the participation of the inhabitants. This means that wherever neighbourhoods are planned, the future inhabitants must be identified and included in the process. It also means that in existing neighbourhoods we must allow for a kind of user appropriation, which implies the transformation of the project initially framed by the architect, planner, client, or regulator. We can and should let users alter and adapt their habitat in all kinds of ways, as they always did until institutional control was tightened. How a project evolves over time is unpredictable, and planning for such unpredictability is probably the toughest challenge facing cities and planners. Far from meeting this challenge, however, municipal authorities routinely deprive users of the possibility of improving their own habitats. In Dharavi, residents have been barred from rebuilding their homes as the area awaits a large-scale redevelopment project that has been in the works for decades.

The problem is not with planning per se. Civic authorities are needed to support the implementation and management of infrastructure, promote safe construction practice, and safeguard environmental standards. The issue comes from the unwillingness of policymakers, planners, and architects to recognize and engage with processes at work. On the other hand, citizens themselves must learn how to produce plans that are compatible with the city's rules and regulations.

Architecture for the present

Historically, architecture has been a hands-on, context-sensitive practice as much as a specialized skill. The architect Camillo Sitte, writing in 1889, blamed the poverty of urbanscape on the fact that architects designed from their studio instead of conceiving 'in natura'.[18] What seems to make sense on a plan – placing objects at straight angles, creating symmetry, or placing a sculpture at the centre of a square – may feel very different on site. Indeed, it seems that we are still stuck with an architectural practice that sees what can be drawn on a computer screen as correct, and the reality of the site for which the design is intended as secondary.

On the contrary, we see architectural design as a lingua franca that can express a world of potential at the intersection of the realities of the user, builder, regulator, financier, and the context in which they operate. If architecture can tell the stories of all these actors, then new pathways can be opened up for all involved in that world.

The architect can be attracted to the physicality of the mason's work; the mason can be enriched by the projection skills of the architect; the contractor can contribute to a realistic evaluation of the process of construction. This mutually beneficial collaboration can help in evolving a professional space that is at once pragmatic and holistic. Such a recalibration of practice is necessary for more projects like Doshi's LIC Colony and Correa's Artist Village to become mainstream. We conceptualize such a professional, who works in natura and can communicate across specializations, as an *architectisan*: someone who combines the skills of the architect with the patience of the craftsman.

This kind of professional is not being trained in academic institutions today, which tend to shield students from the real world. Sitting on architecture juries, one sees the most futuristic and visionary images of how the cities of tomorrow should look. Freed from the constraints of context, students are supposed to be at their most creative. The projects seem to float in space, ideas for an abstract world. Yet visions produced in a contextual vacuum usually lack originality. The architectural future is smooth and shiny, made of high-speed transportation (monorails and flying cars), protective domes with rich ecosystems, stellar skyscrapers connected by bridges. Nothing that B-grade science fiction did not invent a hundred years ago. Artificial intelligence will not save us from these retro-clichés but rather remix them in a tasteless manner.

Even talented architects who have the ability to imbue meaning and beauty into their work often get frustrated when it comes to inserting their visions in a piece of urban reality. They would prefer abundant finance, empty plots of land, obedient workers, passive users, and rich clients to buy into their fantasy. Unfortunately, since these conditions are not available in the world where most of us live, such visions end up in galleries, biennales, and classrooms where the messiness of life can be kept at bay. The same talented and embittered architects sometimes become teachers, inculcating new generations of students with a certain scorn for the world they are supposed to contribute to building.

The mismatch between the world out there and the way architects are trained has produced a bizarre volume of speculative drawings that have no connection whatsoever with anything real. For the most part, architectural education assumes that the tabula rasa – the empty plot – is an available condition. The tabula rasa is the original architectural utopia. In reality, every place has a pre-existing ecology and history, as well as ongoing social dynamics. The desire to reproduce the condition of the white page where the creative input of the architect is supposedly unconstrained has led to a cult of starchitects, who seem to be the only ones with enough aura to impose their grand-design visions onto the world as it is.

On closer inspection, however, even starchitects such as Rem Koolhaas or Frank Gehry are constrained by the power structures above them. Their agency is always tempered in ways that would damage ideal visions. This is why most starchitects cannot afford to be purists; they are well aware of the trade-off between winning grand commissions and creative freedom.

It is common to see students of architecture take their learning from the university into the world, only to find out that their skills do not quite match. In a highly competitive professional environment, aspiring architects often find that work is scarce – and yet the amount of construction going on around the world is enormous. In fact, a lot takes place outside the radar of known professional choices. Millions of people build their own homes with the help of local construction workers and without architects, simply because architects are not willing to negotiate complex factors such as the conventions of construction, the clients' occupancy status, or the political location of these settlements.

It is also true that students of architecture and urbanism have developed an interest in favelas and slums. There is an important role to play for academia, to radically interrogate and transform the practice. However, slums should not be used as a backdrop for feel-good theoretical projects that are disconnected from ground-level realities. A meaningful place to start is to reorient notions of what means to be an architect in a context where construction is ad hoc and relational.

The practice needs a rethink, not only to find relevance in homegrown neighbourhoods but also to take full advantage of the possibilities offered by a world in rapid transformation. These days, urban environments are located in the interstices of many new configurations and fault lines. The virtual, spatial, and temporal collapse of experience has become part of everyday reality.

A small contractor working in a homegrown settlement in Mumbai has access to unlimited knowledge via the web, some local finance, and enough support to start a project. An office in distant Turin or Rhode Island can connect with him to start a conversation that might soon become a wholesale professional arrangement. A *pedreiro* from São Paulo may want to visit India and compare construction techniques. Researchers working on new-material technologies in Boston can experiment with live applications where it matters most. A practising architect from anywhere can participate in all these conversations.

We've been involved in many similar experiments, but for such practices to become a mainstream reality, architects need to have a deeper engagement with diverse contexts. They need to locate themselves and be inspired by the multitude of urban forms that actually exist but don't always find formal expression. The only reason architects have not stepped into those spaces with more confidence is that they are constrained by conventional professional and economic considerations – which prevent them from developing collaborations and partnerships with millions of residents around the world who do very similar things – finance and build homes.

The tools for reaching out to this world are already there. Why not shape and sculpt an architectural practice specifically for the living world? Maybe the only reason more are not jumping on this bandwagon is lack of imagination. This is where architectural practice as we know it today is trapped: a timeless zone, firewalled from the living present, which is a reality for millions of people around the world. To escape such a predicament, all one has to do is what now comes naturally to most of us: get connected.

Yet connecting to the lived world is not as easy as it sounds, especially for those in the architectural professions who have taken comfort in their labs and studios. Connection means establishing a relationship that could destabilize certainty and explode comfort zones. This is because feedback from the field – from real people – is less polite than a like on LinkedIn and more real than a mid-term jury. The kind of connected practice we are envisioning is based on the realization that knowledge flows in more than one way and that there is a tremendous amount of intelligence to be gathered in worlds that were once considered too distant, hopeless, or backward.

For architectural practitioners, this demands another facet of their creativity. It is not about imposing one order onto another or bringing more rationality to an existing local practice of construction. The authority of the architect as an expert in design, material, and structure can only be useful when it is blended with the knowledge of collaborators who are rooted in their imminent reality. What happens otherwise is mutual dismissal. The context and residents reject architectural design as being incompatible with their reality; the architect meanwhile rejects the context as lacking the proper channels for the expression of their professional expertise. This is a loss for all involved.

Why should architectural practitioners have to reproduce the same inflexible and directive approach, only to find themselves frustrated by the fact that they don't have the means of imposing their vision in a defiant context? What would an architectural practice that acknowledges the depth of any departure point and the nonlinearity of the process look like?

This would not be a utopian architecture. It would instead be something between pragmatism, boldness, optimism, and playfulness, emerging and drawing inspiration from whatever exists. Connecting to the context would mean more than using physical reality as a backdrop for clever designs. The context, however problematic, is ultimately the most creative and challenging of social, economic, and psychological canvases.

The biggest threat for established architects when engaging with such a live process is that one can never be sure of the outcome. If the outcome is a built object, then one has to accept that the way it looks in the end may not be quite what one initially had in mind. Some ideas may be reinterpreted along the way and become something else altogether. This means that the architect's agency should no longer be limited to producing a design that must be precisely executed; instead, the agency of

others interacts with that of the architect. But these inputs are not something that must be suffered as an imposition; rather, they are objective
and subjective forces that one must compose creatively. The respect and
non-hierarchical relationship that such a process promotes are at once
ethical, creative, and pragmatic. They are based on the recognition that
mere imposition of a design is neither desirable nor possible.

12

The Natural City

The world we make

We have no choice but to engage with the world as it is, no matter how corrupt and polluted. It is simply the only one we have, the only reality we can deal with. This means we must leave aside urban utopias and lofty plans. It is at the ground level that we best understand what can improve. We use whatever is there already and we work with it. We clean up, we repair, we organize – we make the new out of the old.

Change comes through practice, and good ideas come from interacting with the world, not shielding oneself from it in a gated community, ashram, research lab, or remote island. It is through local engagement that we can attempt to detox our urban environment and ourselves. While humans have been responsible for endless destruction, we have also at times been great custodians of nature, turning deserts into forests, increasing biodiversity, and developing symbiotic relationships with many species. We have the capacity to do much more.

In many ways, this is what generations of residents in Dharavi and other homegrown neighbourhoods around the world have always done. They have continuously improved a formerly hostile environment, consolidated their houses and streets, invested in developing their skills and economic activities, and built schools and businesses. They put plants in their windows, planted trees, and cleaned up their streets. This process could continue, turning Dharavi into a continually better version of itself, if only there were enough vision and empathy among municipal leaders. Its planned destruction by the authorities will not only wipe a monument to humanity off the map but also chop down a process of self-empowerment that's deeply rooted in the land and which branches out all the way to the city and the countryside.

The Hungry Tide by Amitav Ghosh is unexpectedly relevant to Dharavi's history. It is an account of power and space that unfolds in the dense mangrove forests of the Sundarbans in Bengal, dragging into its intense narrative flow all of the Indian state's contrary feelings towards its own people, its neighbours, and its continued fidelity to arcane categories, especially those that revere nature and forests while being contemptuous towards those who live directly off them. We draw from it a powerful lesson for Dharavi (beyond the mangrove connection – Dharavi too grew out of the marshy lands that surround the city). There is a moment in the novel when a schoolmaster revolutionary first encounters the community of recent settlers in the mangrove forests and is completely disarmed by their ability to reorganize their lives:

> What had I expected? A mere jumble, perhaps, untidy heaps of people, piled high upon each other? … But what I saw was quite different from the picture in my mind's eye. Paths had been laid … little plots of land had been enclosed with fences; fishing nets had been hung up to dry.
>
> There were men and women sitting outside their huts, repairing their nets and stringing their crab lines with bits of bait and bone. Such industry! Such diligence! Yet it was only a few weeks since they had come.[1]

The protagonist goes on to document his thrill at seeing 'the birth of something new' – the creation of a world not by a single visionary but one dreamt up by 'the very people who were trying to make it real' – not 'by those with learning and power but by those without'.[2]

At the simplest level, this response echoes those typical of many who encounter habitats such as Dharavi for the first time. Numerous reports and accounts by journalists and travellers describe surprise and shock at the level of organization and activity, in sharp contrast to the standard perspectives – from the authorities and uninformed public opinion – that usually reach their ears first.

Prejudice also manifests itself in violence, as depicted in the novel: in the destruction of the intricate social and economic resources that are embedded in the neighbourhood – connections as intricate as those between the Sundarbans and the lives of its settlers. The category *refugee* is tied into similar condensed prejudices, such as illegal migrants, encroachers, or simply slum dwellers.

The Hungry Tide can be seen as a larger commentary on administrative categories and mythic constructions that make and break habitats. It shows how nationalism and its accompanying discourses of legitimacy and illegitimacy translate into questions of development that play vicious games in the name of the environment and its unarticulated and equally constructed antithesis – urban space.

The preservation of the forests as an end in itself goes hand in hand with the demarcation of the city – and the rigid rules of demarcation are rigidly enforced in both directions. In this popular official perspective, a city as the epitome of civilization must not show any signs of wilderness.

Conversely, following this logic, wilderness must never show signs of industry. Anthropologist Suresh Sharma describes the travails of the indigenous Agaria community in colonial India.[3] The people of this community, from the forests of central India, were adept at smelting iron and were treated coldly by colonial authorities, who preferred to characterize them as primitive forest dwellers. When the Agarias responded with enthusiasm to the arrival of the railways – which they saw as an extension of their iron-rich cosmos – they were viciously reminded of their social location. Instead of harnessing their enthusiasm and working with their industrial presence in the forests (where they would shallow-mine iron ore in an ecologically sound way), they were criminalized and stripped of their traditional rights over forest land – which the authorities proceeded to mine unsustainably or zone out as exclusive nature preserves in which the Agarias had no place.

The need to demarcate pristine forests from civilizational space – the compulsion for categorization and zoning – runs very deep. A village in a city will eventually be considered anachronistic and must either be gentrified or lose its identity as a village. In Mumbai, almost all the biggest slums have a nucleus that once was a recognizable village. Thanks to a rigid administrative framework, they were quickly downgraded into slums. After this downgrade, all their potential to improve – all the skills that could create new habitats – were drained away.

A healthy and innovative urban policy needs to reverse this trend. It must transcend such old-fashioned ways of seeing and learn to use whatever means are at hand, even if it means giving up some cherished habits. These habits are often connected to ideological frameworks that run across the political spectrum and are hard to transcend.

Yet, given the context we live in today, such transcending of polarities is proving more and more urgent. A healthy, locally relevant urban policy needs to harness local resources as well as make the most of state agencies. It needs to deal with the real anxieties of those who are vulnerable to conspiracy theories and other manipulations. It needs to look beyond political dogmatism to work with local markets, while seizing the opportunities provided by regional and global markets. Global players need to respect local management of resources for the sake of environmental goals, which are best managed by local actors – as has been repeatedly demonstrated. A grounded urban policy that works with local resources does not close itself off to larger flows of capital from regional and global contexts – provided there are limits placed for all.

This takes effort and huge political will. A few countries, notably in Northern Europe, have demonstrated tangibly how to balance these multiple scales of operation across local, regional, and global realms. Their efforts may not easily fit into rigid ideological frameworks – but that does not matter.

Engagement with an imperfect world involves some form of negotiation. Those who hold high moral standards and critique the waywardness of the world from afar may offer relevant viewpoints, but if they impose simplistic responses onto complex realities they only make matters worse. The best way to counter dogma and moralizing is to encourage these cheerleaders to become involved in some form of practice: it is in the doing that things acquire meaning – form follows process.

No other community represents the integration of what seems to be irreconcilable opposites better than the Koli – the fisherfolk of Mumbai. Dharavi Koliwada is situated between the land and the sea, village and slum, tradition and modernity, nature and urban space. In our view, the Koli have internalized the kind of syncretism required to overcome the destructive binaries that cities such as Mumbai have been stuck with for so long.

The biggest threat to the city's fragile ecosystem comes from perspectives rooted in old-fashioned evolutionary narratives that consider a Koliwada in Mumbai – with its dual commitment to traditional fishing activities and modern occupations – as unacceptable. It is this lack of understanding which made every historical move to modernize the city into a battle against a lifestyle it considered redundant. Whether it was the sea-reclamations, the filling in of the islands, the blocking of creeks and rivers – the central vision that motivated civic authorities was based on the conviction that the presence of the Kolis and their connections to outmoded occupations such as fishing – had no place in the future of the city.

Even when the Kolis continued to demonstrate their willingness to become part of the growing middle-class of the city by becoming architects, engineers, doctors, but without totally sacrificing their connection to the sea and the activity of fishing, the city simply didn't have the capacity to accommodate their sentiments.

This is a typical example of urban policymakers refusing to acknowledge the specificity of a place, who instead try to force-fit it into a preconception.

Considering the particularity of a place does not imply a restriction or narrowing down of choices. Rather, specific local contexts invariably express an awareness of other places – neighbours, regions, and the nation – that exist around them. They are infused by the different scales of operation in which they evolve. These have their specific institutional arrangements that together constitute the concreteness of that specific local reality.

We must be cautious about reducing local contexts to one end of the spectrum that privileges the regional, national, and global as ascending identities. This reductionist approach treats the local as a subset. In reality, localities are not fenced off, independent units at the bottom of a scale; rather, they are frontiers of engagement and practice that make it possible for all scales to operate. Even the most global arrangements operate in specific places – whether a generic office complex belonging to a multinational corporation or a global airport terminal. They are all situated somewhere. In a neighbourhood, the local context is a resource that's being continually produced by its inhabitants, without whom no urban practice is complete.

Institutionalizing participation

Why is it that, even with the rhetoric of citizens' involvement in urban affairs being so prominent in cities around the world, most people these days feel that the evolution of their habitat is absolutely out of their hands?

Many cities have put participatory budgets in place. There are an increasing number of schemes and processes aimed at opening up planning to stakeholders and the public at large. Public consultations, roundtable discussions, and participatory workshops are popular in South Korean, Japanese, European, and American cities. Concerned parties seem to have real enthusiasm. Residents, who are now better informed than ever, have become increasingly vocal, challenging the rule of experts. At urbz, we have been involved in organizing dozens of participatory projects, mandated by municipal authorities, international organizations, and local associations in Europe, Asia, and the Americas. In many parts of the world, the notion that users' knowledge and collective intelligence bring value to a project is well accepted.

Even real estate investors are starting to recognize the value of participatory processes as a way to reduce opposition and add relevance to their projects by anticipating users' needs and aspirations. Elected representatives increasingly promise their constituencies more openness and participation. Some see this as a new dimension of the democratic process, which extends far beyond the right to cast a yes/no vote.

Yet on the ground, planning departments don't find it so easy to translate users' consultations into participatory action. There seems to be some resistance to a full embrace of the participatory-planning paradigm. This becomes obvious when participatory processes produce non-standard projects, which don't fit neatly into the regulatory framework and require a special effort to navigate norms that are often out of sync with the reality of the context.

Bureaucratic resistance stems partly from procedural impatience with the subtler and context-specific aspects of urban life: existing uses; specific needs and aspirations; particularities of the landscape and inhabitants' personal attachment to some of these aspects; relationships with neighbours; the history and identity of a place; circumstantial opportunities; and so on. These are intrinsic to residents' lived experiences and have a direct impact on their quality of life. When these dimensions are abstracted from a place leaving only lines on a plan, we impoverish places instead of developing them.

At a discursive level, everybody agrees that it is necessary to value the characteristics and intricacies of specific contexts. Yet when they become part of the official proceedings of a participatory process, they appear misshapen and awkward. They seep out of administrative categories and land up either vanishing between the lines or being rejected outright. Consequently, people feel that their knowledge, interests, and views are not being given the consideration they deserve – even when all the boxes of the participatory-process checklist have been ticked.

Notwithstanding the high-decibel rhetoric around institutional participation, what we see on the ground is a more organized mobilization of residents – especially against imposed official plans. This is not the usual agitation of confrontation (though that continues to happen in the time-honoured tradition of resistance, with solid reasons in most cases) – it is something more challenging.

New forms of mobilization are hard-wired into transformations of knowledge systems, mainly due to the higher and more distributed agency that decentralized and collective media networks generate. Local groups engage with technical and legal questions with professional rigour. In many cases, such groups are a force of proposition, not only of opposition. This makes conversations across official tables more complicated – it demands a genuine shift from rhetorical posturing to real listening and working together.

We increasingly find that in most places there are people with local expertise in matters relevant to planning, community building, and neighbourhood management: architects, social workers, builders, masons, health workers, locality archivists, businessmen, journalists, anthropologists, lawyers, party promoters, shopkeepers, or artists. This diversity of demographics has become increasingly important. Residents hold expert knowledge of their environment through use, and they are also increasingly experts in planning it.

They are experts because they have been practising in their neighbourhoods for years, and they know what works and what does not. We must take on board that people now have knowledge, not only opinions, which means the ballot box is indeed too narrow a form of expression. They are able to organize themselves and take action; they have the skills and capabilities to engage with the process of planning and building. This, indeed, changes everything.

Many professionals have integrated the notion that participation is not simply good on moral grounds. Participatory processes also increase the quality, feasibility, and value of urban projects. Initiatives such as PlacemakingX, initiated by Fred and Ethan Kent, have become global phenomena, enticing a new generation of professionals from different fields of practice.[4] The core idea of this movement is that successful public spaces usually follow a specific set of principles, the most important being the involvement of users in the creation and maintenance of these spaces.

For these ideas to start impacting our cities, we need a genuine opening up of the administrative imagination of planning departments, which must go beyond participatory rhetoric and managed consultation. Real engagement with inhabitants as players on the field requires a culture change. Participation cannot be massaged into existing processes; instead, a deep rethinking and rewiring of urban development is required. Within planning departments and private organizations, we find people who are genuinely committed to expanding this process. Many of them would like to do more but are caught in a structure that leaves them very little scope for action. Some cities, however, have managed to turn their urban planning culture around. We were lucky enough to work with the metropolitan authorities in Nantes, France, which managed to integrate notions of 'citizens' inspiration', 'citizens' pacts', and participatory processes into administrative procedures and systems. As a result, Nantes has some of the most interesting and innovative urban projects in Europe.

In Switzerland, the cooperative housing movement is successful in producing affordable housing and innovative typologies, reflecting residents' aspirations and lifestyles. Cooperative housing projects typically bypass classic real estate operators and reduce the scope for profiting from rising property value – actively preventing speculation. Non-profit housing cooperatives in Switzerland have adopted a charter laying down progressive guiding principles such as 'no speculative profits, good-quality affordable and sustainable housing, integration of disadvantaged households and tenant participation and self-determination'.

Swiss authorities actively support housing cooperatives by providing them with low-interest loans or guaranteeing bonds issued for their development. But it remains extremely difficult to navigate the regulatory framework that constrains the participation of people who are not specialized lawyers or architects. Because of this we have witnessed the emergence of large cooperatives that are themselves highly institutional bureaucratic actors.

In addition, existing rules and incentives limit the emergence of new housing typologies – for example, by supporting vertical densification rather than low-rise, high-density typologies. As a result, cooperative housing tends to reproduce generic architectural forms: a rectangular prism sitting on a plot. All resident inputs are directed to interior design or common spaces within the boundaries of the plot. From an urban planning point of view, these innovative objects often fail to connect to the neighbourhoods where they stand and to the city at large. They tend to create inward-looking communities. The urban dimension of the project is usually lost in a utopian microcosm, turning its back to the city.

Planning departments have an important role to play in fostering meaningful relationships and connections between buildings and the neighbourhoods where they stand. The larger scale they deal with is precisely the neighbourhood scale – this is where civic life unfolds. The case of Nantes – or Tokyo for that matter – serves to remind us that we need urban planning and management departments which engage with people and context in the planning phase, and which leave scope for initiatives and evolution in the management of built habitats thereafter.

A major challenge for contemporary urban planning, which is rarely articulated as such, is the idea of community itself. At the simplest level, community refers to the impulse to live with people with whom one identifies. In this sense, it seems to have a universal basis. Communities, as such, are frequently considered as internally homogeneous and exclusive, even if a discerning eye will always see complications. What is undeniable, though, is that this sense of belonging has shaped the identity of some of the most fascinating neighbourhoods in cities around the world – from Chinatowns and Jewish quarters to Dutch streets and gay enclaves.

The cooperative housing model follows the same logic of imagining communities as enclaves or zones of sorts. This model is used in cities around the world to allow people who identify as a community to participate in the planning of their habitat. In contemporary contexts, these groups could be ecologically minded individuals living in Basel or Zurich, successful creative types in New York or Berlin, or conservative vegetarians in Mumbai. Their desire to regroup and live together may be understandable, especially in a larger celebratory context of inclusivity and diversity.

At the scale of the city, and given the challenges of modern urban living, however, we have come to understand the limitations of such spaces. In fact, the impulse today is to prevent the creation of gated enclaves, which do, in fact, reinforce social tensions between insiders and outsiders. The ideals of community living and participation in urban planning cannot translate into a multiplicity of divisions. The city is not a cake for different communities to slice and share, but an intertwined tapestry of the commons. Being able to move through it, following a network of streets, sidewalks, parks, and squares, is an experience that must belong to all.

As a rule, new developments should contribute not only to the well-being of their future residents but also to the general welfare of their neighbours. The idea of a neighbourhood is predicated precisely on the existence of neighbours at different scales – implying co-dependence and exchange rather than the management of boundaries.

In practical terms, this means allowing urban spaces, neighbourhood after neighbourhood, to be criss-crossed by connections and cross-connections. This translates into incentives for building infrastructure and public amenities that allow passers-by to walk around and through them. The addition of urban pieces must create the ensemble that we call a city. The whole is made greater than the parts thanks to permeable pedestrian neighbourhoods that welcome visitors rather than a series of walled enclaves that keep them out.

For walkers, there is nothing more enjoyable than a street that radiates with not only one strong cultural identity but with many. It is always comforting to know that the place that one walks through is diverse, and therefore tolerates strangers and otherness. It is in this sense that city life today can fulfil the endangered modern values of inclusion and diversity. This is a city which stores and transmits identity in the form of architecture; which allows a high level of local involvement; where the political ideals of democracy are actualized in everyday life through civic participation; where placemaking happens through daily uses. It is a city where communities are embedded in their neighbourhoods, not mutually exclusive or segregated, thereby creating a network of multiple possibilities for community living in an endless series of combinations; and where this multiplicity is connected to practical issues of neighbourhood living with infrastructures and amenities that support these impulses.

Historically, many cities have allowed diversity of habitat to emerge by failing to control urban development. A field is divided into small plots, which are sold individually; houses are built on them by their future inhabitants – each according to their means. These houses may also host economic activities: a shop, a clinic, a hostel, a restaurant, or a tea stall. Houses consolidate and grow over time as families grow and reinvest in their homes. Land gains value as the inhabitants add storeys to their houses. From time to time a few small plots are consolidated into a large one and large buildings get constructed. A first step towards a more diverse urbanism is simply to recognize and validate habitats that have emerged through such incremental and piecemeal processes.

The issues associated with low-rise, high-density settlements are well known, and they have given rise to massive reconstruction drives such as the Haussman plan in Paris. The Congres Internationaux d'Architecture Moderne (CIAM) was based on the ideal of another kind of city: one that would be orderly, organized on a functional basis, spacious and hygienic, connected by road and rail.[5] While these intentions were justified, especially in the context of rapid urban growth, we must also acknowledge that large-scale urban plans have often denied people's right to the city and taken over land occupied by the poorest on the pretext of making it more rational or beautiful. The driving forces behind the realization of plans for modern settlements were often speculative and characterized by a will to control rather than a demonstration of welfare, concern, and improvement.

We also know now that cities and neighbourhoods that are master-planned following a single architectural logic are difficult for users to appropriate. Christopher Alexander's distinction between 'natural' and 'artificial' cities come to mind.[6] Artificial neighbourhoods are not usually adept at adapting to unforeseen circumstances. Built as self-contained systems, they leave out what they were not planned to integrate. The classic case is, of course, Brasília, where the thousands of workers brought to the middle of the Amazon jungle to build the capital also built shelters for themselves, where they finally settled with their families. This settlement was the first favela of Brasília; it came as an unplanned, organic outgrowth of the master-planned city.

The city, like many other human creations, may be structured around opposing drives to control and create, but essentializing the slum as a place without planning or control is not a helpful strategy. Likewise, it would be reductive for Alexander to make a distinction between natural and artificial cities if he thought of natural cities as totally unplanned. Many artificial neighbourhoods have become naturalized over time, and many natural neighbourhoods have been consolidated internally and integrated into a city-planning framework.

The important distinction Alexander makes is between cities that allow for emergence and specificities and those where the spatial control limits appropriation by the users. Some historical cities are so well protected that they also leave no scope for appropriation; they become beautiful dead objects. The spirit of a place – its *genius loci* – resides in the dynamic relationship between an existing built form and its creative appropriation by successive waves of users.

Alexander, along with Turner, Illich, and Jacobs, were all part of a hopeful generation who identified ways in which the government and architects could support the work of inhabitants – industrious user-producers – who have for centuries provided for their own housing needs. They thought that the parts of the city residents could appropriate and consolidate over time were more vibrant and interesting than those that are master-planned by bureaucrats and real estate developers. The real worry is not the slum-studded future described by Mike Davis, but rather a global cityscape full of dismal, grey, vertical buildings, economically sterile and socially dysfunctional, generated only by mis-placed anxieties, high-tech surveillance, mediocre urban policies, and unchecked greed. For many people, this is not just a version of the future, but the place where they live today.

Ultimately, describing the city only in terms of extreme polarities doesn't help. This is why we are advocating for a city that is tolerant of a variety of urban forms, where the homegrown neighbourhood and the high-rise are both accepted as valid typologies, and where, most importantly, we recognize the huge variety of possibilities between these extremes. Likewise, when it comes to urban planning and management we need efficient public services and infrastructure, reaching even the most remote or densely populated part of the city – and at the same time, we must allow people to leave their mark on the city, and let successive generations reshape it according to their needs and sensibilities.

This is not achieved by getting rid of the urban planning departments, but by opening the process of urban development to inhabitants – with the understanding that this fundamentally changes how we design neighbourhoods. Importantly, we must recognize the fact that shift-ing from technocratic urban planning to participatory planning means that spatial arrangement is no longer the end goal of urban planning and design. Instead, it puts the onus on relationships between people and their habitat. For too long, urban planning and design have been practised reductively, as if it were all about arranging spatial objects to make them look neat in two dimensions. This 'compulsive desire for neatness and order', reflects a reductive understanding of order – spatial and imposed from above.

In the relational paradigm, order is emergent. It doesn't need to be designed as much as recognized. It is generated by the way different elements function together – how they relate to each other. Space no longer constrains relationships, instead it is shaped by the relationships, planned or spontaneous, between elements of the urban system.

Designing communities

Relationships with people and the environment are an essential dimen-sion of the human experience. Hearing the wind blow through the branches of a tree, walking back from school with a friend, sharing a recipe with the elderly person next door … These are some of the simple things that make us feel alive and connected. We shape these relationships unconsciously through habit and consciously through design.

The importance of connecting with people and nature cannot be overemphasized in a world of increasing social isolation, communitarian division, and environmental degradation. In the networked age, when distance has lost meaning as far as information and data are concerned, we seem increasingly removed from our corporeal life. The ease with which we navigate the digital realm contrasts with how poorly we deal with the social and material reality immediately around us. We know that obstacles to communication cannot be reduced to time and space – such obstacles are also social and cultural. It is easier to talk to a friend who is miles away than a neighbour whose mother tongue and world-views are different. This is why the principal challenge of participatory projects is to design communicative processes that have the capacity to generate common goals and outcomes at the local level, where we have to deal with familiarity and proximity.

Sometimes, it is the very technologies which bring us virtually closer that create a sense of distance. Writing in the 1960s, Melvin Webber described cities as gigantic switchboards. He defined urbanity as a phenomenon and experience connected to the density and variety of human interactions.[7] It soon became obvious, however, that the infrastructures and technologies that enable cities to become efficient communication systems also reduce the space and time available for more immediate forms of interactions. Think of the classic image of the highway taking us faster from here to there at the cost of severing all possible relationships with the landscape it cuts across.

Withdrawal from neighbourhood life has become a pervasive reality for many people. The *Economist* recently coined the term 'hermit consumer' to describe an enduring post-COVID tendency in the rich world.[8] People spend less time and money than before on personal services such as restaurants and hairdressing, and more on home entertainments, computing goods, and delivery services. Hermits can have rich social and professional lives online or at at distance, and at the same time feel isolated at home. Locality itself has become disjointed as it increasingly finds itself at the confluence of many flows or *scapes* which may be connected to far-away communities, institutions, and mythologies. This condition, which was perceived by Arjun Appadurai in the 1990s, is now a pervasive reality that urban designers must reckon with.[9]

De-sign means to mark out, to point out. It can be a roadmap or a vision. It is aimed at sharing ideas and showing the way. Yet, one shouldn't reduce design to the expression of an intention to be realized in the future. A printed plan is not itself the design, but merely a tool in a broad, evolving, and adaptive scheme. Design must be understood as a communicative act, just like speech, which is at once context-driven and context-generating.

Webber reminds us that it is 'no linguistic accident' that 'community' and 'communication' share the Latin root *communis*, 'in common'. It is our ability to communicate that provides us with meaning and a shared sense of purpose. Design considered as a communicative act can help reduce the distance between people, filling the social gap and even encouraging us to overcome our inhibitions. It can reveal potentialities built into our environment and provide us with the means of activating them. Shaping and nurturing our habitat is one of the most natural and creative ways to feel alive and part of something larger than ourselves.

Participatory urban design can rewire spaces that are in close physical proximity but outside our comfort zone, and make them truly ours. There is no greater comfort in life than feeling connected and at peace in one's surroundings. Finding this peace can be the fruit of an investment in one's own habitat, or it can mean finding an environment more adapted to one's needs. Either way, it indicates an understanding of one's relationship with the surrounding environment and the intention to engage with it.

If design is a conversation with the environment, it must include non-human entities as well, not only as protagonists but also as co-narrators. What do birds, the mountain, and even that industrial ruin tell us about the world we live in? How do we co-exist? Amitav Ghosh demonstrates how stories have the power to connect humans to each other and to other life forms.[10] The places we shape as designers, planners, and users are already inhabited, not only by fellow humans and non-humans but also by narratives, which exist in a realm beyond time and space. We are not the only ones speaking: the world also speaks to us, if we only care to listen. The new stories we write are only stronger when we weave them into the context. Rootedness does not take anything away from creativity. On the contrary, it has the potential to bring inspiration, relevance, and durability to our schemes.

The rupture with the tangible and physical aspects of life is particularly obvious when it comes to environmental and ecological consciousness. We find ourselves developing a high degree of virtual connectedness in the context of our concerns about nature and the environment. We may have deep knowledge about the environment through school and the internet – maybe we vote for our country's green party – and at the same time, we could remain oblivious to the material reality that surrounds us and live in a world of abstraction where we relate to nature as a passive backdrop, instead of something that speaks to us and affects us in every possible way.

Environmental awareness cannot happen without engaging with the material realm. Developing a strong environmental knowledge base through information sharing and data transmission is of course important – it helps us get the larger picture, shapes policies, and guides our choices. Yet if it is not matched by our ability to judge the material deterioration of air or water, social or mental health, or food quality, ecological consciousness will be limited to audits and austerity measures and can only operate on an abstract level. To transform our environmental concerns into concrete action, we must accentuate our senses and our ability to become conscious and engage with the material world as a species, and as citizens whose lives are embedded in our habitat.

The overlapping worlds of the immediate and the abstract, the here and the elsewhere – intersections that we inhabit so casually – need a conscious and deliberate strategy of engagement. Design belongs to the world of symbols. It is a mediation – a passage through abstraction, but a performative one, with the capacity of bringing people together and leading them to action. Design can bridge the gap identified by Henri Bergson between intuition and intelligence, just as it can help us to share our perceptions and coordinate action.

If we accept that interpersonal and inter-species communication are essential aspects of design, we must ask how design can support social communication. How can design give us the means to create what Appadurai calls a 'structure of feeling'?

Urban design as a communicative and participatory practice has the potential to gather local agents towards a shared vision, the elaboration of a plan and direct engagement with our habitat. Without participation there can be no shared meaning and no shared intent, and urban design becomes one more imposition from above on communities that struggle to unite around the space they share. The biggest contribution of participatory processes is the coming together of people who have a common interest in improving their shared environment. Sharing perspectives and ideas is also a moment of community generation, which has value in and of itself.

Many mansions

As we write these words, we are concerned about the fate of homegrown neighbourhoods around the world that are threatened by large-scale re-development projects. In many ways, this book advocates for places such as Dharavi and thousands of others around the globe that are unfairly dismissed as irregular slums in need of clearance. We want to locate these places in a continuum of habitats which have existed throughout human history and which continue to be part of the landscape everywhere they are not actively repressed.

Our intention is to demonstrate that there is nothing inherently wrong with homegrown neighbourhoods, and that in fact, in comparison to the kind of developments that typically come to replace them, they have qualities that are worth recognizing and building upon. One of the most important of these qualities is that they are built from within. They are social constructs as much as spatial ones. This puts them on track to develop a local economy and a sense of place, two qualities that most master-planned housing projects sorely lack.

We have identified *spreadsheet urbanism* – taking the form of poorly built mass housing for the lower and middle classes alike – as a greater threat than the proliferation of homegrown habitats. We have argued that homegrown habitats have this advantage over mass housing: they can improve over time, if only the authorities support the process and bring in the kind of services and infrastructure that every neighbourhood must be equipped with.

We have described what is universal to Dharavi and other homegrown settlements. What we have learned and continue to learn from Dharavi has become part of our practice, not only in Dharavi but also in many other places around the world that have evolved in totally different environments. We have tried to demonstrate how much the case of Dharavi resonates with the recent history of Tokyo, which provides powerful clues about how homegrown habitats can be integrated in the modernization of a metropolis.

What worries us most about spreadsheet urbanism is that it already covers so many parts of the world – so much so that it has conquered the global imagination. It has become the only ideal to which we can aspire. Rectangular blocks, whether they are lying on their long edge or standing up on the short one, are all we seem to be allowed to dream about in Geneva, Bogotá, or Mumbai. Are these blocks the only places where all humanity is destined to live and work? Are these the only places where we are supposed to develop a sense of belonging that we pass on to future generations? While we have nothing against rectangular buildings in principle, what we find highly problematic is that there seems to be no other horizon left for dense cities. This singular skyline, shared across Manhattan and Moscow, has become the generic ideal of our global urban future. It imposes itself on the reality of cities that are intrinsically as diverse as Mumbai and Geneva.

Against the mechanistic reproduction of a unique model of urban development in cities around the world, we once again evoke Geddes, who proposed the concept of eutopia (the good place) to counter utopia (no place).[11] Real estate utopias, like the one which is being forced upon Dharavi today, are of the second type; they project a future that requires a total erasure of the present. The plan imposes itself upon reality – and the process becomes secondary. The new must replace the old *by any means necessary* – even when the process of building a new neighbourhood on the ruins of the old one involves evicting and displacing hundreds of thousands of people, breaking their social networks, and annihilating their sources of income.

In our view, the planned destruction of Dharavi is the opposite of modernization. Instead of representing Mumbai as a proud, forward-looking metropolis defining the future in its own terms, it proposes a city that reproduces urban utopias that belong to the twentieth century. The city of high-rises and highways is a backward model of development that has lost currency even in China, which had embraced it more than any other, besides the US where it originated. Far from celebrating the entrepreneurial spirit of the city, plans for the makeover of Dharavi show a public sector unable to protect the interests of its citizens, including those who work hardest to make Mumbai the industrial and service powerhouse that it is today. At a time when cities are struggling to retain or recreate an industrial sector, it does not make any sense to demolish a neighbourhood of tool-houses teeming with activity, only to replace it with the same old housing towers that decay in a matter of years. Instead of making Mumbai shine on the global stage, it will simply make it obvious that the city is being broken apart by real estate greed.

What could the alternative look like? Quite simply, a better version of the present. The good place, Geddes's eutopia, is not an unreachable dream. It is not an ideal or a perfect place. It is a place within reach for the people who live there now. It is a process more than a form – a journey more than a plan. The journey to eutopia starts with a hard look at present conditions and focuses on how they can be improved.

Geddes began every project with a 'regional survey', which aimed at producing 'a complete description of the community's foundations, its past, its manner of working and living, its institutions, its regional peculiarities, and its utilization of physical, vital, and social resources'.[12] It emphasized

> the natural characteristics of the environment, as they are discovered by the geologist, the zoologist, the ecologist – in addition to the development of natural and human conditions in the historic past, as presented by the anthropologist, the archaeologist, and the historian. In short, the regional survey attempts a local synthesis of all the specialist 'knowledge'.[13]

Contrary to utopia, eutopia starts from an assessment of context, in all its complexity. And what matters most in this process is not what each specialized form of knowledge has to say, but how these different dimensions of the place in question come together to produce its uniqueness, and how these characteristics can be used as resources to fulfil a place's potential.

Utopia sets an objective regardless of the context and relies on external resources to impose itself onto the present. Eutopia sets its objectives on the basis of the present context and local resources. The Dharavi redevelopment project, like all other slum-clearance projects and real estate development projects generally, imposes a cheap, generic utopia upon a rich and diverse reality, destroying everything that stands in the way. These projects justify their ignorance of the places, histories, and ecologies they wipe out by claiming that these are illegitimate, irrational, or inefficient. In short, they claim to replace disorder with order, and in doing so they reveal their own biased and simplistic conception of order, as well as their lack of consideration for the existing order, which is present but which they refuse to see.

When we state that *form follows process*, we are also saying that we must reclaim the processes that generate our cities using all available forms of knowledge as well as our imagination. Developing a shared understanding of what could make a neighbourhood a better version of itself is part of the process. It seems uncontroversial to say that the people who live in a place must be involved in the process of improving it, because they hold precious knowledge about it and because their own future is at stake. We believe that these questions, which become urgent in the context of Dharavi, are universal.

At the time of writing, we remain deeply involved in Dharavi's own evolution, where we work closely with the Koli, the oldest organized community in the settlement. With them we are developing a plan for the incremental improvement of the dense urban village of Koliwada, which involves restoring historical structures, installing lights in some of the darkest streets, producing a water sanitation plan that doesn't involve destroying homes, and designing a garden with a jetty along the Mithi River. We hope that the work we do there will inspire decision makers, developers, and community leaders to reconsider their approach to urban development in Dharavi and beyond.

We work in contexts as radically different as India, Switzerland, and Colombia. In each of our projects, we build on our experiences and strengthen our methodology through recognition, participation, community, and open-ended processes. The most exciting aspect of our work is that it is grounded in realities that are always unique, and so the outcome can never be predicted in advance.

Rather than places, we design ways of engaging with the context and the people that inhabit them. Our first task is always to bring together a multitude of different perspectives, identifying points of convergence and divergence. We call these *creative tension points*. Sometimes they can be resolved, and sometimes they just need to be acknowledged and worked around. Either way, they provide a sense of structure and help to identify the contours of a shared vision. This shared vision is developed through an iterative process that involves testing the story with as many people as possible and consolidating it a little more each time through the inclusion of feedback. This process has the power of bringing together actors as diverse as residents of different age groups, investors, city officials, environmentalists, and advocates. Out of this vision we generate a programme, with objectives that serve as moving targets towards which the process unfolds. The community of users and stakeholders then becomes a central resource in the realization of the objectives set by the vision. Such an approach is much more sophisticated and qualitative than the standard master-planning approach, but it is also more pragmatic, less destructive, and not necessarily longer. Master plans create so much bad blood and opposition that they are susceptible to failure. The incremental and participatory way is embedded in existing processes and is therefore much more likely to sustain and yield results.

This is why similar approaches in distinctive contexts lead to outcomes that cannot be anticipated. Each process is simultaneously rooted and creative – and its outcome is homegrown in the most fundamental way. As Geddes said, in the kingdom of eutopia there will be many mansions.[14]

Acknowledgements

A large part of co-authorship in this book is invisible. We are scribes and signatories for the thoughts, exchanges, and experiences of a multitudinous collective – one that is made up of our teams interacting with the many inhabitants from the neighbourhoods we have worked in – in cities as varied as Mumbai, Kochi, Goa, Tokyo, Seoul, Bogotá, Cali, Rio, São Paulo, Geneva, Lausanne, Paris, and Nantes, over the past sixteen years or so.

We would like to thank several more people, but in a journey so long, where each conversation is special, it is impossible to acknowledge them individually. There have literally been a couple of hundreds of associates, interns, and visitors who have enriched our offices over the years, contributing skills, ideas, effort, and goodwill.

We thank each and every one of you, even though we are not in a position to name you individually.

We are deeply indebted to our present partners in Mumbai, Geneva, and Bogotá – Bharat Gangurde, Samidha Patil, Kareena Kochery, Jai Bhadgaonkar, Eesha Pethe, Amin Khosravi, Gabriela Jeanrenaud, Leonardo Vimos, Andres Sanchez Arias, and Anushka Samat, whose illustration we used for the cover of the book. Our journey in this form would not have started without Geeta Mehta, who supported the setting up of our Mumbai office in 2008 and remains a vital part of our team from New York.

Ramchandra (Bhau) Korde is our 'Yoda', the wise old man who invited us to set up base in Dharavi, which we never left. Our advisor Yehuda Safran joined us in so many adventures, stepping over drains and stumbling over pipes participating in every workshop he could, while enriching our understanding of architecture and urbanism through his razor-sharp contribution. He remains our philosopher in residence, whom we cannot do without.

Matt Karau and his students from New York University, Abu Dhabi, are virtually fellow travellers, working intimately through our handstorm workshops year after year.

Our friends, supporters, and partners in Geneva: Vincent Kauffman, Luca Pattaroni, Gary Waechter, Nathalie Havinga, and Françoise Le Goff; in Paris: Clarissa Pelino, Isabault Maniglier-Sotiropolos, Simon Chabas, Pierre Kirk Jensen, Emmanuel Grimaund, Arman Le Berre, and Come Salvaire; in Bogotá and Cali: Melissa Martinez Cañadulce, Nicolás Ayala, Jairo Velasco, and Catalina Riascos; in New York: Raphael Garnaith, Joseph Setton, and Sunny Setton; in Vienna: Itai Margula; in Tokyo: Kimura Kazuo. Our friends in Mumbai – Ketaki Tare, Larson Vaiti, Prince Koli, Joseph Koli, Digambar Koli, and the Kenny family – and in Goa – Cecil Pinto – continue to strengthen us in our ongoing activities and we remain hugely grateful.

In the field of urban practice we were lucky to interact with luminaries in different capacities – those who agreed with us or not, they all made an impact: Sheela Patel, Rahul Mehrotra, Arminio Ribeiro, Anita Patil Deshmukh, Charles Correa, the Charles Correa Foundation, Sylvie Landrieve, Christopher Gay, Stefano Boeri, Ricky Burdett, Anush Kapadia, and Amita Bhide, among others.

We were fortunate to have in-person conversations throughout the years, with intellectual giants whom we quote often in the book. They have guided us, helped us grow, provided constructive critiques, and encouraged us in ways they may not be aware of: Arjun Appadurai, Amitav Ghosh, Keith Hart, and Shunya Yoshimi. We thank them with gratitude. In the same vein we owe special thanks to our editor, Leo Hollis of Verso, who needs to be given an award for patience. He had faith in us that is immeasurable and it would not be an exaggeration to say this book would not exist if it had not been for him.

Some of the chapters in this book have been previously published in different forms and we would like to thank the original editors and publishers. These include Richard Hu, ed., *Routledge Handbook of Asian Cities*, Routledge, 2023; Nancy Brooks, Kieran Donaghy, and Gerrit-Jan Knaap, eds, *The Oxford Handbook of Urban Economics and Planning*, Oxford University Press, 2011; Frances Holliss, Howard Davis, and Shalini Sinha, eds, 'Homes that Work', special issue, *Built Environment* 49, no. 3, 2023. The Forum for Mobile Lives, Paris, commissioned our study on circulatory lives on urban–rural connections in India, forum-viesmobiles.org, and our arguments on informality were developed in conversations at the Max Planck Institute for the Study of Religious and Ethnic Diversity, Göttingen.

Our families have been the most important foundations, the proverbial bedrock, of our idiosyncratic life choices; they have allowed us to do what we've done all these years and continue to do so. To them we owe everything.

Finally – the people from the neighbourhoods with whom we had the most stimulating conversations, who taught us so much about buildings, construction, making a community, about dreams and aspirations, who reaffirmed time and again, in every part of the world, that there is genuine talent, skill, brilliance, and willingness to transform lives all around us. Urban practitioners of every shade and inclination have the best partners available to work with in every corner of the world – they just have to make a move and reach out.

Since we firmly believe in process over product – a theme that echoes through the text – we see the acknowledgements as a list of associations, networks, and intellectual kinships we hope will keep sharpening our practice. They will guide us as we keep these exchanges ongoing, between ourselves, with our partners and colleagues at urbz and others. Our practice is experimental, shaped by experience and animated by the people who are part of it. Writing *The Homegrown City* is an ongoing discovery of all the elements of our urban practice – a journey we will continue to describe, methods that we will continue to refine, and a place that we will continue to return to.

Notes

1. The Cities We Build, the World We Live In

1 Vinicius Peripato et al., 'More than 10,000 Pre-Columbian Earthworks Are Still Hidden Throughout Amazonia', *Science* 382, no. 6666, October 2023, 103–9.
2 Roland Strobel, 'Before the Wall Came Tumbling Down: Urban Planning Paradigm Shifts in a Divided Berlin', *Journal of Architectural Education* 48, no. 1, 1994, 25–37.
3 Caner Gizem and Fulin Bolen, 'Urban Planning Approaches in Divided Cities', *ITU AZ* 13, no.1, March 2016, 139–56.
4 Barbara Engel, ed., *Mass Housing and the Socialist City*, Berlin: DOM, 2020.
5 The World Bank refers to this in several reports like this one on its official site. 'Slum Rehabilitation Scheme, Maharashtra, India', Public-Private Partnership Resource Center, ppp.worldbank.org.
6 Jurgen Habermas, *The Theory of Communicative Action*, vol. 1, *Reason and the Rationalization of Society*, Boston: Beacon Press, 1984.
7 Bruno Latour, *We Have Never Been Modern*, trans. Catherine Porter, Cambridge, MA: Harvard University Press, 1993.
8 Arjun Appadurai, 'The Production of Locality', in *Modernity at Large: Cultural Dimensions of Globalization*, Minneapolis: University of Minnesota Press, 1996, 178–99.

2. Speculative Versus Intensive City

1 Rahul Mehrotra, *The Kinetic City and Other Essays*, Berlin: Architangle, 2021.
2 Kevin Lynch, *City Sense and City Design: Writings and Projects of Kevin Lynch*, ed. Tridib Banerjee and Michael Southworth, Cambridge, MA: MIT Press, 1990.
3 Donald Richie, *Tokyo: A View of the City*, London: Reaktion Books, 1999.
4 Saskia Sassen, 'The Informal Economy: Between New Developments and Old Regulations', *Yale Law Journal* 103, no. 8, 1994, 2289–304; Manuel Castells, *The Informational City*, Oxford: Blackwell, 1991.

5   LSE Cities, 'Urban Age Cities, Mumbai', December 2012, urbanage.lsecities.net.

6   Mike Davis, *Planet of Slums*, London: Verso, 2007, 206.

7   Stephen Trinder, 'Capitalism with a Human Face: Neoliberal Ideology in Neill Blomkamp's *District 9*', *Film-Philosophy* 23, no. 1, February 2019, 1–16.

8   Matias Echanove and Rahul Srivastava, 'Taking the Slum Out of "Slumdog"', *New York Times*, 21 February 2009, nytimes.com.

9   United Nations, *The Millennium Development Goals Report*, New York: United Nations, 2005, un.org.

10 Jim Kunstler, 'An Interview with Jane Jacobs, the Godmother of the American City', *Metropolis*, 4 May 2016, metropolismag.com.

11 Achille Mbembe, *On the Post Colony*, Berkeley: University of California Press, 2001, 2.

12 Nauzer Bharucha, 'Dharavi Remake Plan a Land Grab, Says Panel', *Times of India*, 8 July 2009.

13 Nauzer Bharucha, 'Move to Postpone Dharavi Bid Opening Raises Eyebrows', *Times of India*, 31 July 2009.

14 These are changing figures that are constantly negotiated. For a sense of this dynamism, see redevelopmentofhousingsocieties.com. The figures need to be compared and updated by referring to the official portal of the government in charge of redevelopment: sra.gov.in/en.

15 Amita Bhide, 'Resettlement or a Silent Displacement?', *Mumbai Reader 2008*, Mumbai: Urban Design Research Institute, 2008, 302–29.

16 Martin Anderson, *The Federal Bulldozer: A Critical Analysis of Urban Renewal 1949–1962*, Cambridge, MA: MIT Press, 1964. See also Herbert Gans, 'The Human Implications of Current Development and Relocation Planning', *Journal of the American Institute of Planners* 25, no. 1, 1959, 15–26.

17 Bhau (Ramchandra) Korde is a lifelong resident of Dharavi and has been an advisor to urbz since its inception in 2008. This quote emerged in a personal communication that has become an important reference in our work and in presentations.

18 Adam Smith, *Theory of Moral Sentiments*, pt I, sec. III, ch. II, 1759.

19 Charles Correa, *A Place in the Shade: The New Landscape and Other Essays*, New Delhi: Penguin, 2010.

20 Liza Weinstein, 'Mumbai's Development Mafias: Globalization, Organized Crime and Land Development', *International Journal of Urban and Regional Research* 32, no. 1, March 2008, 22–39. This article provides a darker twist to this assertion, but one that is even more accurate.

21 Ivan Illich, *Tools for Conviviality*, London: Marion Boyars, 2001.

22 Edward Seidensticker, *Tokyo Rising: The City Since the Great Earthquake*, Cambridge, MA: Harvard University Press, 1990.

23 Bombay First and McKinsey, *Vision Mumbai: Transforming Mumbai into a World-Class City*, New Delhi: Cirrus, 2003, mumbaifirst.org.

24 Tarun Khanna, *Billions of Entrepreneurs: How China and India Are Reshaping Their Futures and Yours*, Boston: Harvard Business School Press, 2007, 75–6.

25 'China's Economic Crisis Claims More Victims: Companies', *Economist*, 10 October 2024.

26 David Epstein, *Brasilia, Plan and Reality: A Study of Planned and Spontaneous Urban Development*, Berkeley: University of California Press, 1973.

27 Sassen, 'The Informal Economy'.

28 Martha Alter Chen, 'Rethinking the Informal Economy', *India Seminar* 531, November 2003.

29 Christopher Alexander, *The Nature of Order: An Essay on the Art of Building and the Nature of the Universe*, Berkeley, CA: Centre for Environmental Structure Publishers, 2002.

3. The Road from Illegitimacy to Recognition

1 John F. C. Turner, *Housing by People: Towards Autonomy in Building Environments*, New York: Pantheon, 1976.

2 Jane Jacobs, *The Death and Life of Great American Cities*, New York: Vintage, 1961, 4.

3 Amartya Sen, *The Argumentative Indian*, London: Allen Lane, 2005, 36.

4 Slavoj Žižek, *Plaidoyer en faveur de l'intolérance*, Paris: Climats, 2007, 73.

5 Peter van der Veer, 'Who Cares: Care Arrangements and Sanitation for the Poor in India and Elsewhere', lecture at the Tata Institute of Social Sciences, Mumbai, September 2012.

6 The exact figures for the specific breakdown of different communities are never clearly expressed in most statistics. These figures have to be estimated by scrutinizing the numbers indicated with specific reference to the scheduled caste and scheduled tribe figures. The last official statistics available are in *Slums in India: A Statistical Compendium, 2011*, New Delhi: Government of India, Ministry of Housing and Urban Poverty Alleviation, National Buildings Organisation, 2012, nbo.gov.in.

7 Swaminathan Anklesaria Aiyar, 'Slums Are Hubs of Hope, Progress and Dignity', *Times of India*, 31 March 2013.

8 Ibid.

9 Pietro Garau, Elliot Sclar, Gabriella Carolini, and UN Millennium Project, 'A Home in the City: Improving the Lives of Slum Dwellers', London: Earthscan, 2006, digitallibrary.un.org.

10 United Nations, 'Sustainable Cities and Communities', in *The Sustainable Development Goals Report 2023: Special Edition*, New York: United Nations Publications, 2024, unstats.un.org.

11 The Maharashtra Slum Areas (Improvement, Clearance and Redevelopment) Act (1971: Mah. XXVIII], text as on 7 August 2024.

12 Darshini Mahadevia, *Inside the Transforming Urban Asia, Processes, Policies and Public Actions*, Delhi: Concept, 2008, 549–89.

13 Lisa Björkman, 'Becoming a Slum: From Municipal Colony to Illegal Settlement in Liberalisation Era Mumbai', in Gavin Shatkin, ed., *Contesting the Indian City: Global Visions and the Politics of the Local*, Chichester: John Wiley & Sons, 2013, 208–40.

14 Björkman, 'Becoming a Slum'.

15 Henri Bergson, *The Creative Mind: An Introduction to Metaphysics*, New York: Dover, 2010.

16 Vijay Govindarajan and Christian Sarkar, 'The $300 House: A Hands-On Lab for Reverse Innovation?', *Harvard Business Review*, 26 August 2010, hbr.org.

17 Matias Echanove and Rahul Srivastava, 'Hands Off Our Houses', *New York Times*, 1 June 2011.

18 Ananya Roy, 'Slumdog Cities: Rethinking Subaltern Urbanism', *International Journal of Urban and Regional Research* 35, no. 2, 2011, 231.

19 Ibid.

20 Sheetal Chabbria, 'The Aboriginal Alibi: Governing Dispossession in Colonial Bombay', *Comparative Studies in Society and History* 60, no. 4, October 2018, 1096–126. This essay challenges many narratives that drive the popular political narratives of Mumbai, especially those related to the history of the fishing community referred to as the Koli. Her essay shows how 'only once the Koli became marked as aboriginal and treated as privileged petitioners by the early twentieth century did they garner protections with regards to the allocation of urban space that nominally exempted them from market-based redevelopment projects in the neighborhoods of Bombay' (1097). This template continues to be deployed with modified narratives by other vulnerable groups in the city, and is visible in their attempts to negotiate rights when faced with new real estate development projects.

21 Roy, 'Slumdog Cities', 231.

22 Mike Davis, *Planet of Slums*, London: Verso, 2007.

23 Matias Echanove and Rahul Srivastava, 'Taking the Slum Out of "Slumdog"', *New York Times*, 21 February 2009.

24 Marilyn Strathern, ed., *Audit Cultures: Anthropological Studies in Accountability, Ethics and the Academy*, London: Routledge, 2000.

25 Matias Echanove and Rahul Srivastava, 'When Cities Are Imagined as Excel Sheets', *Hindu*, 2 February 2019.

26 Mike Davis, *Ecology of Fear: Los Angeles and the Imagination of Disaster*, New York: Metropolitan Books, 1998; Amitav Ghosh, *The Great Derangement: Climate Change and the Unthinkable*, Chicago: University of Chicago Press, 2016.

27 'Adhocracy' is a term coined by Warren Bennis in *The Temporary Society*, New York: Harper and Row, 1968. It was popularized by Alvin Toffler in *Future Shock*, New York: Random House, 1970. We were introduced to it by Joseph Grima at the Istanbul Design Biennale in 2012 (see 'Adhocracy', Space Caviar, spacecaviar.net). '"Adhocratic" is the creative response to "bureaucratic" and refers to a process or structure that is adaptive, flexible, and creative. Futurologists in the seventies, like Toffler, predicted the dominance of adhocratic procedures, which today can be seen most clearly in the internet revolution; and primarily in the way in which communication distances have collapsed, changing many of the rules governing organizational structures, work procedures, administrative methods, and business practices.' Rahul Srivastava and Matias Echanove, 'The Design Comes as We Build', *International Journal of Ekistics and the New Habitat: The Problems of Science and New Settlements* 80, no. 2, 2020.

28 For an engaging discussion on this city, see Sanjay Srivastava's *Entangled Urbanism: Slum, Gated Community and Shopping Mall in Delhi and Gurgaon*, New Delhi: Oxford University Press, 2015.

29 Turner, *Housing by People*.

30 'City as Home / Home and Urban Infrastructure', PIIRS seminar, Princeton, NJ, 16–17 November 2012.

31 Keith Hart, *The Memory Bank: Money in an Unequal World*, London: Profile, 2000, 145.

32 Ibid., 151.

33 Ibid.

34 Keith Hart, 'Bureaucratic Form and the Informal Economy', in Basudeb Guha-Khasnobis, Ravi Kanbur, and Elinor Ostrom, eds, *Linking the Formal and Informal Economy*, Oxford: Oxford University Press, 2006, 21–35.

35 Michael Fei, 'Forming the Informal; A Conversation with Cecil Balmond', *Dialogue. Architecture+Design+Culture Magazine* 67, 2003.

36 For an engaging discussion on the idea of informal form, see Anush Kapadia, 'Is the Informal Economy a General-Purpose Machine?', paper presented at the American Anthropological Association Conference, San Francisco, 2012.

37 Fei, 'Forming the Informal'.

38 Georges Bataille, 'L'Informe' (Formless), *Documents* 7, 1929, 382. See also Georges Bataille, *Vision of Excess: Selected Writings, 1927–1939*, ed. Alan Stoekl, trans. Allan Stoekl, Carl Lovitt, and Donald Leslie Jr, Minneapolis: University of Minnesota Press, 1985.

39 Laurent Thénevot, 'The Plurality of Cognitive Formats and Engagements: Moving Between the Familiar and the Public', *European Journal of Social Theory* 10, no. 3, 2007, 413–42.

40 Georges Bataille, *Acéphale*, 24 June 1936.

41 Henri Bergson, *The Creative Mind: An Introduction to Metaphysics*, New York: Dover Publications, 2010.

42 Arjun Appadurai, *Modernity at Large: Cultural Dimensions of Globalization*, Minneapolis: University of Minnesota Press, 1996.

43 Indira Munshi, *Patrick Geddes' Contribution to Sociology and Urban Planning: Vision of a City*, New Delhi: Routledge, 2023.

44 Patrick Geddes, *Cities in Evolution*, London: Routledge, 1998, 397.

4. Homegrown Neighbourhoods

1 Volker M. Welter, *Biopolis: Patrick Geddes and the City of Life*, Cambridge, MA: MIT Press, 2002, 93. See also related observations in his own words: Patrick Geddes, *Cities in Evolution: An Introduction to the Town Planning Movement and to the Study of Civics*, London: Williams, 1915.

2 Raffaele Pernice, 'Images of the Future from the Past: The Metabolists and the Utopian Planning of the 1960s', *Journal of Civil Engineering and Architecture* 8, no. 6, June 2014, 761–71.

3 Joseph Giovannini, 'Arata Isokazi: From Japan, A New Wave of International Architects', *New York Times*, 17 August 1986, Section 6, 26.

4 Nicolai Ouroussoff, 'Future Vision, Banished to the Past', *New York Times*, 6 July 2009, nytimes.com.

5 Christopher Alexander, 'The City Is Not a Tree', reprint from *Design* 206, February 1966.

6 Ibid.

7 Kevin Lynch, *A Theory of Good City Form*, Cambridge, MA: MIT Press, 1981, 89–98.

8 Welter, *Biopolis*, 93.

9 Ibid.

10 John Kelman, *The Interpreter's House: The Ideals Embodied in the Outlook Tower, Edinburgh*, Edinburgh: Oliphant, Anderson & Ferrier, 1905.

11 Welter, *Biopolis*, 154.

12 Global Jurix, 'Foreign Direct Investment in Real Estate', globaljurix.com.

13 Pierre Frey, *Learning from Vernacular: Towards a New Vernacular Architecture*, Arles: Actes Sud, 2010, 45.

14 Ibid., 74.

15 John F. C. Turner, *Housing by People: Towards Autonomy in Building Environments*, New York: Pantheon, 1976.

16 Judith Butler, *The Judith Butler Reader*, ed. Sara Salih with Judith Butler, Malden, MA: Wiley Blackwell, 2004.

17 Michel de Certeau, *The Practice of Everyday Life*, Berkeley: University of California Press, 1984.

5. Form Follows Process

1 Andre Corboz, 'Respecter les ensembles', *Journal de Geneve/Samedi litteraire*, 10 October 1964.

2 Louis Sullivan, 'The Tall Office Building Artistically Considered', *Lippincott's Monthly Magazine* 57, March 1896, 403–9.

3 Jackie Craven, 'The Looshaus Scandal in Vienna: Architect Adolf Loos and the Shocking Goldman and Salatsch Building', *ThoughtCo*, 16 May 2019, thoughtco. com; see also Adolf Loos, 'Two Essays and a Note on the Michaelerplatz House', *Building on the Built*, buildingonthebuilt.org.

4 Adolf Loos, *Ornement et crime*, Paris: Payot & Rivages, 2003, 124.

5 Ibid., 78 (translated from French by the authors).

6 Umberto Eco, *The Open Work*, trans. Anna Cancogni, Cambridge, MA: Harvard University Press, 1989.

7 Jaqueline Tyrwhitt, ed., *Patrick Geddes in India*, London: Lund Humphries, 1947.

8 Arjun Appadurai, *Modernity at Large: Cultural Dimensions of Globalization*, Minneapolis: University of Minnesota Press, 1996, 181.

9 Ibid., 184.

10 Ibid., 181.

11 Amitav Ghosh, *The Nutmeg's Curse: Parables for a Planet in Crisis*, London: John Murray Press, 2021.

12 Appadurai, *Modernity at Large*, 48–65.

13 Loos, *Ornement et crime*, 83.

6. Design Comes as We Build

1 M + Museum, Hong Kong, presents our work at their website, mplus.org.hk.

7. Mess Is More

1 Mary Douglas, *Purity and Danger*, London: Routledge and Kegan Paul, 1966.
2 'Can Tokyo's Charms Be Replicated Elsewhere?', *Economist*, 24 November 2022, economist.com.
3 Donald Richie, *Tokyo: A View of the City*, London: Reaktion Books, 1999, 25–6.
4 Kevin Lynch, *A Theory of Good City Form*, Cambridge, MA: MIT Press, 1981, 89–98.
5 Ibid.
6 Hidenobu Jinnai, *Tokyo: A Spatial Anthropology*, trans. Kimiko Nishimura, Berkeley: University of California Press, 1995.
7 Kishi Kurokawa, *From the Machine Age to the Age of Life*, London: BookArt Ltd, 1998.
8 Ryue Nishizawa, in discussion with the author, 2007.
9 Hirohisa Kohama, *Industrial Development in Postwar Japan*, London: Routledge, 2007.
10 Hugh Patrick and Thomas Rohlen, 'Japan's Small Scale Family Enterprises', Working Paper No. 3, Center on Japanese Economy and Business, Columbia University, September 1986, academiccommons.columbia.edu.
11 André Sorensen, *The Making of Urban Japan: Cities and Planning from Edo to the Twenty-First Century*, London: Routledge, 2002.
12 Theodore Bestore, *Neighbourhood Tokyo*, Redwood City, CA: Stanford University Press, 1989.
13 Yoshitsugu Kanemoto, Toru Ohkawara, and Tsutomu Suzuki, 'Agglomeration Economies and a Test for Optimal City Sizes in Japan', *Journal of the Japanese and International Economies* 10, no. 4, December 1996, 379–98.
14 Ann Waswo, *Housing in Postwar Japan: A Social History*, London: Routledge, 2002.
15 André Sorenson, *Uneven Geographies of Vulnerability: Tokyo in the Twenty First Century*, London: Routledge, 2011.
16 Waswo, *Housing in Postwar Japan*.
17 Takeshi Hayashi, *The Japanese Experience in Technology: From Transfer to Self-Reliance*, Tokyo: United Nations University Press, 1990.
18 Sorenson, *Uneven Geographies of Vulnerability*.
19 Yoshiyuki Mizukoshi, *The New Illustrated Building Code*, Tokyo: Shinnippon Hoki, 1978, huduser.gov.
20 Ibid.
21 Hidenobu, *Tokyo: A Spatial Anthropology*, 131.

8. The Tool-House

1 Ivan Illich, *Tools for Conviviality*, London: Marion Boyars, 2001.
2 Charles-Edouard Jeanneret (Le Corbusier), *Towards a New Architecture*, trans. Frederick Etchells, New York: Dover, 1986.
3 Frances Holliss, *Beyond Live Work: The Economy of Home-Based Work*, New York: Routledge, 2015; Howard Davis, *Living Over the Store*, Abingdon: Routledge, 2012.

4   Frances Hollis, Howard Davis, and Shalini Sinha, eds, 'Homes That Work', *Built Environment* 49, no. 3, September 2023.

5   Philipp Rode, 'Mumbai: The Compact Mega City', in Ricky Burdett, ed., *Urban India: Understanding the Maximum City*, London: Urban Age, London School of Economics, 2009, 45–6.

6   Smita Srinivas, 'Urban Labour Markets in the 21st Century: Dualism, Regulation and the Role(s) of the State', *Habitat International* 32, no. 2, June 2008, 141–59.

7   The names of residents and users in this section have been changed for privacy.

8   The Shalimar restaurant no longer exists.

9   Antonio David Cattani, Jean-Louis Laville, and Keith Hart, *The Human Economy*, London: Polity, 2010, 6.

9. Beyond the City

1   Auguste Tano Kouamé, 'Gearing Up for India's Rapid Urban Transformation', World Bank Group, 30 January 2024, worldbank.org.

2   Ashis Nandy, *An Ambiguous Journey to the City: The Village and Other Odd Ruins of the Self in the Indian Imagination*, New Delhi: Oxford University Press, 2001.

3   See 'Urbanization in India', Town and Country Planning Department, Government of Uttarakhand, tcp.uk.gov.in.

4   M. G. Parameswaran and Kinjal Medh, eds, *India 2061: The Future of India*, Mumbai: Cogito Consulting, 2013, cogitoconsulting.com.

5   Anthony Leeds, *Cities, Classes, and the Social Order*, Ithaca, NY: Cornell University Press, 1994.

6   The study was done with the Forum for Mobile Lives, Paris; see 'À la fois en ville et au village: Les vies circulaires des Indiens', forumviesmobiles.org.

7   Dipankar Gupta, 'Beyond the Metropolis', *Seminar India* 629, 2012.

8   François Ascher, *Métapolis: Ou l'avenir des villes*, Paris: Odile Jacob, 1995, 50–1.

9   Ibid.

10 This section uses real names. The family has participated in an exhibition, 'Mumbai' Return, presented by urbz at the Dr Bhau Daji Lad Mumbai City Museum, Mumbai, 1 July – 13 August 2017.

11 Neil Brenner and Christian Schmid, 'Towards a New Epistemology of the Urban?', *City* 19, nos 2–3, 2015, 166.

12 Ibid., 169.

13 Neil Brenner, ed., *Implosions/ Explosions: Towards a Study of Planetary Urbanization*, Berlin: Jovis, 2015.

10. Accommodation Versus Housing

1   Avikal Somvanshi and Anumita Roychowdhury, *Building Sense: Beyond the Green Facade of Sustainable Habitat*, New Delhi: Centre for Science and Environment, 2014, 173.

2   'Affordable Housing Shortage to Reach 31.2 Mn Units by 2030: CII-Knight Frank Report', *Times of India*, 4 December 2024.

3 Somvanshi and Roychowdhury, *Building Sense*, 175.

4 Rajnarayan Chandavarkar, *From Neighbourhood to Nation: The Rise and Fall of the Left in Bombay's Girangaon in the Twentieth Century*, Cambridge: Cambridge University Press, 2009.

5 Daya Pawar, *Baluta*, trans. Jerry Pinto, New Delhi: Speaking Tiger, 2015.

6 Rajnarayan Chandavarkar, 'From Neighbourhood to Nation: The Rise and Fall of the Left in Bombay's Girangaon in the Twentieth Century', in Meena Menon and Neera Adarkar, eds, *One Hundred Years, One Hundred Voices: The Mill Workers of Girangaon, an Oral History*, Calcutta: Seagull Books, 2004, 7–80.

7 Shreyashi Dasgupta, 'The Accommodation City: Private Low-Income Housing and Urban Space in Dhaka and Mumbai', PhD thesis, University of Cambridge, 2020; Annemiek Prins and Shreyashi Dasgupta, 'Shifting Peripheries: Dhaka's Rickshaw Garages and Mess Dormitories as Spaces of Work and Movement', *Society and Space* 41, no. 2, 18 April 2023, 231–52.

8 Based on field interviews done by Shreyashi Dasgupta. A more detailed analysis can be found at Shreyashi Dasgupta and Annemiek Prins, 'City Liveability Rankings Tell a Biased Story – Our Research in Dhaka Explains Why', theconversation .com, 14 July 2023.

9 Rajdhani Unnayan Kartripakkha, public agency for coordinating Dhaka's urban development in Bangladesh.

10 These observations emerged through an urbz co-supervised master's thesis by Simon Chabas, 'Affordable Housing in Mumbai: An Accommodating Narrative on Accommodation', Sciences Po, 2015.

11. Back to the Future

1 Indira Munshi, 'Patrick Geddes, Sociologist, Environmentalist and Town Planner', *Economic and Political Weekly* 35, no. 6, 5 February 2000, 485–91.

2 Ibid.

3 Indira Munshi, *Patrick Geddes' Contribution to Sociology and Urban Planning: Vision of a City*, New Delhi: Routledge, 2023.

4 Geddes, cited by Volker M. Welter, 'The 1925 Master Plan for Tel-Aviv by Patrick Geddes', *Israel Studies* 14, no. 3, 2009, 106.

5 Patrick Geddes, 'Town Planning in Kapurthala: A Report to H. H. the Maharaja of Kapurthala, 1917', in *Patrick Geddes in India*, ed. Jacqueline Tyrwhitt, London: Lund Humphries, 1947, 26.

6 Karthik Rao-Cavale, 'Patrick Geddes in India, Anti-Colonial Nationalism and the Historical Time of "Cities in Evolution"', *Landscape and Urban Planning* 166, October 2017, 71–81.

7 Geddes, 'Town Planning in Kapurthala', 24.

8 Ibid., 26.

9 Ibid.

10 Rao-Cavale, 'Patrick Geddes in India: Anti-Colonial Nationalism'.

11 Ibid.

12 Vikram Bhatt et al., *How the Other Half Builds*, vol. 3, *The Self-Selection Process*, Research Paper No. 11, Montreal: Centre for Minimum Cost Housing, McGill University, 1990.

13 Daniele Ronca, 'PREVI, Lima, Peru: By Aldo Van Eyck, James Stirling, Atelier 5, Georges Candilis, Charles Correa', Architectuul, 17 July 2017. architectuul.com.

14 Andrea Testi, 'Exploring the Relationship Between "Sites and Services" Projects and Urban Adaptability: A Case Study of Charkop (Mumbai)', *Habitat International*, 139, September 2023.

15 Stuti Pandya and Marie Moors, 'The House as a Work in Movement, The Living Heritage of LIC Housing by B. V. Doshi in India', in Anna Rubbo et al., eds, *Design for Resilient Communities: Proceedings of the UIA World Congress of Architects Copenhagen 2023*, Cham: Springer, 2023, 749–65.

16 Charles Correa, *The New Landscape: Urbanisation in the Third World*, Singapore: MIMAR Books, 1989, 55–62.

17 Clara Lewis, 'Give 64 Acres in Mulund for Rental Homes for Dharavi Squatters, State Tells BMC', *Times of India*, 18 January 2024.

18 Camillo Sitte, *City Planning According to Artistic Principles*, New York: Random House, 1965. Originally published in German as *Der Städtebau nach seinen künstlerischen Grundsätzen*, 1889.

12. The Natural City

1 Amitav Ghosh, *The Hungry Tide*, London: Harper Collins, 2004, 171.

2 Ibid.

3 Suresh Sharma, *Tribal Identity and the Modern World*, New Delhi: Sage, 1994.

4 E. Kent, 'Leading Urban Change with People Powered Public Spaces: The History, and New Directions, of the Placemaking Movement', *Journal of Public Space* 4, no. 1, 127–134.

5 CIAM, Congrès Internationaux d'Architecture Moderne, founded in Switzerland, 1928.

6 Christopher Alexander, 'The City Is Not a Tree', reprint from *Design* 206, February 1966.

7 Melvin Webber, ed., *Explorations into Urban Structure*, Philadelphia: University of Pennsylvania Press, 1964.

8 'Welcome to the Age of the Hermit Consumer', *Economist*, 22 October 2023, economist.com.

9 Arjun Appadurai, *Modernity at Large: Cultural Dimensions of Globalization*, Minneapolis: University of Minnesota Press, 1996.

10 Amitav Ghosh, *The Nutmeg's Curse: Parables for a Planet in Crisis*, Chicago: University of Chicago Press, 2021.

11 Lewis Mumford, *The Story of Utopias*, New York: Viking, 1962, 267.

12 Ibid., 280.

13 Ibid., 279.

14 Ibid., 305.

Index

Page numbers in **bold** refer to figures.